362.784
Ay7g

120908

DATE DUE			
Apr 30 '82			
Feb 13 '81			
Mar 14 '83			

WITHDRAWN

Growing Up Handicapped

Also by
E V E L Y N W E S T A Y R A U L T

Helping the Handicapped Teenager Mature
You Can Raise Your Handicapped Child
Take One Step

Evelyn West Ayrault

GROWING UP HANDICAPPED

A Guide for Parents
and Professionals to Helping
the Exceptional Child

A Continuum Book | *The Seabury Press* | New York

Second printing

The Seabury Press
815 Second Avenue │ New York, New York 10017

Library of Congress Cataloging in Publication Data

Ayrault, Evelyn West, 1922–
Growing up handicapped.
(A Continuum book)
Includes bibliographical references and index.
1. Physically handicapped children. 2. Child development.
3. Physically handicapped children—Psychology. I. Title.
HV903.A9   362.7'8'4   77-13447
ISBN 0-8164-9319-7

For
WILLIAM HAROLD PARSONS, M.D.,
whose patients are privileged to benefit from his compassion,
sense of understanding, and medical skills.

Contents

Appendices

ACKNOWLEDGEMENT

Without the devoted, loyal help
of Patricia Ann Meeker this book could
not have been completed.

Foreword

It becomes a refreshing event when an old hand like myself, presumably knowledgeable in the problems of children with handicaps and their families, can be reminded of something he had forgotten. This occurred when I read the first sentence of the introduction of Dr. Ayrault's comprehensive and practicable book *Growing Up Handicapped*. I had forgotten the phrase *to have a disability is not necessarily to be handicapped*. The guilt feeling that emerged because I recognized that over the years I had begun to take too many things about handicapped children for granted prompted me to read the entire text carefully. It was worth reading!

The range of topics in this book encompasses virtually every conceivable aspect of growing up, whether handicapped or healthy. The book is written in such a fashion that it can meet parents' needs and still fulfill professional expectations.

The range of problems that accompany growing up differently, including family feelings and relationships, and what to do about it, are handled superbly. Parents are told what to look for from the assessment team and how to interpret the findings. A directory of services for the handicapped is included in this smorgasbord type of book. I'll be referring parents to it often because it deals with practical problems requiring ready solutions. I'll see to it that I read it regularly as well, lest I forget *basics*.

ERIC DENHOFF, M.D.
Medical Director,
The Meeting Street School
Children's Rehabilitation Center
Providence, Rhode Island

Introduction

A *disability,* whether it be physical, mental or social is one that an individual can acquire as a result of a birth injury, an accident, or a disease. A *handicap* is the limitation that the person feels his disability imposes upon him and prevents him from doing what he wants to do or becoming what he wants to be. *To have a disability is not necessarily to be handicapped.* A disability only becomes a handicap when the effects of it limits the individual from fulfilling a task or role at a specific time or place. It is only as big a handicap as the person makes it. He can sit back and do nothing to improve his condition or he can, under the guidance of a rehabilitation team, work to improve his abilities and his handicap will grow smaller.

Rehabilitation seeks to restore the child's and adult's degree of physical and mental abilities. Doctors, therapists, social workers, vocational counselors, special education teachers, and psychologists all make up the rehabilitation team. Their efforts are coordinated to help the disabled person attain his highest degree of self independence. He may need treatment requiring physical therapy, speech therapy, occupational therapy, or perhaps all three. However, major emphasis should be placed on basic daily activities that the handicapped person can learn to do for himself.

I have spent thirty-five years in private practice as a clinical psychologist, as well as serving as consultant to various community agencies throughout the country that serviced all types of handicapped children. From this experience, I know some of the many needs these children and adults have. Among these is the great need for a school curriculum that would be child-centered and concerned with developing educational and personal activities for the brain-injured child who has a disability in learning. From this realization I have drawn a concept of a school which I hope to put into operation sometime in the future. Physical, intellectual, emotional and social needs would be integrated into a program to give each child the opportunity to become master of himself.

I am also very conscious of the great need for good counseling of the parents of any child with a problem, be it emotional, physical, or intellectual. Parents should not be forgotten people. In my work I have found that a child, or any individual, cannot make significant progress improving himself and overcoming any problems he may have, unless his family is interested in how he copes with his problem.

Sometimes the first step toward this type of rehabilitation is the most difficult for both child and parent. Seeking help takes a great deal of courage. During my professional career, I have seen parents bring their child or teenager to me for the first time. I have watched them take hesitant steps toward my office then take a deep breath in anticipation of what psychological verdict I might make on their daughter or son. I can feel the heartache and bravery which has brought them to this point.

I discovered also in my practice that parents of troubled children need reading material related to the child's problem that the parents can easily understand. Because of this, I wrote three books: *Take One Step,* (the story of my own life), *How to Raise Your Handicapped Child,* which should be helpful to the parent with a handicapped child between birth and ten or twelve years of age, and *Helping the Handicapped Teenager Mature* which also touches on some problems encountered by the young handicapped adult. This present book is intended to be an extension of those three. I hope this book will make the problems of the troubled child more understandable not only to parents but also to the many different types of professional people that handle the child when he is outside the home.

My practice as a whole has been interesting. My experience over the years has ranged from helping the most severely mentally and physically handicapped child up the ladder to treating adults with marriage, social, or job problems. My practice has spanned nearly all the problems common to human nature. While dealing with the physically and mentally handicapped is heart-searing, it is just as searing to deal with a perfectly "normal" teenager who is on drugs, or who is having a great deal of difficulty finding himself in our society today.

One case comes to mind: A girl of seventeen, a senior in high school, with grades above average, most physically attractive, and yet her question to me over and over again during twelve counseling sessions was "I don't know what is wrong with me. I do not feel easy with other people." How sad. And, at the same time, how gratifying it was to have her look at me after twelve counseling sessions and say, "Miss Ayrault, you saved my life. Thank you."

The reader will notice that the word "normal" is used throughout this book. Therefore, a definition is in order. The first fact is that no one is really normal. The handicapped has his particular hangups, just as the non-handicapped. Normal, as used in the following chapters, refers not only to the non-handicapped, but rather encompasses all individuals. For example, it is normal to laugh, cry, be hungry, have to go to the bathroom, and so on. This is true not only of the physically normal child and adult but also of the handicapped. Furthermore, both the handicapped and the non-handicapped may also have the same hangups. Both may get jealous, angry, have feelings of inferiority, and be hostile toward their environment.

Many of the points made in this book are from case histories. All names, ages, and sexes have been changed to protect the actual person who has a particular problem.

For the material used in Chapter 8, "Learning Disabilities," I am indebted to *The Child With Minimal Brain Dysfunction,* published by the American Occupational Therapy Foundation.

I hope that the chapters which follow will introduce parents and professionals to the basic philosophies of raising, training, and handling the handicapped child through adolescence and into adulthood.

EVELYN WEST AYRAULT, M.A.
Clinical Psychologist
Erie, Pennsylvania

Growing Up Handicapped

1

Your Child Is Handicapped

Why Me?, cries out many a parent. Why is God punishing me? These feelings can affect the child's whole future.

After the first horrible heart-stopping moment, and the sickening shock of discovery, questions begin to rush through the parents' minds. Anger, guilt, fear and self-pity—all of these emotions center on themselves. For days, weeks, and months, even years, these feelings may never change. The world stopped when the doctor said, *Your child is handicapped!*

Before anything can be done to start the rehabilitation of the child, parents must begin to understand their own feelings. During pregnancy, the mother and father look forward to their baby's arrival with pride and joy. They are going to share a most precious process—the re-creating of themselves in a new life. The child is to be their gift of love to each other.

But the gift, when it arrives, is not perfect and all their hopes become twisted into shame and hate and despair. They are drawn into a vicious circle of feelings they often can neither control nor understand. Their thoughts may be ugly, selfish, and belittling. If the child's handicap stems from a birth injury, there is great temptation to blame the other mate. The family tree is examined microscopically to find some ancestor who might be responsible for the criminal genes. If the handicap results from a disease contracted in childhood, a parent may consider the affliction punishment for some misdemeanor. A mother may shoulder a burden of guilt for some fancied lack of care. Other parents see it as Divine Punishment. These unreasonable explanations are the frantic search for an answer—any answer! They do not realize that such feelings may be the seeds of destruction for the rest of their family.

In the beginning, each parent may feel terribly alone and isolated. It is probably the most bewildering experience they have ever encountered. Consequently, the first step must be taken immediately after a diagnosis has been made by a competent doctor. If the parents and the doctor can discuss openly what the child has, the causes (if known) and some of the avenues for treatment, the parents will be making an important beginning. Now, there is promise that they can develop positive attitudes toward their child and toward themselves.

Parents will approach this kind of talk, and the problem as a whole, in light of their own particular characteristics. No two parents develop exactly the same attitude toward their handicapped child, but certain general patterns have been observed. By being aware of their own true feelings, they can begin to evaluate their own emotions in a more realistic framework. Great strength and courage is required to look beyond the tragedy of the moment.

Parents are often frightened by their own attitudes because they have feelings which have been labeled as sinful since the beginning of civilization. A parent may feel hostile, he or she may wish to abandon the child, or even kill it. Some may adopt the role of the martyr, and others may simply try to pretend the problem doesn't exist. Each parent of a handicapped child will experience some of these feelings at different times and in varying degrees. However, it is possible to develop new attitudes from their original feelings. The healthy reconstruction of the family begins in understanding.

How Do You Measure an Infant's World?

Consider the baby's world at birth and his physical limitations in dealing with that world. He cannot speak, or move about. He relies on what he can hear and feel and sense to establish his climate of security or insecurity. From food, warmth, a firm hand, and gentle sounds accompanied by comforting acts, he soon understands that all is well in his world. Discomfort, pain, sudden noises, brusque tones, or rough handling, all alert him to be on the defensive.

Most parents of normal children who have done some reading and talked with their doctor, find it reasonable and not at all difficult to establish a warm, loving attitude with their children. They come to the task affirmatively, resolved to be model parents. At such times it would be hard to convince a parent of a mildly or severely handicapped child—as one ultimately must be convinced—that the cultivation of a constructive relationship between parent and child is as important as any effort to improve the physical condition of the child. It is inevitable that what he comes to expect of you and those around him in his earliest days and months will affect his ultimate evaluation of society and his place in it. It is imperative that the father and mother and doctor forthrightly discuss exactly what it is the child has, the known causes if there be any, the implications of the handicap, the avenues of care and treatment, the financial aspects, the effect on other members of the family, and the areas of responsibility. This kind of discussion can be charged with emotion because it comes at a time when parents are engulfed in feelings of disappointment, even shock. But if they can take the first step, there is promise of developing a good attitude toward their child. Formulating ideas and plans helps them see positive aspects. It reduces the monumental job ahead to smaller, manageable tasks that can be divided among the family members so that no single chore is overwhelming. Parents will approach this kind of talk and the problem as a whole in light of their own particular characteristics. Because people are complex, they cannot always recognize the motivation for some of the things they do. The object is to anticipate some of the problems if you can, and avoid much trouble later on.

The Rejecting Parent

One of the most prevalent attitudes is rejection. This attitude exists among the parents of both disabled and non-disabled children. However, handicapped youngsters often are the easiest for the parents to shun. Many parents do this unintentionally, and it may take a subtle form. In some homes, rejection is shown by laying down rules designed not so much to keep the child out of harm's way as to keep him out of the parent's way. When rejection occurs in the parents of normal children, it is likely that the problem lies within the parent and is deeply rooted. The parent of a handicapped child rejects him for more obvious reasons, which are equally as deeply rooted.

The father may have painful questions about his own virility. His pride may be hurt to think he has sired an imperfect baby, particularly if it is a son. He may think there is something wrong with him and may toy with the thought of abandoning both child and wife. Or, he may blame his wife entirely and think of taking another wife to prove he can father a normal child. The prospect of the financial burden may also terrify him or he may fear that the care of the child will take too much of his wife's time. Rather than acknowledge his feelings as jealousy, the father may say that he is considering sending the child away so he can keep his wife's complete interest, and spare her heartache.

The mother has a special problem. During pregnancy she is usually proud to have fulfilled herself as a woman, particularly if it is her first child. She anticipates praise from family and friends, and looks forward to the pleasure of showing' off her new baby. Even before birth, her maternal feelings are awakened, creating an emotional bond between her and the unborn child. But, when the child is born, and he is not what she expected, the mother feels cheated. The child may not be able to swallow, his legs may be rigid or his movements conclusive. The mother had expected to present her husband with a baby who would be everything he wanted it to be. Now she feels guilty that she has failed as a wife and as a mother. As some realization of the future begins to emerge in her thinking, she wonders whether she is capable of the patience and time it will take to teach the child the things that other children learn to do by themselves. It is not uncommon for her to resent the thought of the things she will need to do for her child that other mothers will not have to do. She unconsciously fights to free herself of the responsibility of training and caring for the child.

Perfectionist Parent

Sally, an eight-year old, was able to walk and use her hands; however, her major problem was poor speech. Despite the fact that she had difficulty in making herself understood, Sally was accepted in public school because she could get around by herself and was above average in intelligence. The teacher treated her as she did her other pupils, and called on her to recite and read aloud. But, when Sally stood up in front of the class, she would either cry or wet herself—a source of deep embarrassment to her.

It was at this point that I had a talk with Sally's mother, an attractive, stylish woman. She revealed her true feelings by saying: "I want Sally to do things better than I did in my youth." She was obviously trying to erase the child's handicap by pretending it didn't exist. For instance, she insisted that Sally speak distinctly. "I keep right after Sally to pronounce every word correctly. When she reads aloud to me and I can't understand what she is saying, I make her read it over and over again. She knows that I don't want to listen unless she pronounces every word so I can understand it," she further said.

Was this mother making a contribution to Sally's development? Was Sally speaking better because of her mother's insistence on repeating the words until she said them perfectly? The answer, unhappily, is no. Sally's speech was already good for her degree of handicap, but she might have been more fluent without the fear of criticism by her mother.

Discussion with Sally, apart from her mother, revealed that she cried in school or wet because, "I'm afraid they'll laugh at me if I don't speak clearly, and mother says if I don't read nicely the other children won't like me. And, I want them to like me."

Sally's severe emotional strain created tension in her mouth muscles that contributed to worsening her speech. The crying and wetting were a reaction to unreasonable pressure put on her by her mother who believed that she was doing good for Sally.

In a counseling session, I encouraged this perfectionist mother to talk out the feelings she had toward her child. The object was to get her to accept the fact that her child would never have normal speech. She was helped to see Sally first as a child, and then as a handicapped child. Once she had adjusted to this fact the mother began to understand that if her child felt perfection to be the only acceptable performance and her only assurance of love, she would soon refuse to read or recite aloud and would retreat into herself. This could result in developing an increased disinterest in reading and a reluctance to speak and socialize with others as she progressed from childhood into adulthood.

There is a fine line between going too far and going far enough. Sally needed to be encouraged in her speech. She also needed to be commended for her efforts, praised for her improvement, and have her limitations accepted by her mother. The least important aspect of this mother's education was an explanation of what Sally's speech problem involved. From a speech therapist the mother learned that tightened muscles, as well as tense jaw muscles, made it difficult for her child to enunciate clearly. To press beyond her maximum ability was not only to indulge in unrealistic wishing, but to create tensions that heightened and emphasized Sally's speech problem.

Passive Parent
The attitude of passive parents influences the child's outlook on life. From a very young age, he views the world as gray colored and neutral. From the behavior of his parents, he may conclude that he is uninteresting and feels no desire to grow or participate in what appears to him a drab uninspiring world.

Passive parents are not to be confused with irresponsible ones. The former arrange for the education of their child, see that he is cared for, seek out the necessary therapy. They do everything except *give of themselves*. In their flight from reality they develop a superficial relationship with their child. They see nothing charming or interesting in him. They function out of duty and with little love. The effect on the child is devastating. In an atmosphere devoid of emotion the child soon relinquishes any claim to affection and resorts to immature emotional behavior.

These parents rarely seek out and find the special gifts and talents that make each child unique—the sunny smile, the soft skin, the bright blue eyes, the well-shaped fingers. By withholding their interest in the child and showing him no love, it becomes impossible for the child to perceive himself apart from his handicap. They open up no possibilities in him. As a result, the child develops no true individuality. He becomes an enigma to himself and to those around him. The hazard facing these parents is that they may perform their round of chores in behalf of their child meticulously and never know that they are failing as parents. They are likely to bridle at the suggestion that their handling of the child is destructive.

Overindulgent Parent

Ten year old Jane wore braces and could not walk unassisted. Her family was wealthy enough to afford a maid, a chauffeur, and a governess to teach and care for her, and her life was made as comfortable as money could make it. Most of Jane's waking hours were spent in a wheelchair. Without any conscious effort to exploit the household staff who attended her, she made free use of their services and counted on them to do errands and chores at her command. If she wanted a book that was out of reach, she had only to ask for it and it would be handed to her. Although her family yearned to see her walk, they made no attempt to press her when she refused to try. "I feel," said her mother, "that Jane should be given everything she wants since we can afford it, because she has such an awful burden to carry."

Without motivation, without any incentive and without the conviction that someone believed she was capable of helping herself, Jane not only was retarded in walking but also was slow in her emotional and personality development. She knew nothing about self-discipline and its rewards. With everything she could want at her beck and call, she was on the way to becoming a human vegetable.

In counseling sessions, I helped the parents to understand that their overindulgence was hindering rather than helping Jane's emotional, social and physical development. They soon understood why it was important to encourage her to wait on herself as much as possible, and they were receptive to carrying out a suggested program designed to make her independent. Her toys and books were put within her reach in her bedroom. A tubular bar was installed around the wall of the room to help her move about with greater assurance. Low hooks were put on the back of her closet door so that she could hang up her clothes. Jane came to know the unique experience of moving her legs by herself by holding onto the bar, and sliding one hand after the other, heading toward something she wanted to get herself. She discovered the pleasure of deciding what she wanted to read, what she wanted to wear. In time she acquired self-confidence because she sensed the new confidence of those around her and believed her parents when they commented to a visitor, "She can do it herself." And, in the inevitable pattern that emotional security weaves, her growing confidence made it possible for her to do more and more.

Overindulgence takes many forms and occurs for many reasons. Among parents of normal children it is commonplace. Some parents overindulge because they have guilt feelings about spending too much time away from their children or because they hope to buy affection. Other parents need to show proof of their material success by showering their children with gifts.

Perhaps parents of a handicapped child can more readily rationalize their tendency to overindulge their child. Yet, when shown the crippling effect of their indulgence, they are shocked to think that they have been in some measure responsible for retarding their child. If properly oriented to the child's limitations, parents can separate what must be done from what a child with training and motivation can do for himself. A program of self-help that does not demand more of the child than he is capable of giving at the time can be set up with trained therapists.

Adjusting Parents

Parents who make a rapid adjustment to their child's condition are considered to be most desirable. Yet such parents need to be cautioned. There is a danger that they will couple their "adjustment" with the assumption that their child can, with determined effort, cope alone. These parents may show the utmost respect for their child's individuality as a person but stand aloof, making a point of not coddling or praising him. Their attitude is that in the world the child must get along as he is and therefore the parents can best help him by treating him as a physically and mentally normal person.

Normal children and adults have many periods of self-doubt. They experience valleys and peaks of security and insecurity. Good mental health and a well functioning body enable them to level off and go their own way. The handicapped child must face times when he is doubtful of the world's possibilities for him and fearful of the tyranny of his handicap. The fact that he walks or talks differently from those around him creates these feelings. The physical and emotional impact of his handicap makes him feel more insecure than his non-handicapped friends.

There is no parent who can *accept* his handicapped child entirely. He has to aim at *adjusting* to the child's condition. To do this is never easy. Some of the things that will help are parent counseling, knowing your child better through a psychological evaluation and finding a physician you trust.

Fearful Parent

Parents of normal children live with all manner of fears—fear that their young babies will suffocate, that their toddlers will fall or run into the street, that their school age children will get sick, and on and on. Fears are a part of life, and no child can be completely protected. The handicapped child faces many dangers, and his parents too, must live with some fear. How the child reacts to danger will depend on how his parents react. For example, he may have many falls before he learns to walk. To shield him from these falls, you would have to keep him from trying to walk, and surely you would not do this. You may be anxious and afraid, but if he is to gain confidence in himself, he must believe that you believe in him. It takes a kind of courage only parents have.

Martyr Parent

Though friends and neighbors may marvel at the selflessness of parents who devote themselves to the complete care and training of the handicapped child, it would be better for both child and parent if the parents made a more reasonable allocation of their time and interest. Sometimes such excessive devotion is penance for what parents consider wicked thoughts—the desire to destroy or abandon their child. A mother may diligently carry out a home training program to the letter, but her reasons for doing so are not always good ones—that is, to enable her child to develop to the maximum of his capabilities. Often the reason is an inverted form of rejection in which she thinks of her child as a poor helpless thing. A close examination of her feelings is likely to reveal that what she is really thinking is *poor me*.

The Urge to Kill

Rejection manifests itself in many ways. Perhaps the most difficult emotion parents of a handicapped child have to understand is the urge to kill. An unspeakable feeling, for such an act is not accepted in any society.

During a counseling session a mother confessed to me, "I want to kill him. He can't learn fast enough, he makes ugly faces all the time and he drools like a baby. No one could really love him. I don't want to live the rest of my life saddled with such a queer child. But I don't want to be a murderer because of him."

Her son was a six-year-old with an attractive personality, even though he could not yet walk or speak intelligently. And he was thought to be educable. Yet none of this was a consolation to the mother. It was doubtful if she was really aware of these things. Her real reason for rejecting the child was plain enough: "Just to have him around me every day reminds me constantly how I have failed my husband."

Each one of us possesses some innate animal instincts. If sufficient control is not exercised when shock or passion or fear stimulates the wish to kill, then a killing occurs. The handicapped child's parent who thinks momentarily of killing him is reacting as an animal might to an imperfect runt in a litter. An animal mother may refuse food to her imperfect offspring or may try to kill it by trampling it to death.

A human parent, however, endowed with intelligence and reason can and should exercise control. Though he might try to rationalize death as a painless, peaceful end to what he interprets as a life of suffering, he can be helped by understanding his true motives. What he really wants to do is to wipe out his mistake and start life anew. He is hoping to free himself of a handicapped child to whom he has not yet learned to adjust. With proper guidance from a skilled counselor, parents can learn to adjust to their child's condition and his place in their lives.

The Urge to Abandon

Another form of rejection, akin to the wish to kill, is the urge to abandon. Both acts have one meaning for the parent—release from unpleasantness and responsibility. Because it is less violent and less contrary to the parental instinct, more parents think seriously of abandonment. However, few think of it as that in their own minds. Institutionalizing a child may be the socially acceptable form this rejection takes. Without probing too deeply into his own reasons, a parent may justify abandonment on the basis of the well-being of the spouse or other children in the family. At that time, it seems better to dispose of the "problem" and to go on living exactly as before.

No one should rush to blame parents for their feelings. Many handicapped children require an unreasonable amount of service and attention. Why shouldn't parents give serious thought to institutionalizing their handicapped child? It is reasonable to suggest that training a handicapped child can be a challenging venture with great rewards.

Perhaps the answer lies in the fact that the relationship between parent and child is like that of husband and wife. The pact is for better or worse. And it only becomes better when a genuine effort is put forth to make it work. Parents of a normal child accept him willingly even though they know nothing of what lies ahead. Yet most will have their share of pain and disappointment along with the pride and joy of the child's growing up. They have at least as many hazards to anticipate and possibly less control over them. The future is unknown, even for the parents of normal children! For the parents of a handicapped child, the future is much more predictable.

Hostility in Parents

When a normal child misbehaves, the parent becomes annoyed or angry and responds by scolding, yelling, or a slap. These reactions are acceptable because they are prompted by a specific misbehavior of the child. The parent of a handicapped child can just as certainly be expected to react to some specific act of disobedience or misbehavior. But, when a parent consciously or unconsciously finds fault with almost every action of his child, when he criticizes him before others, when he shows annoyance at any unsuccessful effort his child makes, when he consistently demands a level of performance of which his child is not capable, he is evidencing a deep-rooted hostility. This parent actively resents the problems that have been created; he has not adjusted to his child and he has not faced squarely the permanence of his child's handicap.

Such hostility can do serious damage which will have a tragic effect on development. There are some children whose handicap characteristics may grow more pronounced the older they become. Drooling or poorly coordinated body motions of a five-year old may irritate a hostile parent but are easier to accept at five than when the child approaches his teens. It is not necessarily that the condition has worsened, it is simply less acceptable in an older child.

What is most distressing about hostility is that it is infectious. Others, including the child, can take their cue from a parent's tone and manner. If the child hears or senses that a parent is angry with him, he may turn on himself to oblige the parent. Unchecked, this child can come to hate himself. One could almost offer it as a formula: show a child that you are angry with him and have no love for him and he will be angry with and hate himself.

Hostility simply cannot be concealed from a child, however much you think you are controlling your feelings. It is evident in the touch of your hand, the tone of your voice, the tenseness of your body. Hostility cannot be controlled from without. You have to come to terms with yourself and your child if you are to resolve your hostility within. Unless this can be done you can expect serious trouble ahead.

2

Family Relationships

The family with a handicapped member is a handicapped family.
No statement was ever truer. Having a handicapped child in the
home directly affects the other members of the family. Once the
parents have made the first painful attempts at understanding their own
feelings toward their handicapped child, they must shoulder the additional responsibility of insuring his acceptance within the family
group. The place the child assumes will ultimately depend on their attitude toward him.

What happens can be likened to a play. The parents are the directors who set the stage. The other members of the family—siblings,
grandparents, aunts and uncles—are the actors who perform their roles
as they are directed. Their reactions are the unconscious response to
the directors and attitudes they display develop at the directors' insistence. This may seem to be a cold blooded analogy, but I have seen
the basic truth of this in family after family that I have counseled.

If the parents are tolerant and undertanding of the handicapped child
growing up within the family group, the brothers, sisters and grandparents will be more likely to treat him with tolerance and understanding. If the parents are apathetic or oblivious to the problems
which face the child during his infancy, childhood and young adult
years, then the other members of the family may not offer him the affection and attention he needs.

Which way the pendulum swings depends upon the parents. In their
role as directors, the parents must strive to integrate the child into the
family. At the same time, they must make every effort to draw the
non-handicapped brothers and sisters into the life of the disabled child.
Family harmony cannot exist otherwise. Any other approach will result in one or the other of the children being neglected and unloved,
drifting through life without the bulwark of parental guidance.

All children, regardless of their physical or intellectual capabilities, need discipline and thrive with love. The parents are the only source for this. Both handicapped and non-handicapped children depend almost entirely on their parents for guidance, so it it up to the parents to set the stage and provide the direction.

Siblings

Not only what the parents say but also what they do affects the attitude of the other children in the family toward the handicapped member. Sometimes non-handicapped children are the forgotten ones. So much care is given to the handicapped child that those without a handicap are left on their own. Then there is the other side of the coin where the nonhandicapped child is the star in the family and the disabled child ends up at the bottom of the family totem pole.

How many parents think of their handicapped child as a "teacher" to the rest of the family? Not many. Yet this can be true. The child who seemed to be short-changed by life may well bring a special gift to his family, to young and old alike. He can teach compassion, understanding and tolerance. Helping him with the day-to-day business of living can be a priceless learning experience.

This does not mean they should cater to all his whims. But it does mean they should encourage him to do as much as he is capable of doing for himself. The family of thirteen-year-old Robert worked out an ideal solution by setting up a weekly schedule. Each knew what Robert could do and could not do for himself. A typical week's plan included everyone in the family. His fifteen-year-old brother helped him get his coat buttoned to go to school in the morning. At mealtime, his eleven-year-old sister made sure that his food was cut up so he could handle it easily. His mother helped him get his braces on and off in the morning and at bedtime. So that Robert could get out and meet the neighbors, his father accepted the responsibility of taking him out in his wheelchair.

In this family the handicapped child was no burden to any of them. At the end of each week, they switched roles. Robert was the teacher in this family. His brother and sister were learning at young ages what it was like not to be able to do everything you wanted to do for yourself. And this training transferred into their relationship with their friends.

In the case of twelve-year-old Carrie, the situation was very different. Her ten-year-old sister was the star of the family. She was a pretty child with a fetching personality, and everybody adored her. She didn't have to overcome a handicap and was a straight "A" student. Carrie had assets too, but they were not recognized by her parents.

When the doctor recommended braces and crutches for Carrie, her mother told the doctor that they could not purchase them right away because they planned to send the sister to a summer camp. Carrie had to wait six months before she could start using the braces to help her get on her feet.

The position of the handicapped child in relation to other siblings often affects the parent's attitude as well as the brothers and sisters. When the handicapped child is the oldest, the younger child does not have a typical child to identify with. He must look to his playmates or friends at school for learning normal patterns. The parents, too, have no experience with raising a non-handicapped offspring. They are elated at having produced a normal child and may tend to favor her as in the case of Carrie's parents. At some point in his or her development the younger child will surpass the handicapped child, causing him to question his own ability, and perhaps contribute to a feeling of inadequacy.

When the handicapped child is the youngest in the family, the other members may tend to baby him. He may be overindulged by his parents and by his older siblings. They may wait on him constantly and try to gratify his every wish so that he makes little or no effort to do for himself. In a situation of this type, the normal learning process is slowed down to the detriment of the handicapped child.

The child with a handicap may present emotional difficulties for his normal brothers and sisters. Adults often do not recognize how sensitive youngsters are toward their handicapped sibling. They may develop feelings of guilt, anxiety, and even hate, as they run off to play, leaving the handicapped child behind. Again, the parents are called upon to help the child without a handicap cope with his feelings and to acknowledge that such feelings exist.

Grandparents

The role of grandparents varies from family to family. Some eagerly anticipate the day when they will be blessed with grandchildren; others resent the thought, believing it is a sure sign of old age. Regardless of their personal feelings, all hope that their children will have a physically perfect baby.

When the grandchild is either born handicapped, or becomes handicapped as a result of an accident, the grandparents are often as shocked and upset as the parents. Grandparents are usually not silent partners; they tend to be very vocal. They may indulge in medical and psychological diagnosis, usually without qualifications.

At the time of discovery, they too may try to put the blame on the in-laws, saying hurtful things such as "If you hadn't married him (or her) this wouldn't have happened."

They may rush in with free advice about medical care and how to handle the child. Some may have strong opinions about the question of institutionalizing the child if he is severely disabled. Others, however, adopt a supportive role by trying to do constructive acts like taking care of the child for an afternoon or by making helpful suggestions. Grandparents are always on the safe side if they realize that the handicapped child is not their own and that the ultimate decision about his welfare is up to his parents.

Although they can be extremely helpful in caring for the child as a relief for the parents, they should never become full-time babysitters or assume the complete care of the handicapped child. Very often parents will give the handicapped child to the grandparents to raise. To the parents it is a socially acceptable escape from the chagrin of having a handicapped child. By placing the child with the grandparents, i.e. keeping him in the family, they reduce their own feelings of guilt. The danger, of course, in the grandparents raising the child is that they are more likely to be doting and overindulgent, depriving the child of the stimuli which encourage his progress toward independence or semi-independence.

Aunts, Uncles and Cousins

The handicapped child is a member of the whole family clan. Aunts, uncles, and cousins too, must adjust to him. Sometimes they are hesitant about including the family with the handicapped child in get-togethers or reunions. They do not know quite what to do with him or about him.

Cousins the same age as the child with a handicap very often stand off in wonderment. They do not know whether to include their handicapped cousin in their play or not. How this works out depends a great deal on how the parents of the child and the aunts and uncles handle the situation. If the child's condition is carefully explained to the cousins, he has a better chance of being accepted by them.

To insist that the cousins accept the child into their play groups often results in estrangement. The cousins are afraid of the handicapped youngster and the handicapped youngster feels unwanted.

As the cousins grow up, they often grow out of wanting their handicapped cousin in their group. He either becomes a burden to them or someone they must cater to. Often enough, they bypass the handicapped cousin by entering careers or getting married. By now the handicapped cousin is classified as "my aunt and uncle have a handicapped child and I remember growing up with him." Now the handicapped teenager or young adult is only a cousin by name. Often he is on the outside looking in to the family clan.

One way to avoid this becoming too difficult for parents and the child is to take special care in his grooming. If he is of average intelligence see that he has some of the luxuries that others his age have, and invite non-handicapped relatives over for dinner or other get-togethers. To make the problem larger than it really is would be for the parents of the handicapped individual to go to family functions and leave the handicapped relative at home. A good motto that the family could use with relatives is, "You accept our child and invite him or we do not go."

Husband and Wife

The mother and father in a handicapped home also must adjust their roles as husband and wife. Having a handicapped child, adolescent or young adult in a home can either make or break a marriage. Statistically, this has been proven over and over.

In most cases the primary difficulty is that the care and treatment of the handicapped child is often left totally to the wife. In such instances, while the marriage may not be totally destroyed, it may have some mighty wide voids in it. If the disabled person requires a great deal of personal care from the mother, she has little time left to devote to her husband. To offset loneliness, he may resort to alcohol, other women, or to his business which becomes all-consuming.

By sharing the care and treatment of the handicapped member of their household, the husband and wife are involved in a joint venture. One mother put it very well: "I found it less difficult to take my child to the doctor because each time I went my husband would say, 'I'm thinking of you and I'll be home from work as soon as I can and talk it over with you.' " Sharing decisions and care of the handicapped member enables the parents to continue sharing other facets of their life. Together, for instance, they can decide when they can take off for a few hours, or even a weekend, for relaxation and fun.

For every member of the family—parent, sibling or grandparent—I believe there are certain basic attitudes toward the handicapped member that, if practiced to the best of their ability, will create a happy, harmonious and gratifying home.

The Ten Commandments

Thou shalt:

1. Adjust to him as he is with love and respect.
2. Give him a feeling of security—both physical and emotional.
3. Help him to do the best he can do in learning how to live with his handicap.
4. Encourage him to be dependent on himself and to assume as much responsibility as he is able.
5. Protect him from fear and frustration where possible.
6. Never push him to do more than he is physically or mentally capable of doing.
7. Realize that his wishes, opinions and ideas are evidence of his growth.
8. Show an interest in his activities, however small they may be.
9. Praise him for what he accomplishes.
10. Encourage him to adjust to himself as he is rather than as he wishes he could be.

3

Image of Self

Why do some people stare? What do they think?

The picture a handicapped individual, as well as a non-handicapped—develops of himself is formed in his early childhood. Unless people help to change his idea of himself, he grows into adulthood reflecting his childhood image.

For instance, Danny cannot get about by himself. He is in a wheelchair and has only a few playmates. He is around his parents all day and exposed to their ideas and attitudes toward his life. Thus he may develop a narrow self image. He may not have an opportunity to hear how people regard him. If he is to develop a realistic idea of himself, one he can live with all his life and adjust to by not running away and trying to hide from it, those around him are responsible for giving him good food for thought about himself.

Escape from Self Image

The handicapped child is told, accept yourself as you are. Parents are told, accept your handicapped son or daughter. It is difficult for one to *accept* permanent damage to the human body. For example, a dent in a car fender, or a broken leg on a favorite chair cannot be accepted. They are usually fixed as soon as possible. These examples are quite different from impairments caused by brain injury, infections, or accidents. Gross injuries to the human body usually cannot be repaired as easily. The individual may have to live with the injury the rest of his life. Rather than accept it, he must learn to *adjust* to it. This is not easy. Many adults with no physical impairment never achieve the maturity to adjust to themselves.

There is no choice for Carol. She may try to run and hide to avoid facing the truth because she can't adjust to herself. She may take refuge in a make-believe world that has no relation to reality. She thinks of herself as a perfect human being, physically and mentally able to do everything her non-handicapped friends can do. She is trying to escape the real image of herself. Then one day she must face the truth. This could result in developing feelings of inferiority. These feelings could keep her from pursuing goals she might have achieved such as walking in braces, getting about in a wheelchair by herself, or maybe even walking by herself. Negative feelings she may develop might be so destructive as to retard her social, emotional and intellectual development.

Reaction for Renee may be just the opposite. She may become aggressive, obnoxious, and demanding in behavior. She may try to deny her handicap by pretending she is someone else. She may be hostile, all steamed up to lick the world. She envisions herself as strong and unafraid. No one can hurt her. Let her friends laugh at the way she walks. She doesn't care, she tells herself. She is strong and unhurtable. But deep down inside she does care.

For Larry the impact is still different. He sits and stares sullenly into space, and acts like a zombie. He does nothing, not because he cannot, but because of the image he has of himself. He is convinced that if he cannot do things as well as others, why do them at all. He thinks he is unable to feed himself, button his coat, or take care of his personal needs. He feels like yelling at everyone, "What's the purpose of life for me? Look at me! I cannot do anything." He hasn't any dream world to wallow in, escape to at will; nor has he the trumped-up joy of being "cock-of-the-walk." Instead, his image of himself stands naked before him, and he is drowning in his handicap. Any of these patterns of "escape from reality" reveal how the handicapped person can conceive of himself. They are warnings of the bad concept-of-self that can develop as years go by.

There is much to be gained by the disabled individual who draws healthy attitudes from those around him as he matures. This can help him *adjust* to the fact that he *is* handicapped in some manner. It will help him to feel more secure within himself. As he grows older he will not be afraid to ask himself, "Who am I? Of what significance am I?", and he will feel that he has the capacity to do as much as he can within his physical and mental limitations. With confidence, he will be able to ask himself, "What can I do?", and honestly answer that he can do only so much and no more. When he can say, "This day I accomplished more than yesterday," he has begun to develop a self-image-philosophy of life.

The incentive for the handicapped is motivation. This *must* be coupled with the conviction that someone believes him capable of doing something, however small. Such convictions can encourage the handicapped to shift from a defensive attitude *against* himself, to a more pleasing respect *for* himself. It can help him reduce to a minimum the problems which have obstructed his development and emphasize his positive accomplishments.

Disciplining of Physical Self

Having a good image of oneself is fine. However, it is important that one be able to discipline it. Everyone likes a self image he can control. For example, he can learn to be disciplined about entertaining himself. Developing an interest in the stock market, daily news broadcasts, or favorite TV shows can help him to be master of himself and not have to depend on others for entertainment every minute of the day. This helps him develop a sense of personal dignity. He realizes that every part of his mind is something he can master, and he can be proud of this accomplishment.

Development of Social Self

As each individual grows older, he wants to mingle with people. He wants to feel he is a part of society. If he is to be something other than a human lump of flesh sitting in a wheelchair or walking on crutches, he must develop an image of his social self. If he does he will give a cheery "hello" when met or a "thank you" when given something. If he lacks a social image, he is a nobody to himself, is treated as such, and may be socially ostracized.

The knowledgeable handicapped person feels wise, aware of people and things around him. If he feels socially insecure he squirms and hangs his head. He fears being hurt, and feels threatened by those around him. Yet, in his breast hotly churns the desire and need to join in the fun. But this does not often occur. The individual may sit passively as an "onlooker," never a participant in activities going on around him. This can be as true when he is at home as it is when he is away from home.

Environmental Retardation

The environmental maturity of the individual begins in the home. A normal crawling baby explores every accessible corner of the house, and, as many a dismayed mother can report, will open every drawer that yields. Such a child usually greets visitors who come to the door, hears a variety of voice tones, sees expressions on faces about him, and tastes everything within his reach.

The handicapped person often cannot reach out for things. They often have to be brought to him. To stimulate him intellectually, socially, and emotionally he must be exposed to activities of everyday living. The more interest he can take in his environment, the more he will have to talk about with his friends. If this is not done in his early childhood, he will show marked evidences of environmental retardation when he reaches adulthood.

Emotional Image

"From little acorns big oak trees grow" describes well how a childhood image can become magnified in adulthood. The image of self a child forms is the "acorn" from which his adult image—the "tree"—will sprout ten or twenty years from now.

It is not uncommon for the handicapped to act out his infantile and emotional patterns. In many cases, the mother is the prime object. Dependency of this nature forces the handicapped to ask advice of a parent or another adult and act on that advice without thinking through his problems himself. He accepts values from others without question. He lives passively, never making independent judgments. He spares himself anxiety. He thinks of himself as helpless. His image of himself is nil. Perhaps this can best be described in the case of Dotty.

Dotty's Childhood Image

Dotty, a seven-year-old with poor speech and hand coordination, showed an active desire to harm herself. She wanted to harm her body, disfigure it, do away with it. For example, whenever she was asked to button her coat or tie her shoes, she became unduly emotional and had temper tantrums. She dug her teeth into her arms and cried as soon as she met with any difficulty doing these tasks. "Bad, bad, bad! You don't do what I want you to. You make mommy mad at me. I don't want you on me," she would say to her hands as she struggled to do these things. If she was punished for her failure to do tasks or for her temper tantrums, she ran into the kitchen, grabbed a bread knife, and tried to cut off her arms and fingers. When her mother tried to stop her, she cried, "Let me alone. You hate me because my hands don't do what you say they must. They're no good!"

In Dotty's more controlled moments, she made great effort to please her family. She offered to wash dishes, make beds, even do the impossible in her case—carry steaming hot dishes of food to the table. If she was stopped in trying to do these tasks, she screamed and struck out at anyone near her. "Let me do it!" she would yell, "I want to do it for you so you will love me." Her compulsive desire was to prove herself, make herself noticed, and assure herself that people needed her. One of her basic fears was that she might not be liked, shunned by playmates, ostracized by her family. As a result, she was aggressive. She demanded that everyone (children or adults) take her into their circles, cater to her, praise her efforts in her various awkward, but still accomplished skills. Her image of herself was very low and distorted. All these characteristics carried over into Dotty's young adulthood stage of development.

Dotty's Adult Image

In desperation, Dotty's parents brought her to me for evaluation and counseling. Psychological tests revealed that Dotty, at age 22, felt that her environment was made up of people and things that could harm her. Because she lacked conscious control of her emotions, Dotty burst into hysterical fits and went into deep depressions.

"When I get undressed and look at my body, it looks like any other girl's body, but I do not feel like other girls feel. I am ashamed of my body because it won't act normally. My hands shake when I try to do something for someone else, and I cannot talk so that other people understand me. I just can't stand this."

She had carried over from her childhood her poor self-image and her compulsive desire to prove herself. She hoped this behavior would attract attention to herself, and bring concern from others. Dotty was emotionally reactive to her inner world of fears. She was preoccupied with her own problems and unresolved conflicts.

Dotty spent a great deal of time feeling sorry for herself and was unable to adjust to being handicapped. She denied herself joys in life because she felt she had no right to enjoy them. "That is not for me. It is only for those who can do things," was her answer when I suggested that she attend a community recreation center for young unmarried men and women her age. Dotty's difficulty was that she had so much negative emotionalism—fears, unsatisfied desires, unhappiness—in her makeup from childhood, that she anticipated the same for her future adulthood. Age made no difference. Who was she? Of what worth and significance was she to herself or to anyone else, she pleaded. She did not have these questions adequately answered at the age of seven and at the age of twenty-two she still had no answers to them. Thus, her image of self remained at an immature level.

This is a classic example of what can happen to any disabled person if he is not trained early in life to develop an awareness and control of self. He is apt to view things in his life with extreme caution, being afraid to become involved in life's pattern, and may prefer to hide behind his mother's skirts. He may be fearful of his surroundings. He may become so emotionally upset that he will lack control himself. Why? He has no image of self. He needs help to develop one, a strong one, a realistic one. The fact that he may be on crutches, braced from head to toe, or live hour after hour in a wheelchair is no excuse for him to display such behavior. Developing controlled behavior is not accomplished by a crutch, a brace, or making the wheels of a wheelchair turn, but is controlled by one's frame of mind. It must come from within the individual and he must work on developing and controlling it as he grows older.

4

Behavior of the Child

A misbehaving child is harder to accept.

All children have behavior problems. The handicapped child's behavior problems are more involved. For example, the palsied child may have impairments that prevent him from having a good walking balance or a good sitting balance. Another child may have impaired or retarded speech. A third child may have learning disability in school. These problems can cause such children to be aggressive, hostile, and difficult to handle. And because of this, handicaps may become more pronounced.

Why Does He Act That Way?

"Why does Jim act that way when we encourage him to drink out of a cup by himself?" or, "Why does Mary have temper tantrums when she is asked to try to wash her face or get undressed for bed?" Parents, teachers, and therapists ask this in exasperation. The answer to their questions lies in an understanding of the physical and mental development of the child and the relation of that development to frustrations he has experienced in the past.

Frustration is the key word in the makeup of most handicapped children. If the handicapped child cannot suck at birth, he experiences frustration. A baby at the breast or bottle will become agitated if he cannot get enough milk. If the milk begins to flow more easily he settles down to satisfying his hunger.

The six-, seven-, or eight-year-old child may reflect original frustrating experiences. Since he was thwarted in his first attempts to satisfy hunger, automatically he tolerates feelings of frustration as he grows older. The more difficult he finds it to suck or to read or to

24

speak, the more difficult he may find it to grasp his first toy, eat, balance himself, stand or walk, because of early fixed frustrations.

This is the reason that caution should be used when asking the child to do more than he is physically or mentally capable of doing. For instance, some parents urge this son or daughter to feed himself the minute he shows any sign of handling a spoon. This could have many repercussions. The child could become fearful that he will not get the food into his mouth to satisfy his hunger. He might become physically and emotionally tense. His frustrations could overwhelm him. He might feel that other people consider him worthless.

It is better for him to engage in activities he can enjoy and accomplish. When a physical handicap is severe, a boy at age eight may never kick a football or ride a bicycle. It should be explained to him why he cannot do this like other boys.

I advise parents to offer a child alternatives. "You may not go into the water, but you may play in the sand." "You may not have candy before dinner, but how about a carrot?" When you tell the child he cannot play football or dance, follow it up with a statement of what he *can* do. "You can't play football, but I bet you're the only one who knows the name of all the Rose Bowl teams!" Or, "You can't dance, but I think you've got the best scrapbook of dancers!" The object is not to kill the child's interest in the activity because of his limitations, but to channel it into areas he can pursue.

Aggressive Behavior

The type of aggression exhibited by a child is determined by the problems he has to solve as he grows up. Signs of this behavior appear in all children because of periodic needs to satisfy goal-seeking drives. The older aggressive child teases or strikes his playmates and is jealous. His aggressive behavior differs from that of the handicapped child in intensity. Fear of being considered weak may impel him to prove his worth. He has a driving compulsion to establish his worth as a person in the eyes of others. This grows stronger as he grows older. Aggression is one way for the child to gain attention.

The problems that a ten-year-old child is solving are frequently so overwhelming that he approaches them with a negative attitude. If he is pushed to do something that is too difficult for him and in which he may fail, he reacts with negative aggression. In cases where a child has difficulty in speaking, aggression may be shown in a subtle manner. Bed wetting or spitting out food are common behavior examples.

For the intelligent handicapped child who has not the strength or physical coordination to act out his aggressive feelings, these may become techniques he uses to control those around him. He may not be able to say what he is thinking, but he can act in a unmistakably aggressive manner that draws attention to him.

Daydreaming

Handicapped children who are unable to compete with the non-handicapped, frequently daydream. Since they cannot do what they see others doing, they withdraw from reality into their own private world where life seems easier. They conjure up images of the self they wish to be. They see that self running up and down, playing, doing all the things other children do.

Eight-year-old Tom's mother successfully handled such a problem. Tom refused to go outside in the yard in his wheelchair. She invited three or four neighborhood children to the house and encouraged them to ask questions about Tom's handicap. To questions, "Why is he like that? Why can't he walk the way we do?", they were given answers that they could understand. The reasons why Tom wore braces were clarified by taking them off so they could see that he could not stand up alone without them; that his foot turned in unless the brace kept it straight, that his legs were not strong enough to hold him. The demonstrations aroused much interest. The children commented freely and admired the ingeniously constructed braces. Their interest did a lot for Tom, since it was focused all on him. He felt important. He became more willing to go outside, sit in his wheelchair and watch the others play ball in the street or ride up and down on their bikes. On occasions, some of the children pushed his chair. If a strange child asked about him, his young friends answered all questions proudly. Even Tom, who had poor speech, would try to explain about the braces. When Tom finally refused repeated offers to be pushed down the block by his mother to get an ice cream cone because he preferred watching his friends playing ball, he had adjusted to his handicap realistically.

Daydreaming retards learning. A child then exerts only superficial efforts on therapy or school work. The daydreamer concentrates poorly and retains little of what he is taught. Regardless of the severity and type of handicap, a child must be encouraged to become self-entertaining and independent. He must be provided with food for thought to give him healthy thinking habits. A busy mind has little time to escape into distorted unrealistic daydreams.

Withdrawal

A child who has not been helped to adjust to the fact that he is different from other children can easily be shocked into withdrawal from the world. If he has been assured that he can do everything other children do, that he is no different from other children, his parents have not given him protection against the day when he realizes the full impact of his handicap on his life. When this day comes, the jolt can make him withdraw completely or become embittered and hostile. He may suddenly decide there is nothing good about him. He may try to make himself completely objectionable because he wants to be ostracized from group living.

When I was counseling ten-year-old Beth, she was hostile in every group she was in. She said, "I know I'm not wanted by them because I walk and talk this way. I can't keep up with them anyway. And I know what they were going to say about me before they even said it . . . so I spit on them. They told their mothers, and now when they see me they say I can't play with them. I'd rather play alone anyway because then no one sees these legs that don't act right, and if my hands jerk I don't have to worry about kids laughing at me."

It is not only the child with a severe disability who withdraws. A child with a mild handicap suffers the same ridicule. Parents can easily fall into the trap of discounting their child's mild impairment and pressing him to perform as well as a normal child. This only pressures him to try and act beyond his capacities. This became evident in the case of Susan.

Susan was an only child, whose family gave her everything. They expected her to do as well or better than the physically and mentally normal child in all her activities. Although Susan's handicap was mild, she had difficulty writing with a pencil and coloring with crayons. Before sending her to school, Susan's mother spent many hours each day teaching her to color outline drawings. The task was difficult for Susan because her hand jerked frequently. Every time she did not color within the lines, her mother took the picture away, tore it up, and gave her another one. She hoped that constant practice would make Susan color as well as her friends.

This method of training had repercussions when Susan entered school. When the teacher passed out pictures for coloring to the thirty or so children in the class, Susan made no effort to do hers. It was only after several days of urging by the teacher that Susan admitted that she did not want to color because she was afraid to let the other children see her messy work. She told the teacher that her mother had said that if she did not color as nicely as the other children, they would not like her. Her teacher asked Susan what she wanted to do about it. Typically she chose to withdraw. She chose to color by herself at a table in the corner of the room where the other children could not see her.

The teacher knew that such withdrawal tendencies could develop into a habit affecting Susan in later life. To help avoid this, she urged Susan to show her work to her classmates. When she did, the teacher made a special point of praising Susan's efforts. By explaining Susan's problems in drawing and coloring to the other children, the class developed the habit of commenting on how well she did a picture and began inviting her to color and draw at their tables. When it was discovered that Susan colored easily on wide areas, she was assigned the job of coloring in the wide space of green fields on a wall mural the class was working on as a project. Her pride in this assignment gradually minimized her fear of working with her classmates. Soon she wanted to join her classmates in coloring as well as other class activities.

Behavior then is the product of a child's early fears and his feelings about himself. When parents understand these fears and teach the child who he is and what his worth is to himself and those around him, he will be given the greatest gift ever.

Frustration at Mealtimes

Hunger is one of the three basic drives in man that demand satisfaction. If a handicapped individual who is feeding himself spills his food before he can get it to his mouth, he may find it difficult to control his temper after repeated failures. This can be minimized by gauging how able he is to feed himself and how much help and encouragement he may need to keep trying. Too much pressure and frustration has the same effect that an unpleasant emotional scene has on a non-handicapped person; the muscles of his stomach tighten, causing poor digestion.

Temper Tantrums

All youngsters at one time or another exhibit temper tantrums. There can be many causes for these tantrums. With the average child it usually is a way of getting attention or an attempt at getting his own way. This can also be true of the handicapped child and teenager.

In many instances, however, the basis for the tantrum can be frustration, a desire to accomplish doing something himself but being physically and/or mentally incapable. In other instances the cause may be a method of trying to make himself understood. In this case the more his wish or idea is misunderstood the stronger the temper becomes. This can be true of the youngest of children as well as in the case of the teenager or young adult. The handicapped individual's temper can become quite potent under certain circumstances. As his level of frustration rises, and should he be unable to speak clearly, he may pound on a table, kick over a chair, scream, or yell.

The best thing to do at such times is not to join in the individual's anger, but to make an effort to quiet him down and try to get him to talk about what point he is trying to get across. This method can be used with all age groups. If temper tantrums are a common occurrence, and the handicapped person will not lend himself to talking out his frustrations, the best thing to do is leave him to himself and let him get it out of his system. Put him in a room by himself and give him a pillow to hit and throw around, or give him two mallets and encourage him to beat them as hard as he can on the floor, or his bed or even on an overstuffed chair. This technique will get across to him that you recognize his predicament and that at the same time you are giving him a chance to beat it out of his system at least for the time being.

Using the Handicap As an Excuse

Excuses! There are few individuals that at one time or another have not tried to hide a fault behind an excuse.

The handicapped individual, be he mildly or severely involved, be he physically handicapped or have minimal brain damage, can usually conjure up a good excuse to hide behind. The range is wide: a child throws his dinner plate on the floor at mealtime, a teenager or young adult does not try to do his best in school or on a job, or takes no pride in his grooming. With the child it might be easy to say, "Stop using your handicap and get down to doing this." But with the older individual it may be necessary to be more direct, to honestly point out his fault and to let him know that his handicap can be no excuse for something you are sure he is able to do. Some individuals hide behind aggressiveness and think that their handicap will cover for them. Other individuals may sit withdrawn and show no effort to help themselves when they are perfectly capable of doing so.

The objective in this situation is to figure out which is real and which is unreal. Can the individual, within his handicapped limitations, do a certain task or not? This usually can be detected easily by drawing him into conversation and asking him what kind of game he is trying to play. The important thing to get across to him is that you want him to do his best and not to hide under any disablement he may have. The aim should be to encourage him to step out of his warped shell and become a part of the world around him.

Toilet Training

The attitude and approach of parents in early training has great impact on the way in which the handicapped child deals with his physical urges and desires. If he is treated with respect and helped to develop a sense of personal dignity and modesty, his toilet training will be comparatively easy to accomplish.

If a child of two, three or even older is permitted or even encouraged to use a toilet chair in the living room or kitchen rather than in the bathroom because it saves steps for the parent, it hardly comes as a surprise that he will have no reluctance to relieve himself anywhere and at any time. Since you have used his handicap to justify toileting him in places other than the bathroom—something you would not tolerate in a normal child—he concludes that his handicap gives him license to relieve himself as he chooses.

The "habit" method, (placing the child on the toilet at periodic times rather than training him to be physically aware of his needs) used with children of retarded intelligence is unfortunately often used with the handicapped child of average or superior intelligence. This can happen when a parent is not informed about the importance of teaching a child to learn and practice voluntary control. Sometimes it happens because parents do not know whether their child has enough intelligence to reason and understand what is said to him. Too quickly, they adopt the "habit" form of response—a substitute for the intelligent response of a child who knows what he is doing—and apply it to walking, talking and other self-help skills. If such a method is fostered and followed, the child can grow up giving the impression that he is mentally retarded or emotionally unstable or immature.

Toilet training for any child should not begin before a child is physically ready. This time varies in individual children and certainly with handicapped children. Catching the child at suitable time intervals is not toilet training—it simply cuts down on laundry. Shaming him or telling him, "Big boys don't wet their pants," is undesirable because by implication it is telling him that he is a baby and that these body eliminations of his are dirty and disgusting. Your own attitude toward elimination tends to carry over into your tone and manner when speaking of it to your child. It is from you that he will learn that toileting is customary, and in time he will learn to use its facilities as other people do.

When you take him to the bathroom and shut the door, it conveys to him without further discussion that toileting himself is a private business and not necessarily for others to see. Thus you encourage him to want privacy, and in so doing you help him develop that sense of self which is essential to everyone and vital to the physically handicapped. Encourage him to say as he leaves the room to go to the bathroom, "Excuse me," or if his speech is unintelligible and you are helping him you might say, "Will you excuse us?" It implies to him that his desire to eliminate must be satisfied in the bathroom or in a room by himself and not in a room filled with other people. It impresses upon him that there is a time and place to satisfy all desires. He is thus encouraged to control and discipline his own body feelings and urges as he grows older.

"Sounds fine on paper," you say, "but it isn't that easy." Of course it isn't. The only consolation is that parents of non-handicapped children say exactly the same thing. Toilet training is a problem in many homes for a variety of reasons. Often it is simply because parents rush their children and want them trained at one or two years of age. Another reason is that the mother's own feelings about the matter are on the whole rather negative. She may dislike handling a full diaper and be repelled by excrement. Inevitably she imparts to the child a feeling of distaste and uncleanliness that makes the project an uninviting one for him. There are children too, who can effectively show their displeasure. Sometimes they wet their pants or fill them because they are jealous of a new baby and compete for the same kind of loving care. Sometimes they perform to express the anger they feel toward a parent for something done that day. The reaction they get when they are detected may not be exactly what they had in mind, but it is a reaction and that is a small satisfaction.

Almost any parent of a normal child will tell you that the greater the pressure and the more admonitions to be a "big boy," the less successful the whole training experience is likely to be. The same rule holds for your handicapped child. He wants to please, just as every child wants to accommodate himself to the wishes of his parents and peers. All that the handicapped child needs is time, patience and understanding of his problems. You need the same.

There are mechanical aids you can provide to help your handicapped child feel physically secure and relaxed in the bathroom and in toileting situations. Bladder and bowels function best when the child feels certain that he will not fall or lose his balance. Following are some suggestions you might try:

1. Place handrails around the basin and toilet area so that your child can grab them to balance while washing at the basin or standing at the toilet or pulling himself on and off the toilet.
2. To give your child sitting balance when it is necessary, cut the legs off a child's armchair, make a toilet hole in the seat, and put grippers on it to clamp over a regular toilet seat.
3. Provide a brightly colored box to serve as a footstool under his feet while he is seated on the toilet. It will give him an extra sense of security if his braced or non-braced feet or legs rest on the box instead of swinging loosely in mid-air.

5

Discipline

A well-disciplined child is easier to accept.

If the care of the handicapped child merely involved feeding and housing him, there would be few problems for parents to worry about. Some handicapped children will have behavior problems not only because they are handicapped, but because they are children.

Disciplining a Handicapped Child

"Should you discipline a handicapped child?" The answer is yes. You not only should but you *must* if he and his family are to live together happily.

Let us begin by understanding discipline, as used here, in a positive sense. It is not punishment, but training designed to help a child learn to control himself. It is the most important thing your child can learn, and with it he can teach himself many skills. He can learn the difference between right and wrong on even the most elementary level. If he doesn't learn this, he may appear to be mentally retarded and act without self control.

Where Does Discipline Start?

Discipline starts in the home. It begins with the parents. Unless the parents exercise discipline they can become so emotionally involved and feel so sorry for their child that they ask nothing of him. Or, they may discipline their child too sternly. Continued use of either technique creates more problems as the child grows older. By asking nothing of the child, parents doom him to immaturity and infancy. By pressing the child unreasonably, tensions are created within him that may cause physical and/or emotional problems.

The child's handicap can present the parents with a multitude of problems. In terms of simple efficiency, it is worthwhile to figure out how both the parents and their child can deal with these problems with the minimum of harrassment and irritation. To do this, the parents must face the handicap squarely, realize the limitations it imposes, the potentials of the child's physical and mental condition, and the disciplines both parent and child must acquire. When parents forget what their child can and cannot do, when they become irritated and lose patience or threaten him because they feel that he is not performing because of stubbornness or laziness, they lose command of the skills they possess to help him. The more undisciplined they permit themselves to be, the more undisciplined they can expect their child to be. The conclusion is all too plain. For the parents to discipline their child, they must discipline themselves.

Uncontrolled Discipline

Uncontrolled discipline, as used here, is defined as a form of punishment that inflicts physical pain on a child. It refers to parents who lose control of themselves and may slap, shake, or deprive their child of a meal.

Among parents of non-handicapped children, there are endless discussions and debates on the advantages and disadvantages of spanking. One can make a convincing case for either side. But, for the parents of a handicapped child, discipline by physical punishment is something that needs to be studied carefully. The need for physical discipline may come when a parent is angered by the unwillingness of a child to perform some simple skill despite repeated instructions. But, why is it of such significance in the case of a handicapped child?

If a child's nervous system has been damaged, fear, frustration, and anxiety affect him physically and emotionally. His stomach ties up in knots, he is less able to exercise self-control, and his whole body may literally start to shake. Physical punishment can give him a feeling of worthlessness and a disgust for his body that can grow as such treatment continues. It can have an effect on how he comes to regard other people. He may reason that if his parents hit him when he does not perform as he is told, other people will want to hit him also. His fear of punishment can make him cower before people and affect his social relationship with them. If he is unable to speak intelligibly, a child harboring degrading thoughts of himself can be in a constant emotional state.

He fears many things. If he has poor speech he is afraid he will not be able to explain why he should not be punished. He may be afraid he will not be able to protect himself from the pain that is about to be inflicted from a spanking. He fears when the punishment is over his parents may not like him.

His growing self-image becomes, in his mind, an object *deserving* of abuse. Continued physical punishment can cause him to ignore the abuse to his body and even to welcome it. Perhaps the most distressing problem resulting from physical punishment is submissiveness. The child develops a growing conviction that he is worthless and may submit to anything he is told to do. He can lose his innate individuality and never become master of himself. This grows worse as he enters into adulthood. He responds only to harshness. Any other approach will seem insincere to him. At school, in a treatment center, or later on a job, he may find it difficult to make adjustments to reasonable, non-threatening requests.

For example, uncontrolled discipline used on a child with cerebral palsy can be devastating. The excitement it creates on the child's nervous system is significant. Speech may become incoherent. The child is too upset emotionally to comply with any directions given him. When this is not recognized, you waste a lot of valuable training and learning hours.

There is but one conclusion: rule out uncontrolled discipline for the handicapped child.

Controlled Discipline

Controlled discipline assures that the parents are taking a constructive approach to correcting the behavior of their child. Instead of showing uncontrolled anger, they deal with the problem in a way that eliminates shock to the child's nervous system, minimizes uncoordinated body movements, and lessens the chance of his developing a feeling of worthlessness.

Controlled discipline calls on a child's reasoning powers and ability, however limited, to explain his behavior. It requires that parents know everything about his physical and emotional capabilities They must not only understand the behavior of the child but the growth and behavior patterns of children of all age levels. For example, a normal child of two and a half or three is at a peak of independence and aggressiveness. Knowing this will help parents understand why their handicapped child of two and a half or three (or the mental equivalent) is behaving badly in a confined situation.

If parents want to motivate and encourage good behavior in their child, it is of the utmost importance that they learn and understand how his body functions, what his reactions are likely to be to various stimuli, and how they can help him move through constructive channels to reach an acceptable level of social behavior. The tools for this are self-discipline, praise and encouragement. The rewards are confidence and improved skills; and with them come self-control.

Let's consider eight-year-old Nancy, who is introduced to the techniques of walking with crutches by her doctor, therapist or parent. At first this may be a terrifying experience for her. She understands that it will give her a chance to get around by herself, but she also is aware that she can fall and hurt herself. She resolves the situation by throwing her crutches down and refusing to use them.

Reason tells Nancy that if she does not expose herself to the danger of falling, she is not likely to get hurt. This is the same reason that her parents must now appeal to her, calmly and without irritation. The parents agree that she might fall, but explain to her that she can learn how to fall and not hurt herself. She can wear a football helmet to avoid bumping her head when she begins to walk. She must learn that it will take practice on her part. Threats and punishment may make Nancy pick up her crutches and try again, but they will never motivate her to try getting around by herself.

The handicapped child, like the normal child, often misbehaves because he does not know how to deal with a problem in a socially acceptable way. He deals with it in the only way he knows, and will continue to do so until he is taught a better way. For example, six-year-old Betty's wheelchair was placed near the dinner table while her mother was preparing the evening meal. Betty promptly leaned over and deliberatively pulled on the tablecloth, scattering silverware, and china all over the floor. Her mother's reaction was to give her hand a good slap. But when Betty persisted in doing this, instead of slapping her, her mother resolved the problem by moving the wheelchair out of reach of the table. It was a solution to the mother's problem, but a poor one for Betty. It did nothing to discipline her. It did not teach her why it was wrong to pull on the tablecloth. It did not help Betty's mother understand why her child repeatedly misbehaved in this fashion. Clearly the situation called for controlled discipline as we understand the term: constructive correction, for the purpose of teaching.

In a counseling session, I reminded Betty's mother that all children generally misbehave for a reason. It may be to attract attention, to prove oneself before others, to gain recognition or to get back at a parent. Whatever the reason may be, there is always a basis for it. Most children would rather behave and win approval from their parents and friends.

In Betty's case, I found that she was being left too long by herself. She resented this and to make sure that nobody forgot her, by pulling the tablecloth off the table, she found a way to remind her mother that she was there. Who can deny that she was successful? It made her mother pay attention to her, even if it was only to scold her, and gave Betty the attention she was seeking.

During a series of counseling sessions, I pointed out to the mother that the solution to this problem was not difficult; and far less so than the problems that would ultimately have been created by repeated physical punishment. Betty's mother was urged to take pains to move her where she happened to be working, and found worthwhile jobs for Betty to do during her busy times so that Betty could appreciate her own worth. Jobs such as folding napkins, sorting silverware, or unravelling a sweater became the solution. When left alone for a time, it was with an activity to keep her interest. A clock ticking away merrily with a pasted arrow on it showing when mother would return, which gave Betty an idea how long she would have to be alone.

Techniques in Discipline

A good technique for parents—and techniques are what parents need to acquire—is to seat the child in his chair away from the others in the group. He should be told that what he did was wrong and why the parents think he did it. The parent should further explain that he is being left to himself for a short time, to give him a chance to think about what he has done wrong. They should tell him that they will be back to talk it over with him in a little while. Angry, emotionally over-wrought normal children are frequently disciplined in this manner except that they are told they must remain in their room. It is an opportunity for them to simmer down, as it is for the handicapped child. After a short time—and I emphasize that it should not be destructively long—the parent should encourage the child to tell why he misbehaved, and listen without interruption. When the parent feels he is ready, he should talk with the child about why such behavior is not acceptable to others. It is a first step in teaching the child to think before he acts and to exercise self-control.

This kind of discipline may have to be repeated many times, for many reasons, and often parents may lose patience. But they will learn self-discipline along with their child because it is the only way that they can help him. It is like the old fairy tale of the prince who magically turns a fish he has caught into a beautiful princess but is warned that if he strikes her thrice he will lose her forever. Each time parents are uncontolled and punish their child in an uncontrolled manner, they lose more of his confidence in them, and ultimately they may lose all of it.

What if a child has unintelligible speech and cannot explain what is bothering him? Parents must speak for him and ask him to gesture in some way: by raising his hand, blinking his eyes, and so on, to answer a question relating to his misbehavior. For example, the first question to Teddy might be: "Do you know why you did this?" Even though Teddy may not be able to answer clearly, the question requires that he think and then answer yes or no in his own way of communicating. Should he gesture yes, the next question might be: "Do you think you should be punished for doing this?" In most cases Teddy may answer *"No!"* If this is the case, his parents need to ask him questions that take a yes or no answer and that will explain why he thinks he should not be punished. Just because his parents think he should be punished does not mean that Teddy agrees with them. In his terms, what he did might be fully justifiable. To find out what he is thinking, they might ask: "Did you do it to get mother to come near you? Were you lonely? Do you want to make more work for mother? Are you mad at mother? Did I make you angry by doing such and such?" Was it this, or that? The parents may ask these questions, depending on what they know of the situation and how well they know their child. This helps them to understand why he is misbehaving.

Nothing is gained by asking the guilt-inducing question, "Aren't you a bad boy to do what you did?" This only confirms the child's conviction that his parents think he is bad. If parents accept the fact that children misbehave for a reason, they can completely eliminate any identification of the child as being good or bad.

The answers to their questions may be apparent in several of his physical responses. He may display a great deal of hostility in his body motions. He may try to strike or kick at his parents. Or he may jump up an down in his chair, pound his hand on the table and yell. Less dramatically, he may simply pout or frown.

When parents question their child, they should be sure to accept his answers. They may decide that thay are not the true reasons, but that is different from not accepting them. Their child must feel that they believe in him; only then will he make the effort to tell them what is on his mind. If they wave him aside or scoff at his reasons or shout him down, he will soon stop telling them.

It would perhaps be well to offer a word of caution about *controlled discipline*. Parents may pride themselves on their self-discipline and boast that they have never lost their temper or struck their child. The fact is that there are many ways to punish a child cruelly without even laying a hand on him. A slap can do grave damage to a handicapped child, but at least its one virtue is that the sting does not last long. A degrading word about a child, however, can stay in his memory for years and become a bitter hurt for him to mull over. One of the child's hardest jobs is to develop a good opinion of himself as he matures. Parents who call their child bad repeatedly, soon convince him that he is bad. After all, he may reason, they are his parents, and if they say it is so, it must be so. He is apt to adopt his parent's momentary feeling about him as his own permanent opinion of himself—a bad, worthless, handicapped boy or girl.

Maintaining Consistency in Discipline

Parents should give discipline warnings they think necessary and stick with it. If they tell the child he cannot watch his TV program because he misbehaved despite several reminders, no amount of tears or begging should change the parent's mind. The child must not think that he can avoid being disciplined by crying or begging. He will know what his parents expect of him in a given situation and will know what he can expect if he defies them. Parents will find that it will help the child feel more secure. He will know that he can rely on what is said to him. His trust in his parents will be stronger. But remember, give him plenty of warnings. He *is* a child.

Agreeing on the Type of Discipline to Be Used

Generally, it is the mother who cares for the handicapped child most of the day. She spends effort and energy helping the child to learn self-help skills and how to behave correctly. She may not give in lightly when father comes home. The father, on the other hand, has had a hard day at work, but often is more willing to waive the rules of discipline. The result is a confused child. He senses that there is a difference in the way his two parents treat him. This does apply to both handicapped and non-handicapped children. Father often becomes the favorite parent because he does not make the child struggle as much as mother to behave and accomplish skills. Sometimes the child will conclude that the father loves him more, and that his mother is the one who makes him do hard things. His childish interpretations may be that she isn't fun, she doesn't love him, she makes him cry. For this reason he may want to be with his daddy all the time.

As he tries to evaluate each parent and how they feel about him, he is faced with conflicts that create anxiety within. The child cannot respond to two different types of discipline. It is important therefore, that the parents discuss and agree upon the way disciplinary actions are to be handled.

Don't Look for Complete Obedience

How much discipline is too much? This is a question parents of handicapped and non-handicapped children often wonder about. It does not always follow that because the child understands the consequences of certain misbehavior he will refrain from repeating that behavior. Flexibility in dealing with him is good sense. This is not to be confused with indecision and inconsistency. The extent of the child's handicap should serve as a guide. An example might be Kevin, who may find it too much of a problem to ask permission to do a specific thing before he does it. He may reason that if he had asked permission his parents would not grant it. Or, his own reason for doing something might, in his mind, justify what he did. If Kevin's parents consistently punish him for reasons he thinks unfair (because the parents have not made an honest attempt to draw him out and get his explanation) they will lose rapport with him and his confidence.

If Kevin's parents are reasonable in their demands on him, they are less likely to meet with resistance and misbehavior. Asking him to do more than he is capable of doing because it satisfies their needs to show progress and improvement soon creates problems between Kevin and his parents. Kevin needs to succeed in what he does as do all people.

Use a Stern Discipline Technique Where Necessary

Some handicapped children, although average or better in intelligence, have difficulty in thinking things out and making decisions for themselves. They often find it difficult to concentrate on what is said to them. They may be thinking of other things such as wondering whether they are going to fall, keeping up with the others, or be concerned that their uncontrolled arms or legs may accidentally hurt someone or break something. The reasons are valid enough and explain why such a child, distracted by so many problems, is unable to grasp quickly what he is told to do. He is not concentrating on what is being said to him.

To discipline such a child by slapping or spanking him gains nothing. The best approach is a *controlled* technique that will help him direct his thinking towards the specific matter at hand. There are several ways of maintaining his attention. One is to take both wrists, look him straight in the eyes, and ask him to look at you while you speak to him. The grip on his wrists will alert him to listen to you as you explain to him why his behavior was not correct. If you scold him emotionally with such comments as, "I don't know what I'm going to do with you!" or, "Don't you know any better?" he may become excited, angry and more unmanageable.

6

Problems of the Teenager

The teenage years are the most crucial years for any boy or girl. They are years of both physical and emotional change in the growing body. But because of a handicap, their problems may be larger and more serious. One day Sally can be quite a young lady, but let her go under major surgery and she reverts to being Mother's little girl. Johnny can wake up one morning, look in the mirror, see fuzz on his face, start to shave and is sure he can lick the world. Late that afternoon he topples off of his bike, breaks his arm, and is mighty glad to have Mother and Dad around to hear his whimpers of pain. All in all, the teenage years are full of peaks and valleys for any boy or girl.

Boys and girls can be in perfect health, possessing all their physical capabilities, and go through these stages of change; or they can be mildly or severely handicapped and go through the same changes. The only difference is that the teenage growth traumas for the non-handicapped do not usually last as long as they may for the handicapped teenager.

Being Handicapped

Is the handicapped boy or girl prepared for spurts of growth common to teenage years? Many are, and many are not. Some keep nearly abreast with the non-handicapped teenager's growth and development, others lag behind. Which pattern of development the handicapped takes depends upon the manner in which he has been handled in years past by parents, teachers, and others helping him along the way. If he has been babied and coddled, an immature teenager will develop. If he has been given a lot of opportunity to exert himself as much as possible in all areas of development, then a relatively "mature" teenager will emerge.

One of the clues to whether the handicapped teenager is immature or not, is whether he has made a good adjustment to himself. Is he aware of what he can and cannot do? Is he adjusted to the fact that he has certain mental and/or physical limitations? If he isn't, he will find it hard to fit into any group his age. If he has made a good adjustment to his condition, he will be readily accepted.

If he has reasonable intelligence at the age of twelve or fourteen, now is the time to define his handicap to him. Do it carefully. Give him bits and pieces of information. Let him ask the questions about his condition. If he asks whether he will die from his condition tell him we all die sometime. If he asks wheher he will be able to do this or that as Jimmy next door does, do not give him false hopes. If it is quite obvious that he may not walk as well as Jimmy or read or learn as easily as Jimmy, tell him so. Put all the facts on the table. Let him know where he stands as a disabled individual.

No Longer a Child

When the twelfth or fourteenth birthday passes, teachers and parents (as well as the rehabilitation team) must change their ways of thinking. They are no longer handling a child but now have a teenager on their hands. Now he must be treated as such. Talking to him, helping him physically, if he needs it, should be done on a more mature level than it was done when he was a child. Encourage him to act his age, to control his emotions, and to think of people other than himself.

It won't be easy for some handicapped people to mature in a physically limited world. They will have to make the adjustment the best way they can. They will have to figure out ways of finding their niche in life. Sometimes this will be easy, other times it can prove quite difficult. But, the niche must be found if the teenager and young adult is to find any happiness in life. To help him do this is not to raise false hopes.

Another way to help is to guide him to goals within his reach. If Edith has poor speech but reasonable intelligence, and wants to be a teacher, steering her into a more realistic career will save her many a heartache. People with poor speech do not make good teachers. If George has had a learning disability throughout his early years and reading and math are difficult for him, maybe he should not go to college. Perhaps going to a trade school that would train him in a vocation within his limitations would be the best answer for him. Whichever the case, the important thing is that the teenager be guided to enter a field of interest in which he can be successful and reap the rewards of accomplishment.

All teenagers have problems, and the sooner they are recognized and corrected or minimized the better. Some are carried over from childhood, others crop up during the teenage years. One prevalent problem with which I have had considerable experience is the so called "teenage depression" syndrome. The non-handicapped can experience this problem; the handicapped teenager can experience it also. It is usually due to a low opinion of oneself, friction with parents, or difficulty finding his niche in life. Or, it can be a combination of all three problems. Whichever it is, it is frightening to the teenager. Many times it affects his school work and social relationships with his peers. He may withdraw from associating with those around him and spend a great deal of time wondering what is wrong with him.

I have seen this particular problem often among handicapped teenagers. Sometimes they are very emotional; other times they are totally silent. In each instance, the problem is very real to the individual. The best way to help him is to engage him in activities he can do and encourage him to develop relationships with other teenagers his age. This will help him come out of himself and look around, instead of sitting like a bump on a log assuring himself he has no purpose in life because of his handicap.

Sex

Another special problem is in the area of sex.

Ted's parents were concerned over reports from school concerning his sexual behavior. Their complaint was that he was masturbating excessively, and had an uncontrollable curiosity concerning other boys and girls. Pupils reported to the teacher that during recess, or lunch hour, Ted would suggest that the boys take off their clothes so they could compare their sex organs. Ted had also been observed examining his own sex organs in the boys' lavatory. He seemed to exhibit no concern when the teacher discovered him doing this. His response was, "I need to!"

Many thought he lacked the mental ability to control his sex impulses. Others attributed his behavior to the fact that because he was handicapped, such behavior should be expected. Ted's overall pattern of emotional adjustment was flecked with signs of anxiety and inadequacy related to his sex feelings. He had a fear of his compulsive desire to satisy his sex drives.

My analysis of the case revealed that Ted's fear permeated his emotional pattern. This was further revealed in counseling sessions when Ted expressed that *he* felt his daily environment was composed of aggressive, harmful factors directed at him and that he could not adequately handle them. The counseling sessions allowed him to release pent-up feelings of apprehension. Ted expressed these in hysterical emotional outbursts followed by periods of depression. Every aspect of his make-up became concerned with satisfying his sexual desires. My chances of diverting his thinking were very slim.

When discussing his parents, it was revealed that the relationship between them and Ted was strained. He described his mother as unsympathetic and stubborn. She was one of the sources from which Ted's problems stemmed. However, Ted would not accept this fact. He was emotionally attached to her and dependent upon her, and rebelled if any disparaging reference was made toward his mother. But he harbored repressed feelings against her.

His feelings toward his father were tinged with guilt. He avoided him. "He is a crab. He doesn't like me around. If I could do more for myself, Mother would have more time to spend with him. But, she must always be with me. This makes my father mad. He says I should do more for myself. But *I* need mother to help me," Ted reasoned.

Since the father could not get away from his place of business, all the counseling sessions were done with Ted and his mother. Efforts were made to reveal some of the causes for Ted's behavior. The mother was asked a series of questions. Her answers were as follows:

> "Well, lately we have noticed him fooling around with his sex organs. We tell him to stop—that big boys don't do that—but he does not pay any attention to us. And, too, he always wants to come into my bedroom when I'm dressing. If I tell him he can't, he raises a big fuss. One day I locked him out and he got so mad that he kicked at the door until he broke the lock. This behavior is embarrassing to my husband and me. We are afraid it will occur when we are away from home. We don't want to take him anywhere any more. We never know when he might start acting up again. After all, he is fifteen years old! None of our friends' boys act this way."

To the question: How did you feel when you were first told that your son would be handicapped all his life? Her answer was:

"I nearly died! At first I was very disappointed. Then I got mad that it had to be my child. I did not know how I could face the world. Then one day I said to my husband that from that day on I was going to devote my whole life to Ted. I told my husband that I did not want to have any more children. Ted hasn't been out of my sight for a minute—that is, until he entered school. I've allowed no one else to care for him. I cringe every time I think of the days I was disappointed, mad or thought I could not face the world because my child was handicapped. That was wicked of me to have thought that way about my own child."

These were obvious feelings of deep guilt on the mother's part. Questioning her further, she said:

"When he was three years old, a doctor told me he thought that Ted could learn. Then, when he was six years old, I was told that I could send him to school. This was hard for me to do. However, my husband made me send him. Then, all these sex problems began to crop up. I couldn't believe the teacher when she told me Ted had such problems. I did not think he knew enough about such things. For instance, I never believed he could learn. Yet, he is in the eighth grade now. He is so helpless."

When I asked whether Ted could care for his personal needs such as dressing, washing, and toileting, the answer was:

"No! I don't know, I should say I've never let him try. I have always washed and dressed him, and cared for him at the toilet. In fact, I still do. His teacher thinks this is awful but how can you expect such a handicapped child to do these things for himself? The day the teacher made Ted care for himself at the toilet, he came home crying. Why? He didn't know how to take care of himself. He didn't even know how to use toilet paper!"

In a later counseling session, when the mother was asked whether she had explained sex to Ted, amusedly she said:

"Why no! Of course not! He has no sex feelings like other boys. I saw no reason to explain sex to him. As a boy of eight or ten years of age, I kept a "potty chair" for him in the hall. Also, he's always slept in my bedroom and still does. I am afraid I would not hear him if he cried in the middle of the night if he were in another room. When my husband is away on a business trip, Teddy sleeps in my bed with me. My sister was shocked at this. Her boy of fourteen has his own bedroom. But, he is not like my boy. My sister just doesn't understand about Teddy. I would not keep him in my room if he was a normal child. But with Teddy, there is no harm done by having him sleep in my bedroom.''

This attitude often causes twelve-, fourteen-, and sixteen-year-olds to act and often appear immature for their age. When they reach eighteen or twenty-one, they exhibit no self-control over their *normal* sexual desires. As in the case of Ted, too frequently there is a tendency to judge a child as a severely disabled human being, rather than as one with growing body hungers and desires and needing training in self-control.

Sexual adjustment in the child and the adolescent is of concern to parents, and is clearly pointed out in Ted's case. Sex drives are basic in every human being. In the case of the handicapped child, more self-control must be exercised. When this is the case, the child develops a sense of personal worth, directs his own feelings and desires, and is able to better control his physical needs.

If sexual self-control is not taught, the child matures finding it difficult to exhibit control in other areas. He exhibits impulsive behavior. His primary concern centers around satisfying uncontrolled sexual urges. He finds it difficult to develop social relationships with either sex as he grows older.

A case in point is nine-year-old Kenny, who could not take care of himself. He had to be propped up in order to sit; he had to be fed and dressed and toileted, which was done for him by his mother. One day when she came for a regular appointment with me, she said that while dressing Kenny for the appointment that morning, she noticed that he had an erected penis. ''I did not realize that he had any normal parts,'' she said. ''When I saw this I ran to get my husband to show him that our son had one normal physical part. He was surprised as I was and rather proud.''

Parents of girls are often surprised when they discover the first menstrual period of the twelve- or thirteen-year-old. They frequently think something harmful has happened to their daughter. One example was a mother who really was shocked when her daughter began to menstruate. She grabbed the child up in her arms and took her to the emergency room of the nearest hospital. She was sure that the child was internally injured. However, the doctors assured her that her daughter, although handicapped, was not injured but was experiencing her first menstrual period.

These are not uncommon assumptions for parents to make particularly if their child is severely handicapped. All they are aware of is that their child does not physically act like the children of their friends. They need to realize that under the physical handicap, regardless of the severity, there exists a normal human being with normal drives. There is a boy or girl who can be happy, naughty, or good. The solution to this problem depends upon:

1. Parents giving their child sex education at the right age.
2. Recognizing that he possesses all the physical needs and desires of other children his age.
3. Understanding that training in self-control can and must be undertaken by those around the child.
4. Encouraging him to develop a sense of mastery of self.

Entertaining Self

Many problems can be worked out by the teenager himself if he is given the chance. No teenager, unless he is in poor mental health, has to just sit around and do nothing. A little encouragement from an adult usually can put him in the swing of things. A boy or girl does not have to have perfect coordination to keep himself busy. According to his particular difficulty, he should be able to find something to do to entertain himself. A book placed in a book rack gave Tony the opportunity to do a great deal of reading even though he found it difficult to hold a book in his palsied hands. The telephone was Grace's answer. She developed quite a business via telephone while lying flat on her back. Every minute in her day, she was busy taking orders for a cosmetics company she represented.

These two cases show how the teenager can work out problems himself. Tony and Grace hardly have time to be depressed, withdrawn, or unhappy.

Reluctance to Grow Up

All teenagers experience fear at one time or another as they grow older. Acne might create insecurity about how they appear to others. Being too short or too tall creates another fear related to personal worth. Being busty or not busty enough can make a girl wonder if she is attractive. In all, many fears related to the self can become magnified in the teenage years.

The handicapped can experience all the usual fears—even more. Can I make my speech understood? Can I walk well enough that people won't stare at me? And will girls (or boys) want to date me? Such fears piled on top of ordinary fears of the teenage years can become stumbling blocks to the handicapped individual's total development. The best way to help him is to speak directly to him about his physical abnormality. Help the physical handicap become a reality to the teenager. If this is done he is given a chance to place it under his own control. When it isn't done, he may beome sullen and difficult.

The "you take care of me" attitude I have often seen in handicapped teenagers means that the boy or girl lacks the initiative to want to care for himself. He is often content to let those around him cater to his every whim. Bernie may be very capable of zipping up his pants, but refuses to do so because a non-handicapped brother can get hold of the zipper quicker and do it for him faster. Karen, with difficulty, may be quite capable of feeding herself, but it's much easier to have mother feed her. In both these cases what they are actually saying is, "You take care of me." They fear they cannot do it themselves.

What results is that the teenager becomes totally dependent on those around him. He will never discover what he might be able to do for himself. He becomes a family misfit. No one can do anything or go anywhere unless provisions are made to take care of the handicapped member of the family.

7

Adulthood

Acquiring the maturity of adulthood is a challenging part of any young person's life. If the individual is confined to a wheelchair or walks with crutches, walking unaided may seem easy in comparison to such a challenge. However, upon reflection, physical limitations may be a unique opportunity to make a significant contribution to the world. First, though, the individual has to want to make all the contributions to society he can within his limitations. This can be a smile, a laugh, or even a helping hand to somebody who never thought the handicapped adult could do anything for him. It is possible to show "normal" people of the world what life is really about, and by doing so help them in a way they could never repay the disabled person.

Physical limitations can often be used to help others. Loneliness, insecurity, or a lack of human dignity can be too much for anyone to handle. It is important that the handicapped person remember that when things get rough, everybody is watching him. He can help others by the very fact that he can change their lives. They look at the handicapped person and see the courage he has to fight on in life. This in itself can serve the non-handicapped young man or woman.

Everyone needs help in different ways. Each of us has his own disability, his own handicap. The fact that one handicap shows and another doesn't is no reason to think that one is the less burdensome than the other, or less real. The person with the handicap which does not show may need the physically handicapped person's help but in a totally different way. Many times when the able-bodied person sees a disabled person who has the courage to fight his physical limitations, he'll find the strength somewhere within himself to work toward overcoming his own handicap.

First Impressions

"Don't judge a book by its cover," has great meaning in many areas. First impressions are important because often they are how people judge us as social human beings. They often either like us or dislike us based on the first impression. They either want to see us again and get to know us better, or they turn from us and go their own way. What happens depends on the handicapped person.

Impressions consist of pleasing personalities, neat grooming, and a willingness to come out of ourselves and make other people feel comfortable with us. Sometimes this is difficult for the handicapped to do. He may be so involved with his own problems that he finds it hard to give of himself for the happiness of others. He will never learn to "reach out" unless he is given the chance to be with others.

If the individual appears to be carrying a constant grudge, other people will see this and turn from him. On the other hand, if the handicapped greets people with a smile and a warm word of welcome, he will be accepted for what he is—a person who is delightful to know. He does not have to buy his clothes at the most exclusive store to be well groomed. A clean, well pressed shirt or dress, shined shoes, and neatly combed hair is all that is needed to be well groomed. Anything less than this can be a detriment to him. If you are well groomed, smiling, interesting, and kind to yourself and to others, you are beautiful in the eyes of everyone.

Romance

Joys and sorrows, the happiness and frustrations, the winning and losing in love affairs are more times than not the most important aspect of any young person's life. It is often an important part of the young handicapped's life, also. He loses in love affairs more often than he wins. There is no quick and easy answer for him. The fact that he is handicapped makes social success much more difficult.

For most handicapped young men and women, the ages between eighteen and twenty-five are the most difficult. This is the time they begin to look around for someone with whom to spend the rest of their lives. The truth is that everybody is "checking out" everybody else. Each girl or boy with a flaw is put at the end of the list by friends of the opposite sex. Everyone is looking for the one perfect person— Prince Charming or Cinderella.

What is it that most young handicapped men and women look for in a person of the opposite sex? More than anything else they look for companionship—someone with whom to share their life. Most young people find that sharing is what makes a friendship special.

He or she does not have to dance like Fred Astaire; nor do they have to have the figure of a model to show off. Many think this is what brings a male and female together. But, it is not. There must be something more or the relationship will not last. The fact is that if the handicapped is trying to be a hit with somebody but things are not falling into place, all the wining and dining are not going to make the relationship fit together for an eternity.

I believe that if we bring all of the pitfalls of social relations together, we have the sum of the problems we all inevitably face in our attempt to find that special someone. Far more important though, is the joy that comes in knowing we have shared not only what we are, but also what we have, with someone, and that sharing has only begun. It's a feeling without explanation that begins as a simple mustard seed in each of us and never stops growing until it totally engulfs us and becomes a part of our very person each day.

Marriage

Marriage is not for everyone, handicapped or non-handicapped. It carries with it certain vital reponsibilities for both the man and woman. It cannot be a one-way street for either party.

In the case of the handicapped, marriage often seems the epitome of success and social acceptance. It embodies the word ''normal'' in the minds of most handicapped. Many fail to look beyond this point. A handicapped man may fail to realize the role he must play as the financial provider for his wife and very possibly children.

So, it comes down to whether the couple can make a go of it on their own as do their physically normal peers. They can do so if they plan ahead and are willing to realize that jobs may not come as easily to the handicapped person as to one with no disability. For two handicapped people to marry each other is quite acceptable if they can jointly work together to make it a success.

Patty and Jim, both physically handicapped, married in their early twenties. However, they soon discovered that they married not so much out of love for each other, as to legitimize their mutual sex urges. Jim had no job, and it would not be easy for him to find one. Patty had a greeting card business she operated from her parents' home which netted her barely enough for two people to survive.

They were married three months when Patty became pregnant. They were in a bind. Jim was having trouble finding a job, and now with a baby on the way, they had no alternative but to live with Patty's parents. Thus her parents now had to support both Patty and Jim.

How much better it would have been had this young couple intelligently and realistically planned their lives together before tying the knot for better or for worse.

When only one person is handicapped, the outcome is generally better. These marriages generally have as good a chance of being successful as average marriages. When the male partner is not handicapped and can be a reliable source of income for the family, a more successful marriage is possible.

The only possible source of trouble in such a marriage is the possibility that the handicapped partner's condition is hereditary. To be realistic, the couple should sit down before marriage and discuss this possibility. It never pays to go into anything unprepared thinking that time will fix it. The important thing is to talk the whole matter over with a competent physician so that everyone, members of both families included, are prepared for what may or may not happen.

As with all marriages, the choice of a partner should be given careful consideration. The handicapped person may be enticed into marriage by an undesirable man or woman. All handicaps are not seen by the naked eye. I have counseled cases where the handicapped individual has been attracted to a person who is a sexual pervert, homosexual, or finds it difficult to relate to people of his or her social peer group. The timid male, for instance, may be attracted to an attractive handicapped young woman because he feels inadequate to compete with his male peers for a good looking non-handicapped girl. The sad part is when one or the other of the marriage partners discovers the flaw in the marriage and suffers severely as a result.

This is not to say that the handicapped should not enjoy all the joys of a marriage. It does mean that marriage for the handicapped is as acceptable as for the non-handicapped. The only difference is that some minor precautions should be taken before the final step is taken.

Preparing for a Vocation

A vital aspect of the handicapped's life is whether he can be prepared for a job as he grows older. This makes the vocational rehabilitation counselor a vital member of the Rehabilitation Team. He should guide the handicapped person from the time he is sixteen or eighteen years of age through adulthood. He should ascertain that the individual is being trained in adequate ways for a job where he can either work full or part time, or maybe develop a business of his own. In some cases, he helps make the decision whether a boy or a girl goes to college and what he or she will study and prepare to be.

Often this part of rehabilitation has been overlooked. When this happens, a boy or girl reaches the ages of eighteen, nineteen or twenty prepared to do nothing in life. This results in a disgruntled, unhappy individual. He does not know where to go, what to do, or what he can or cannot accomplish. Yet, he may be an individual who, given the opportunity, can make something of his life. By this time he is not looking at doctors and therapists and teachers for help, but is looking to the vocational rehabilitation counselor or job placement specialist for guidance in his future life and what he makes of it.

To be a vocational success, the handicapped person needs to experience association with one or all of the following people:

1. Vocational Evaluator
2. Occupational Skill Instructor
3. Vocational Rehabilitation Counselor
4. A Psychologist familiar with the problems of the handicapped
5. Job Placement Specialist

These are the individuals who can give good training and guidance for a fruitful future vocational life. Following are the educational requirements for each individual:

I. *Work (Vocational) Evaluator*
   Shall meet one of the requirements listed below:
   A. Master's degree in an appropriate field and one year of experience in rehabilitation or other suitable experience.
   B. An undergraduate degree with three years of appropriate experience in such areas as:
   Education
   Industrial Arts
   Occupational Therapy
   Rehabilitation Counseling
   Psychology
   Social Sciences
   Manual Arts Therapy

C. Other combinations of experience and training or experience in industry and completion of specialized rehabilitation related courses which, in the judgment of the survey team, will meet the recommended practices.

II. *Occupational Skill Instructor*
   A. Be accredited by the State Department of Education, or
   B. Qualify as a journeyman through apprenticeship training and have one year of experience teaching a trade, or
   C. Other combinations of experience in industry and completion of specialized rehabilitation related courses which, in the judgment of the survey team, will meet the recommended practices.

III. *Vocational Rehabilitation Counselor*
   Should either:
   A. Have completed a vocational rehabilitation counseling curriculum, or
   B. Have completed a college degree and two years of full service in a vocational rehabilitation agency, or
   C. Have completed a graduate curriculum in counseling and guidance or psychology.

IV. *Psychologist*
   Shall have a master's degree in psychology from a recognized university.

V. *Job Placement Specialist*
   Shall have a bachelor's degree, plus two years personnel work experience or other combinations of experience and training which, in the judgement of the survey team, qualify the individual for the position.*

One of the first steps that has to be taken prior to a handicapped person's vocational training or placement is a history of his physical background, social background, and psychological background. Following are some check lists that may help those who are preparing an individual for vocational training and placement.

Standards for Rehabilitation Facilities and Sheltered Workshops, (Department of Health, Education and Welfare, Social and Rehabilitation Service, Washington, D.C., 1971).

I. *Vocational Readiness and Preparation:*
  A. The employable
      1. Vocational readiness
      2. Personality attributes
      3. Degree of handicap
      4. Possibility of employment
  B. Mental powers
      1. Observation
      2. Imagination
      3. Concentration
      4. Initiative
      5. Perseverance
      6. Ambition
      7. Thoroughness
      8. Will power
      9. Common sense
      10. Competitive feelings out of control
      11. Competitive feelings under control
  C. Is the teenager emotionally and socially ready?
      1. Do a survey
      2. Questions to ask
  D. Parents' attitudes
      1. Trying to predict his employability
      2. The employable
      3. The unemployable
      4. Planning for the future
      5. It is parents' responsibility
      6. Positive feelings
      7. Negative outlook
      8. Effects on your teenager
  E. Vocational needs to fill
      1. Emotional support
      2. Constructive advice
      3. Realistic assurance of success
      4. Faith in his ability whatever it is
      5. Understanding unique vocational problems
  F. Vocational counseling
      1. Injecting realism into it
      2. Adjusting job desires to skill or abilities
      3. The dictates of a handicap

4. Skills to train
5. Choosing a job
6. Developing vocational pose
7. The handicapped in the professions
8. Some professions and their physical requirements
9. The handicapped in the business world
10. Sometimes self-employment is best

II. *Tests That Can Be Used for Vocational Evaluation*
   A. Wechsler Adult Intelligence Scale
   B. Wide Range Achievement Test
   C. California Personality Test
   D. Kuder Performance Scale
   E. Moody Check Lists
   F. Purdue Form Board
   G. Vocabulary Scale
   H. Vineland Social Maturity Scale

Psychological Examination in Preparation for Vocational Placement

Most Bureaus of Vocational Rehabilitation in the country require that clients coming to them in search of employment undergo psychological evaluation in addition to the medical evaluation that the bureau usually offers. These psychological evaluations can give the vocational rehabilitation counselor a comprehensive "picture" of the client's total psychological profile. From this profile, the counselor can often determine whether the client needs vocational training or whether he is employable at all.

The following case of Harriet is a good example of what the vocational counselor needs to know before he can determine how to train her and/or place her in a job.

Name: Harriet
Birthdate: March 31, 1954
Life Age: 16 years
Purpose of Testing: Vocational Guidance

Tests Administered:
1. Wechsler Adult Intelligence Scale
2. Wide Range Achievement Test

3. Kuder Preference Record
4. California Test of Personality
5. Gates Reading Survey—Form 1 (for grades 3 to 10)

Observations:

This young woman dropped out of school (9th grade). Since then she has worked as a waitress. She is the oldest of four children (3 girls and 1 boy). According to her grandmother, with whom I had the opportunity to talk, she was lucky she got as far as the ninth grade in school. She said Harriet appeared to have a strong desire to learn, but had a bad teacher in the first grade.

Her home environment was not too stable. Her grandmother reports that her daughter (Harriet's mother) had an unstable personality. The girl's mother has been under psychotherapy for the past four or five years. Apparently Harriet was never strongly disciplined or encouraged to finish anything she started. However, when she was at her grandmother's house she adjusted well to her schedule and was polite and helpful.

It was my opinion that this young woman certainly was not intellectually retarded. In fact, it was felt that had she been made to remain in school, and had she received proper educational motivation, she may have made a good educational showing upon graduation from high school. The young woman spoke about being self-conscious about her large size for her age. She said her classmates often laughed and taunted her about this. This was one reason she gave for dropping out of school. There was no mention made by either the grandmother or the girl that she had any particular learning difficulty. I accepted this as fact after reviewing her test results.

Findings:
Wechsler Adult Intelligence Scale

On this revised individual test based on deviation IQ and designed to measure intelligence of young adults, Harriet received the following results:

Verbal Scale IQ	100
Performance Scale IQ	103
Full Scale IQ	99

The Full Scale IQ of 99 was at the 50th percentile in terms of the over-all populace and can be described as average. This young woman's general intellectual profile was consistent. Note that it ranges in IQ between 99 and 103. It appears that, due to Harriet's lack of formal education and her unstable home life, it would be best if she were to enter a trade school—preferably one where she could also experience dormitory life with her peers. Her test analysis revealed a good level of general information, average comprehension, average arithmetical ability, a good digit span memory, average speed of performance, and that she observed well important visual details.

Wide Range Achievement Test
This test consists of a battery of three tests measuring abilities in reading, spelling, and arithmetic. Harriet's scores are as follows:

Reading Grade Level	7.3
Spelling Grade Level	Kindergarten—5
Arithmetic Grade Level	3.9

In all three of these learning areas, the young woman rates at the 21st percentile or lower in accordance with her chronological age of 16 years.

Gates Reading Survey
This survey is used primarily to measure reading abilities between the grades of 3 and 10. The areas it covers are speed and accuracy, reading vocabulary, and level of comprehension. Harriet's grade scores on this survey were as follows:

Speed Grade Score	7.0
Vocabulary Grade Score	8.2
Comprehension Grade Score	6.9
Total Average Grade Score for the above	7.4

California Test of Personality
This scale requires the examinee to express his response by marking "yes" or "no" to questions involving personal and social adjustments. Each of the sub-adjustments are then expressed in percentiles and indicative of personality maladjustments, particularly where they may relate to vocational choices.

In the area of personal adjustment, Harriet showed average or above average tendencies. Her only low rating was in the area of sense of personal freedom. This could be directly related to her mother's reaction to her—she is said to either give her children unlimited freedom, or the reverse, very stoic, tight-reined and limited freedom.

In the area of social adjustment, Harriet rated about average. However, she exhibited more inconsistencies in this area than in the personal area. It will be noted that she shows a tendency to be anti-social.

This is not surprising because she gives the impression that she bullies others and participates in frequent quarreling. Her other social deficiencies fall in the areas of social standards and school relations. These low tendencies in adjustment correspond to the personal history taken from her and the grandmother as reported earlier.

However, regardless of the deficiencies, Harriet ranks at the 60th percentile in total adjustment.

Kuder Preference—Vocational

Harriet showed marked elevations in the areas of computational, literary, clerical, and artistic on this scale. To me, it indicates that this young woman may possess more innate potential than she was encouraged to develop during her school years. It is interesting to see that she ranks above the 50th percentile in such vocational areas as: computational, artistic, literary (about at the 75th percentile), and clerical.

Summary:

It must be noted that testing this young woman, was difficult at times. This was not because she could not do the things required, or did not understand them, but that she had a tendency not to apply herself. Once this was evident, I cracked down on her firmly and from then on, she performed well. As she took her test, her tendency to start a job but not complete it became quite evident. In view of this, it is then recommended that, if possible, any training she takes in a trade school be accompanied by motivation from her instructors. They should insist that once she begins a job she complete it to the best of her ability rather than stop in the middle of it just because she is bored.

Workshop Facilities

In the case of individuals who may never work outside in the community, a program should be devised so they can either prepare themselves for future employment in the community or encourage them in homebound work.

Many workshops solicit small subcontract jobs from companies in the community. Efforts should be made to interest the Chamber of Commerce in the community in Workshop Programs. A program should exist for continually placing handicapped persons who have become skilled in some job through a Workshop Program.

Following is a list of definitions which should be adhered to in a sheltered workshop's program:

Job Family: occupations grouped on the basis of similar job requirements such as tasks performed, work experience, training, skills, and knowledge.

Job Tryouts: work experiences, within the facility or in conjunction with outside industry, to assist the individuals to acquire knowledge, develop skills, and/or assess readiness for job placement.

Training in Occupational Skills: a planned and systematic sequence of instruction under competent supervision which is designed to impart pre-determined skills and knowledge with respect to a specific occupational objective or job family, and to assist the individual to adjust to a work environment through the development of appropriate patterns of behavior.

Training Services: the appraisal of the individual's capacity including work evaluation, work testing, providing occupational tools and equipment required by the individual to engage in such training, and job tryouts. Includes payment of weekly allowances to qualified individuals receiving these services.

Work Evaluation: the appraisal of the individual's capacity including patterns of work behavior, ability to acquire occupational skills, and the selection of appropriate vocational goals. It includes "work testing", job tryouts, and self appraisal.

Work Testing: the utilization of work, simulated or real, to assess the individual's productive, physical, psychological, and social capacities to perform in a work environment.

REMEMBER—

Respect yourself! Remember, your body might be disabled, but your mind is not.

Respect other people! Remember, you might be teaching them the most important lesson they ever learn.

Stick up for your rights! Remember, physical might doesn't make right.

Don't shirk your responsibilities! Remember, you have a unique opportunity in life. Don't blow it!

Don't be afraid to ask for help! Remember—everybody's got a handicap; he who helps you might need your help someday.

Be yourself! Just be yourself.*

---

* Henry Henscheild, *View of Life,* (National Easter Seal Society for Crippled Children and Adults, Inc., 1975).

8

Learning Disabilities

"Why can't this child learn like other children?" a teacher or parent may ask.

Many children have learning problems that are due to brain damage—an inefficiency in the working of the brain. Some of these children appear to be quite normal and rate average or better on intelligence tests. Other children may have physical handicaps as well as a learning problem. Both types of children may have difficulty taking in, sorting out, and connecting information from the world around them. They have problems with school work, and their particular type of brain injury can affect just about everything else they do. It can affect their behavior in general, their speech, their play, their ability to understand and get along with others.

There are many names used for this type of disability and the various problems that it causes. Perceptual motor handicap, neurological learning disorders, cerebral dysfunction, dyslexia, hyperkinetic syndrome, and conceptual handicap are some examples. Such learning disabilities are usually caused by certain degrees of brain damage. Other factors also suspected are infection, problems during pregnancy, genetic factors, and early experiences and accidents in the child's life.

Problems of the Child

It is necessary first to determine to what extent the child is brain injured and how it may affect his learning ability. There is no simple clear cut sign that identifies such inability to learn. The first step is a psychological evaluation. This will give the teacher, parents, and the psychologist an idea of what type of learning problem the child may have.

Frequently behavior problems accompany a learning disability. Opposite kinds of behavior patterns can be seen in the child with this disability. He may be physically overactive or underactive. It must be recognized that learning problems and sometimes behavior problems caused by various kinds of brain injury can result in other conditions such as emotional instability and immaturity, or hearing impairments. What is considered a sign of brain injury in an older child may be quite normal for a younger child. For instance, what may be considered a sign of brain injury in ten-year-old Tommy may be quite normal in four-year-old Billy.

Various types of brain injury can be complicated, and not fully understood. Parents and others handling the child should be aware that there is such a condition which may affect learning ability. Children with minor brain injuries often go without special help they need because their problems are either not recognized, or are wrongly assumed to result from laziness, poor motivation, "spoiling", or even mental retardation. Because of such assumptions, many children receive help only after suffering years of failure in learning and being able to get along with others. Such experiences can damage a child's personality development, his confidence in himself, and his ability to be successful in anything he tries to do. As more parents seek professional advice, more children with brain injury will be helped in their important early years.

Common Learning Problems

1. Hyperactivity: Many brain damaged children may be "hyperkinetic" or "hyperactive." Their physical movements are usually more active than other children their own age, and often their activity is without purpose or direction. This can be true of the child who only has a learning disability and no physical handicap as well as of the child who has a physical handicap and some other neurological impairment.

Throughout my practice, I have counseled numerous parents of brain injured children. Some of these children have only had minimal brain dysfunction, while others have been physically handicapped as well. It has been found that in both instances the learning disability has been similar.

In one counseling session with me, the mother of five-year-old Polly stated, "She cannot sit still for a minute. She never walks. She is running and jumping all the time. She is wild! She runs back and forth and touches everything she sees."

In another counseling session, seven-year-old Bill was physically disabled as well as having a learning problem. His mother reported how he pounded on his work table with a block or toy just to keep up a continuing noise and gain attention. Neither Polly or Bill could easily work on an assignment for fifteen minutes; to be quiet long enough to be read to was unbearable for them. Neither child could control themselves for even short periods of time.

2. Hypoactivity: Some children with brain damage are unusually inactive. We see this particularly with the child who has a physical disability as well as a learning disability. He is slow at finishing tasks. Rarely does he get excited over anything. He does not like to move about (or may not be able to move about physically), and seems very lazy. Because of his seemingly low energy, he is usually easy to look after and is thought of as a remarkably "good" child. In this instance there should be as much concern as there would be if he was hyperactive. A "lazy" brain is as big a block to learning as is a brain that causes a child to run all over the place.

3. Problems in Concentrating: The child's attention span may be short and may switch quickly from one thing to another as if everything at once around him were attracting his thoughts. He may be unable to concentrate on one idea at a time, or he may appear to be daydreaming a great deal. This can be observed in the non-handicapped as well as the physically handicapped child who has trouble controlling his physical motions—which can be distracting to him.

4. Irritability: The child with brain damage can be highly irritable. Things such as being touched, bumped, held by the hand, and some sounds and smells, irritate him more than other children his age. He may not be able to tolerate showers, tooth brushing, hair cutting or tight clothing. He may have an unreasonable fear of animals. He becomes easily frustrated and is more likely to explode into tantrums than the average child his age. To sum it up, it can be said that his moods are changeable.

5. Forgetting: Most children may forget how to do things. The child with a brain injury may easily forget how to do things. He may forget how to play a simple game that he learned the day before, or even where his toys are kept. How to follow simple directions can be difficult for him. This is all part of his learning disability and should be given careful attention.

6. Clumsiness: The child with brain damage may be clumsy and uncoordinated. This can range from a minor to major degree. Five-year-old Scott may not have learned to walk until he was two years old or older. In doing simple tasks he may easily become confused as to which hand to use. He may have trouble doing complicated activities such as dressing himself or learning to ride a bicycle. It may be hard for him to play constructively with toys. Such clumsiness may be overcome as he grows older or it may plague him the rest of his life.

7. Lack of Sense of Direction, Position, or Time: Betty may have trouble understanding what is meant by *up, down, behind, left, right, after,* and *before,* long after other children her age have mastered these ideas. This is particularly true in the child whose neurological pathways may require special development so that he can develop a sense of direction, position, or time.

8. Speech and Hearing Problems: Kathy may be slow in learning to talk, and when she does learn her speech may be unintelligible. She may have a hearing loss or a problem distinguishing between sounds. Sometimes with special training this can be corrected. In the case of David, who is grossly physically handicapped, it may be a problem that can be improved upon but will be a handicap to him for the rest of his life.

9. Impulsiveness: More than other children his age, the child with brain damage may seem to do whatever comes into his mind without thinking. His patterns of thinking may be disorganized. For this reason special training, for instance to help him concentrate, is needed at the earliest age possible.

10. Immaturity: Mary may be behind other children in many ways— learning to talk and walk, in her emotional control, and in her understanding. Or, she may show uneven development by being at the average child's level in some things and way behind in others. This may be particularly evident in the child who is unable to walk and get about by himself. However, it is equally true of the child who does walk and only has a learning disability with which to contend.

11. Getting Along With Other Children: As might be expected, the child with a brain damage of any type may not be accepted as a playmate by other children. Normal children may find him too babyish, bad tempered, too rough and spunky, or too slow or forgetful in learning games. These were Peter's problems. Children in his neighborhood did not want him in their play circles. He was left on the sidelines wistfully looking on.

12. Need for Immediate Satisfaction: The child must gradually learn to have patience—to wait when he cannot have what he wants right when he wants it, to keep trying when at first he fails at something he wants to do. To him the lack of immediate satisfaction may be unbearable. He cannot put off having what he wants, or go through the trial and error steps of learning. This he has to learn to do as he grows older.

13. Special Problems in Reading, Writing, Arithmetic: Although psychological tests may reveal the child to be intelligent, he may have serious problems in learning to read, write, spell or do arithmetic. For example, Darryl continued to fail to recognize simple words long after other children his age. He confused the word *was* with the word *saw* and the letter *B* with the letter *D* much longer than other children did. This is one reason why special techniques in educating such children are essential at an early grade level. To ignore the need for special help in learning is only to burden the child with the problem all his life.

We have outlined above how children with brain damage can be slow in learning to do one thing or another. Although a child's development can be judged accurately only by persons with special training, it is important his parents detect unusual delay in his learning to walk, to talk, or to feed himself, etc., and call it to their physician's attention.

Milestones in the Development of Children

The following list may be useful as a rough guide to some of the important milestones in development that can be expected in the preschool years. It should be remembered that every child develops differently and that variations from this guide may not be cause for alarm. Discuss suspected delays with the doctor in case they may be signs of brain injury that should be discovered at the age that learning becomes active.

1. SLEEPING:

About 10 months of age:	Begins to sleep though the night and takes 2 naps a day.
About 15 months:	Usually only one nap.
5 years:	Rarely naps and usually sleeps quietly through the night without wetting or going to the toilet.

2. SITTING:

7–9 months:	Sits on floor without support.

3. WALKING:
   12–18 months

4. RUNNING:
   21–24 months

5. FEEDING:
   2 years: Holds and drinks well from a cup.

6. TOILET TRAINING:
   2½ to 3 years: Can go to the bathroom on his own, manage his clothing, wash and dry hands.

7. THROWING:
   18 months: Throws ball, but only a few feet and with very poor aim.

   4 years: Can throw straight ahead and prefers to use one hand more than the other (he has become "right-handed" or "left-handed.")

8. LANGUAGE: There are great differences among normal children in how quickly their language develops. At two, many use over a hundred words and put together short sentences while others use only a few words. Nearly all children are talking by age three.

   18–24 months: Follows simple directions like: "Bring the ball to mother."

   3–4 years: Understands the differences between *in, on, under, behind, in front of, beside*.

   5 years: Can name colors (red, yellow, blue, green). Can count ten objects.

   6 years: Knows what is meant by "morning" and "afternoon".

9. DRESSING:
   4 years: Dresses and undresses himself with little help, knows which is front and which is back of the shirt, dress, or pants.

   4–6 years: Ties shoelaces.

10. PLAYING:
    18 months: Attention shifts quickly from one thing to another.

    2 years: Attention shifts less rapidly as interest in playing with toys and other objects grows. Begins to enjoy listening to stories and looking at pictures.

    3 years: Increasingly interested in playing with other children (not just alongside them). Shows use of imagination in putting together blocks, ar-

	ranging toy cars and furniture, dolls, etc. Listens to stories for much longer periods. Repeats songs and rhymes.
4 years:	Prefers to play with two or three other children. Will take turns. Interest in creating things with clay, blocks and other materials. Great interest in "pretending", as in playing "house", "store", or "cowboys".
5 years:	Draws and makes objects that are usually recognizable. Likes cutting, pasting, coloring. Shows definite interest in finishing what he has started, even if it takes several days. Plays in groups of two to five.

Seeking Help:

Many kinds of help can be given the brain injured child if his learning problem is recognized early enough. Understanding, encouragement, and various kinds of treatment and training can benefit him. When this is done, his ability to learn is more likely to be developed to its maximum. On the other hand, if his learning problems are not recognized early enough, many may quickly classify him as mentally retarded. His image of himself may be badly damaged.

It can be helpful if the parent, just before going to the doctor's office, tries to recall all problems that make him suspect something may be wrong and describes these to the doctor. A child will often act differently away from home; therefore, he may be on his best behavior in the doctor's office. If so, it will be hard for the doctor to see what the child's true problems are. This is where your list of specific signs will give him the clues he needs.

If after examining the child the doctor feels that a more complete study should be done, he will make a referral to a specialist. This may include specialists in the nervous system of children, in vision, speech, in physical ability, and in hearing and mental abilities. In some cities there are child development clinics, children's hospitals, and medical centers where children with learning problems stemming from brain injury can be examined by teams of specialists working closely together.

After their examinations and discussions, the specialists will decide whether the child needs training and/or treatment, and what kind of training or treatment they should prescribe. Some of the training and treatment that may be prescribed are listed below.

1. Medication: I am cautious about referring a child for medication.

It has been my experience that a well-constructed program of learning can help a child control his behavior without the aid of medication. However, the medication theory varies among professionals treating the brain injured child. Therefore, as a part of the treatment the doctor may prescribe medicine. If the child is hyperactive, medication may help him to calm down, concentrate, and learn more easily. If he is extremely underactive he may need medicine to stimulate him.

2. Sports and Physical Therapy: If the child is not too physically involved, various sports and physical therapy may increase his coordination as well as give him practice in learning to get along with others. For the child with fairly good physical coordination tumbling, baseball, hopscotch, jumprope, and swimming can help him learn to control his arms and legs to the maximum. In different kinds of activities he learns what the words *after, before, behind, on top,* and *below* mean.

When the child has a physical handicap accompanied by a learning disability, activities should be presented to him that he can do within his physical limitations. Throwing a ball behind him, piling blocks on top of each other, putting an object under the table, and placing an object after or before a mark on the table can help him to learn what the words *after, before, behind, on top,* and *below* mean. These activities can be done with two or three other children which will help the physically involved child learn to play, cooperate and compete with others.

3. Arts and Crafts: This type of therapy can aid the child in learning to do certain things in the right order and to remember. They increase his ability to make his eyes and hands work together. Should he be severely handicapped, adaptations of arts and crafts can be made so that he can benefit from them just as much as the child who has better physical coordination. Molding clay, finger painting, and weaving can be used to improve general physical coordination and to teach eye-hand coordination as well.

4. Psychiatric and Psychological Counseling: With failure and frustration facing him, the child with brain injury usually has emotional problems. From the age of ten years on he may benefit from psychiatric or psychological counseling. At a younger age, play therapy might be employed to help him better control his behavior. Counseling and guidance is not only important to him but can be equally important to his parents for better understanding of him.

5. Remedial Education: Some children may have difficulty with academic learning in the classroom. They may need special help with reading, writing, or arithmetic in order to make the most of their abilities. Carol, with little physical disability, may have to learn how to use a pencil to write while Bryan, who was born physically handicapped may have to learn how to use an electric typewriter because his hands are too tense to hold a pencil correctly. The same is true with learning to read. Carol may need help in just reading. Bryan, because of his more pronounced physical disability, may need the same help but may also need a reading rack to hold his book, as his hands shake too much to hold a book steady before his eyes.

6. Language Therapy: Problems in speech and communication with others may require special help. For instance, corrective training may improve Patty's ability both in relating to others and in necessary classroom training. This is particularly true of any child who is born with any type of a speech handicap.

7. Perceptual—Motor Training: This type of training can help the child better identify what he sees, hears, smells, touches, and tastes. It may help John sort out his information and use it in every day situations. Balance and coordination, which are often problems for Jimmy because of the extent of his brain injury, can be improved by playing certain games. Both these boys will learn what and where the parts of their body are and learn left from right. They may learn to use their eyes better by watching a marble move from left to right and top to bottom as it rolls along a track. Puzzles and sorting games may train John to pay attention to one thing at a time.

What Parents Can Do

Parents can do a great deal at home to help the child with a learning disability. The various professional people who examine and treat him will advise them. Their suggestions may include the following:

1. Help the child have moments of success: When the child manages to do something he has been trying to do, he is delighted and encouraged to try some more. On the other hand his handicap may be so severe that it can cause him to fail so often that he may stop trying altogether. To help him learn a game, finish coloring a picture, or learn how to tie shoe laces may take a long time and lots of practice, but when he succeeds he gains not only skill but also encouragement to go on and try other skills.

2. Praise him for his efforts: A child is most responsive when those around him are quick to recognize that he has done something that is hard for him to do. Perhaps it was one of the few times Larry has been able to put away his toys where they belong or button a button, or sit down all through a meal. If he can accomplish these feats let him know that you appreciate what he has done and that you think he can do more if he tries.

3. Try to keep set routines: Dick may learn and get along better with others if his life is kept on as regular a routine as possible. Keep in mind that he does have disorganized thinking patterns. If there are new events and things competing for his attention, remember that he will become more confused.

Some times of the day are especially stressful to the child with a learning disability, and even more so if he has a physical handicap as well. Times such as morning, meal time, and bedtime can be times of stress for the child. Here are a few examples of ways you can make these times easier for him.

Morning routine—The night before, let him help you set out the clothes he is to wear the next day. By doing this he will know exactly what to put on and not have to scramble around hunting for his clothes and trying to decide what to wear. At first the child may have to be told how to wash his face, how to use the toilet, and so on. This instruction may have to be repeated over and over because he may not be able to remember which step follows which for a long time. But by doing it over and over he will soon get the idea of which follows which.

Mealtime—Try to serve meals at the same time each day. If the child is a finicky eater and does not eat well with others, let him eat alone for a short time and then bring him back into the group. He must learn to concentrate on the job before him and to ignore other objects around him such as glasses, dishes, and silverware.

Bedtime—If possible the child should have his own room. If this is impossible try to put him in a room where he will be bothered the least. In the case of ten-year-old Amy, it was found less disturbing for her, for example, to share the same room with her fifteen-year-old sister than with a sister or brother closer to her age. Her parents merely moved the furniture in the room so that the girls were separated as much as possible.

The brain injured child often does not make an easy adjustment to change. Therefore prepare him ahead of time if some change is going to take place in the usual routine. If there are going to be guests for dinner, for example, tell him well ahead of time who will be coming, when, how long they may stay, and what they will be doing while they are in his home. This helps him see how guests fit into the regular routine of his home.

4. Give him one thing to do at a time: If the child is easily confused and has a short attention span, give him only one thing to do at a time. For instance, telling Becky to "brush your teeth, comb your hair, and get your coat," may make her too confused to do anything. She will do better if she is given one thing to do at a time and allowed to successfully accomplish it before going on to a second thing.

5. Be sympathetic, but firm: All children need discipline and the child with a brain injury is no different; but do not belittle him. Just be firm and brief. Do not bribe or threaten him; however, do not give in to his whims. If Tom has outbursts of temper, try to remember that the reasons for them may be stress and anxiety. Remove him from the situation to a quiet place and console him. Sympathy and understanding given him at this time are far more important than words said to him or a spanking. After he has settled down, try to think of what upset him and try to prevent it from happening again.

6. Help your child but don't push him: Just recognizing the handicap as a real problem can change your expectations and take pressure off the child. More is gained if you help him to organize tasks and get started doing them. Do new things with your child, not for him, and avoid pushing and constantly saying "Why can't you . . . ?".

7. Help him learn to get along with others: Rick may have problems understanding and getting along with others. Try to find suitable playmates for him and invite them over, but only one or two at a time. You may have to stay with them most of the time they are together, and actively show your child how to play with other children his age. Also, be sure to limit the time. The child with a learning disability can tolerate activity only so long, then he must be allowed to go his own way for a while.

8. Mothers need help too: Mothers of children who are physically handicapped, have learning disabilities, and who may have other serious behavior problems, are likely to become exhausted because these children need so much attention. If at all possible, the mother should have some relief from child care during each day.

Some parents are lucky enough to find a babysitter who can give good care to a child with a handicap. But there are few sitters who have the maturity, patience and experience needed. Also, the cost of hiring such a person may be too much for the family budget. In this case, other family members mature enough and who understand the child's problem might take over for the mother for a short period.

What Happens When Problems Go Unrecognized?

The learning problems facing the child in his early years, if not checked, will magnify and continue to haunt him the rest of his life. Now they become different in character. The teenager is frustrated, has feelings of inferiority, and has a tendency to "act out" frustrations at his inability to keep up with his peers in school. He often rationalizes acting aggressively, belligerently and sullenly.

Sarah is an example of such behavior. While she had average intelligence, she had minor damage in the learning area of the brain. School work had always been difficult for her from her earliest days and she had always been aware of this. Now at the age of sixteen, she devised her own ways of covering up her deficiencies by trying to control everyone around her, and make them act according to her wishes.

Her parents were at a loss for what to do with her. While Sarah had a basic affection for her parents, she tried in every way she could to outwit them. She was their master, they her puppets. There was a constant hassle between them and to keep peace the parents gave in and Sarah went and did whatever she wanted to do. If her parents made an effort to discipline her by telling her she could or could not do a certain thing they were met with sarcastic remarks.

It was too late now to bring Sarah under control. She had the upper hand with everyone around her. They did as she said or she lashed out at them. In conversations with me, Sarah often spoke of her feelings of inferiority and worthlessness. These feelings were what motivated Sarah to be aggressive towards others. She admitted this to me and also spoke rather gleefully of how she succeeded at controlling this one or that one to her liking.

Although Sarah's learning problem did not result in her being physically disabled, the teenager with a learning problem who is physically disabled can exhibit the same reactions.

9

Fear

One of the most powerful emotions in man is fear. It can haunt the handicapped all his life. It is capable of pushing a child or adult beyond his capacity or severely inhibiting his growth and development. Unresolved and exaggerated fears are coupled with hate of the thing or person that threatens them and are linked with feelings of jealousy and envy.

All children and adults during a lifetime know some kind of fear from their earliest years—fear of noises, harsh tone of voice, pain, the displeasure of those around us, the dark, water, and so on. How the person learns to deal with fears and how much anxiety remains as a result of them determines how stable the person becomes and how effectively he can cope with new problems that arise in his life as he grows older.

The handicapped individual experiences many of the same fears as other people, but not necessarily at the same time, for the same length of time, or with the same intensity. He may feel them longer and more sharply. His need to understand fears and deal with them from the minute they grasp hold of him is important.

The normal child frightened by something, cries and runs away or calls for help. As a rule he is comforted and reassured. If Jean falls and bumps her head hard she may cry, but in time as she discovers that she can stand by herself and walk without falling, she will grow confident about her physical ability to handle herself, and carry that confidence into her future growth pattern.

Many disabled children and young adults are frightened by a physical uncertainty about themselves. The young adult may find it difficult to balance his head. Sudden noises may set Alice's body into convulsive jerking. In the case of Linda, who has poor sitting and standing balance, she may try again and again to control her body motions but meets with little success. The result is that these girls, instead of acquiring confidence about themselves, become more fearful about their ability to exist in the environment around them. In the case of Danny, other fears may build. When next he tries to sit in a chair or get up on his feet to walk, he may bring with him some of the anxiety born of earlier experiences and perform less ably than he might otherwise. Thus it can be assumed that fear can be transferred to each new activity and situation the disabled person attempts as he grows older.

The intensity and impact of fear differs among the handicapped. Doctors have noted that certain types of disabilities generate greater fear and tension than others. For example, a palsied child with a spastic, stiff body, who cannot relax properly is afraid of falling because he may not be able to use his hands or legs to break the fall. Another youngster with involuntary motions tenses up at the thought that he may hurt himself as his body swings from one side to another. The greater his fear and the more anxious he becomes, the more control he loses. Episodes of this type, totaled with embarrassing failures soon make the physically uncertain individual afraid of what may happen and he may react by either doing nothing or behaving erratically. He may hate his body, hate the situation, and anyone involved in it.

If the disabled person's fears are intelligently handled, he can be helped to understand how to deal with them. They may not diminish altogether, even as he grows older, but he can come to adjust to the physical behavior of his body. When this happens he can gain better control over it, acquire confidence that will enable him to take new steps, try new things, and relate more positively and warmly to people about him.

Of course the individual who expresses his fear is much easier to help than the one who, because of a severe speech handicap, cannot express himself. It is safe to assume that even though the individual has never voiced any fears, he certainly has a number of them in varying degrees of intensity.

I have had occasion to work with children and young adults who could not speak but whose fears needed to be brought out into the open. By working out a system of communication, they were eventually able to reveal what fears they felt the most. This was usually followed by reassuring actions by their families to make it clear that they were loved and wanted and as dear and important as any other brother or sister.

Fear of Abandonment

There are few parents who have not experienced an evening scene when they are about to go out. A sitter or Grandma holds a sobbing three-, four-, or five-year-old as they leave reluctantly and with many a backward glance. The child is expressing his fear that his parents may not come back. He is worried about who will take care of him if they do not. He wants to know who will stay with him while they are gone. He is not behaving this way because he is bad, spoiled, or timid. He is responding to a common childhood fear. With sympathetic explanations and assurance by his parents that they will return, such scenes become fewer and fewer. He begins to learn that his parents always return, and eventually his objections should cease.

The handicapped child, and sometimes teenager and adult (as I have said and will repeat many times in this book), have all the fears and reactions of the normal individual. If he is confined to a chair or bed, or if he cannot speak, his fears are greatly exaggerated. He, too, wants to know where his parents are going, when they are going to be back and whether they will return when they say. He, too, may strenuously object in the beginning and make as much of a scene as he is capable the minute they head for the door. Because of his greater dependency on his parents, his fear that they may never come back is a serious one. He may feel that they do not love him enough to want to come back and that he will never see them again. He may feel ill at ease with the sitter they leave him with, or worse, may not even know the sitter and worry about how he will make her understand him if his speech is poor.

Some of the solutions are obvious. The parents should explain where they are going, with whom, how long they will be gone, and so on. Telephoning him an hour or so after they leave to let him hear their voice reminds him that they have not left him for good. A less obvious but equally important step is to teach their handicapped son or daughter to be as independent of them as possible. The best solution is to include in their routine with him as many independent activities as they can. Playing with a toy, looking at pictures, listening to records and stories, playing cards, using crayons, or working on a hobby can be valuable in their ability to keep him absorbed and interested enough to pursue them alone. Fortified by the conviction that his parents love him, and equipped with enough to keep him busy, he will learn to accept their comings and goings.

When non-handicapped children begin nursery school or kindergarten, they often go through tearful periods of adjusting to life away from home. The intensity of each child's fears is correlated to his personality and his home relationships. Handicapped children who begin school, or who are left at a clinic for therapy without mother right at hand, may behave exactly the same or even more intensely. Handicapped children need to know that nothing ever would induce mother to leave them; that they are loved beyond all doubt, whether they are good or bad; that mother (or father) is looking forward to their homecoming; and that the doctor or therapist with whom they are about to come into contact will like and accept them.

Handicapped individuals who have been helped to develop independence and have some command of themselves, approach a new situation with the same positive attitude shown them at home and soon lose their fear of new environments. That Doris may be reluctant, that her parents find it difficult to make arrangements, should not for a moment stop them from giving her opportunities to associate in groups outside her home. If she cannot make herself understood, she should be taught manual signs that others in the group will come to understand after an explanation. She may touch her mouth to show that she wants a drink of water, or put her hand on her head when she has to go to the bathroom, and so on. When she finds that her needs are understood by others even though her mother is not at hand, she will relax and begin to participate.

Fear of Falling

If an individual has difficulty maintaining his balance, the fear of falling makes its appearance in his personality earlier than any other fear. It can affect his concentration, his body control, and be a major block to intellectual growth. He can become so preoccupied with his fear that he has little desire to turn to any form of learning. Even his physical development may become retarded because he is not receptive to physical or occupational therapy that requires him to maintain a sitting or standing balance. Fear of falling can keep him confined to a wheelchair long after he is physically capable of leaving it.

There is nothing bad about changes in one's environment. In fact, it is highly desirable that there be changes. But in the case of many impaired persons, young and old, this requires preparation. For example, if floors are going to be slippery, the handicapped person should be given plenty of time to practice walking on them. He might begin doing so in his bare feet, so he can get the best grip, and then gradually transfer over to wearing hard-soled shoes. If he was not wearing rubber-soled shoes before, maybe it would be a good idea that he wear them now—but only after his orthopedist has approved them for him. If the individual has a fair walking gait, however, it might help him if the furniture was moved about so that he can develop good standing and walking balance in any new environment. If he becomes used to only one type of environment, he will naturally be uneasy away from it and his adjustment to places outside his home may be more difficult for him to make.

This fact is sometimes overlooked: there are far reaching effects of this particular fear. In the case of Doris, a doctor may have told the parents that she should be able to walk. Or, they see another child with what seems to be a comparable handicap feed and dress himself, but their child cannot. They may either question the diagnosis of the doctor or suspect Doris of being lazy or conclude that she is mentally incapable of understanding how to do these things. Few parents associate this inability and reluctance with the simple fear of falling.

A child like Doris may appear to be making no outward effort at all. Inwardly, however, she can busily be reviewing the catastrophes that could occur were she to fall while walking on crutches or putting on her clothes or reaching for a book.

There are individuals whose particular handicap is such that they fall suddenly, without warning. They can come to fear falling and in time fear everything before it happens. They may come to expect failure in all they do. From their fear of falling they conclude that they are personally inadequate, and this prepares a fertile soil for the growth of a host of other fears.

As the meteorite that falls to earth has meaning, the disabled person can learn that falling is a by-product of doing, and that what he does and is has meaning.

Fear of Not Being Liked

Like everyone else, the handicapped child and young adult compares himself to others and is critical of himself. The handicapped child of average or bright intelligence evaluates his limitations and grows increasingly anxious at the thought that his slowness in walking, talking, or his learning in school will make people dislike him. He may or may not understand the implications of his handicap—how lasting it is likely to be and what he can expect to do and not to do. He may take refuge in wishing things were different or building up false hopes about the future.

Fear of Loud Noises

Watch a new baby lying in a crib. A sudden bang of a door and he jerks convulsively, looks startled, and probably starts to cry. A reassuring hug and repeated bangs soon accustom him to the sound. For a time he may continue to respond with an involuntary jerk when he hears the door slam, but it frightens him less and less, and soon he may hardly notice it.

A handicapped baby may respond in exactly the same manner except that his body reactions and motions may be much more exaggerated. It may take a lot longer for him to adjust to any loud noise, but he needs exactly the same assurance and repetition to teach him that he need fear nothing about the noise. With him, as with all babies, physical contact and a warm, comforting tone tell him that all is right in his world and he need not be frightened. When he is older and you have shown him how the wind slams the door or how his brother or sister shuts it hard, he will accept the fact that it presents no threat to him and will better control his reaction to the noise.

Thunder frightens most children (and many adults, too!). You can minimize fear of the rolling noise by contact with your child, by your physical presence, by your reassuring tone. The cartoon character traditionally dives under the bed when he hears the clap and sees the flash of lightening, but your immobile child, who might like to do the same, knows only fear of something from which he cannot escape. Laughing at such fears or becoming angry at a child who shows fright may stop him from saying he is afraid, but will never help him to be unafraid.

Fear of the Mysterious

When something occurs to frighten a handicapped child and no explanation is forthcoming, its impact can be extended to a dismaying degree. For instance, when a toy falls off his table and makes a loud noise, his nervous system may be jolted, causing his body to react convulsively. The physical reaction frightens him and soon makes him eye suspiciously anything that he associates with the toy that was dropped. Or his hand may involuntarily start shaking when he reaches for something, breakable or not. Repeated often enough and frightened often enough, he may end up by fearing to touch anything around him because he is afraid it will cause the shattering sound which starts his body jerking. Later these same fears can make him afraid to handle his crutches because he worries that they will fall as the toys fell. The effects of seemingly mysterious and unexplained events and noises can be minimized if parents explain their source, reassure their child when they occur, and when possible, anticipate them. Toys can be tied on long strings to a table if they are likely to fall. A doorstop can hold a banging door in place. The child should be prepared for what is likely to happen, as in watching fireworks or lightning or listening for the peal of thunder. Consistent efforts along these lines will help him develop a tolerance for the unexpected and better control over his body reactions.

Praise Can Work

Children have a great need for praise. A child may not understand why he cannot do things like other children, but regardless of the severity of his handicap, he clearly understands the tones of praise given his brothers and sisters, and he wants this for himself.

If a six- or eight-year-old handicapped child cannot help with the dishes because his hands are shaky and he might break fragile china, he could be given silverware to swish around in the water, and be thanked for his help. Other things he could do are sort spools of thread in a sewing box, straighten a drawer, watch for the mailman or listen for the weather report. He might tell his mother when the water is boiling or call her when the food timer rings. He could dust the shelves or water the plants. Whatever the job, he can be given something to do for which he can be held responsible, and for which he can truly be praised. He must be helped to feel as worthwhile as his non-handicapped brother or sister. If there are chores for them to do, he must have a chore of some kind also, to help develop a sense of importance and value.

At the age of four, five, or six, children are concerned about how others regard them. Showing off is usual. Soon after a guest enters a house he may be invited to see what they have done, listen to what they can do, and watch how they can do it. Some parents make a show of shooing them away, but it is usual for most to encourage their children to display drawings or a demonstration of block building, a dance, a recitation, a song, or what have you. Whatever the accomplishment, the object and the result is to get praise from the audience. In reasonable amounts, such praise and encouragement contribute to the development of a healthy ego in a child. They make him feel important. He has a better opinion of himself, and he begins to think of himself as a worthwhile member of society.

The handicapped child rarely has this opportunity to show off in hope of receiving praise from those watching. Parents sometimes assume that a handicapped child does not wish to draw attention to himself, when in fact it can be just the reverse. When he is not asked to show off any single thing he can do, it can suggest to him that he has nothing worth showing off.

In a series of counseling sessions, a mother said to me: "Billy can't be jealous! He just doesn't have the normal feelings of other boys his age. He can't do the things they do, and there's nothing he does other people would want to watch. I won't have him making a spectacle of himself. When people stare at him, I feel they're staring at me, too, and pitying both of us."

A second mother confessed: "I never thought of Sally as having any desire to do what she saw other children doing. She's so handicapped and helpless, I never thought of her as having any normal feelings, although now and then I was sure she understood what was being said to her. She did scream and make a fuss when her sister entertained friends by dancing, but we thought it was because she was nervous."

Both comments reveal that the severity of a handicap can mislead a parent into believing that the child feels no emotion. A handicap often so obsesses parents that they cease to look upon their child as a child and see him only in relation to the effect of his handicap on their lives and on society.

"Suppose," you ask in discouragement, "there is very little my child can do? How can I help him build his sense of worth, and give him something to show off?" One way is to find some activity, however small, that he can do and encourage him to do it in front of people other than the family. Perhaps he has learned to crawl up and down stairs. Perhaps he can make marks with his crayon. Perhaps he can move his arms and legs to the same music his sister dances to. Perhaps he has a fish or bird to show off, or maybe he has learned a poem or made up a song. Whatever it is and however slight it might be, he should be encouraged to take pride in doing it rather than brood over what he cannot do.

Words of praise come more easily from guests, particularly when they take their cue from a parent who says, "Good, Tommy! I'm proud of you. You did that so well." If a parent insists the performance be perfect or waves it aside as of little consequence, visiting friends become confused and uncomfortable. It is then they are likely to say: "The poor thing . . . please don't make him do it. It's too hard for him."

A child must feel his efforts to entertain are pleasing and acceptable to his parents and to visitors. If he is fearful that he will not perform to their satisfaction or is jealous because he is not called upon to perform at all, he may resort to crying or tantrums or become shy, submissive, uncooperative. Without help and with repeated experiences of this kind, the child will have difficulty associating with people all his life.

If the handicapped person is to be given a firm foundation on which to build his life, he must be helped to adjust to himself. This has to be made clear to him. Such a firm foundation can be built by emphasizing his abilities and good traits, by admiring all there is about him, by involving him in activities which he is capable of doing and commending him for whatever progress he makes; by demonstrating to him that people like him for what he is; and, by encouraging him to make use of all his mental and physical endowments. These factors will help his feelings of fear in other areas of his life.

10

The Psychological Evaluation

How can you determine the intelligence of a handicapped person? What are his psychological abilities?

Psychologically evaluating the handicapped requires a well trained, skilled psychologist. Gross involuntary body movements and unintelligible speech often can hide learning and reasoning ability. I recognize this and plan my testing programs accordingly.

Psychologists can help parents and the rehabilitation team become more familiar with the mental ability of the handicapped individual and how far that ability may develop as he or she grows older. Parents and others should be made aware of what they can expect mentally, emotionally, and socially. They should know how much he can learn, what his emotional age is, and his social age equivalent at the time of the evaluation.

When Should It Be Done?

The younger the better. Many tests measure mental and psychological development of a child as young as two weeks. Other tests measure abilities from three years to adulthood. Although many tests are standardized for use with the non-handicapped, I frequently adapt these tests for use with various types of handicaps. This however, is not always done easily or quickly. It can take many visits to my office before accurate test results are obtained. The time needed to test each individual depends upon the extent of his handicap and with what physical and mental problems he must cope. Can he write himself? Does he speak intelligibly? Use of the right test is essential to determine problems in the sensory-motor or perceptual areas.

Tests vary in what and how they measure emotional, social, and intellectual abilities. Those used on infants measure rate of mental, social, and physical development. For example, if an infant is eight months old, it can be determined if he is behaving at this age level, or if he is behaving at a lower age level. Is there some abnormal condition causing the child's development to be retarded or slow?

When a child reaches three years of age or older, other tests are used. Some tests use various formboards. Other tests ask simple questions such as, "Show me your eyes." "Show me your mouth." "Show me your hair." or "How many legs has a dog?" Another test may require him to identify by pointing to such objects as a chair, a table, or a bed.

Important Personality Traits

What makes up a personality? Many traits. However, those working and living with the handicapped must be familiar with the many facets of an individual's personality.

Following is an outline of traits that should be developed in the handicapped's personality. Also listed are some of the most prevalent problems facing the handicapped in the categories of social and emotional, personal problems and family relationships.

IMPORTANT PERSONALITY TRAITS*

Trait	Definition
Self-acceptance	An attitude toward oneself and one's personal qualities that are of unique worth to one. An unemotional recognition of one's ability and limitations, one's virtues and faults, without feeling unnecessarily guilty or blaming oneself for that which one cannot help.
Self-actualization	The process of developing capacities and certain talents, of understanding and accepting oneself, of integrating one's motives.
Self-assertion	An ability in social situations to strive for achievement of realistic goals; also, in certain cases, the ability to develop a certain sense of leadership in a group.
Self-consistency	Behavior that conforms to a common pattern determined by individual situations as well as long-term goals; the development of a picture of

* Evelyn West Ayrault, *Helping the Handicapped Teenager Mature* (New York: Association Press, 1971), pp. 57–60.

	self and the progressively greater harmonizing of behavior with the environment around oneself.
Self-criticism	A recognition of behavior patterns that do not conform to those others have adopted; the ability to recognize realistically ones own strengths and weaknesses.
Self-determination	An ability to regulate behavior, not just for immediate circumstances or social pleasures, but by personal initiative for the sake of attaining goals in life.
Self-realization	An ability to balance and harmonize development of all aspects in one's personality and to develop personal potentialities that one is capable of doing.
Self-regard	The sentiment of one who seeks to enhance himself and to develop a feeling of satisfaction when a situation (physical, social, or emotional) is favorable to him.
Self-system	A final choice of potentialities that one seeks to develop and to integrate into one's personality. Not all these tendencies are consciously recognized, and most may be rejective alternatives that are repressed rather than brought to the conscious level of thinking and reasoning.

UNDESIRABLE PERSONALITY TRAITS

Trait	*Definition*
Aggression	He may display hostile behavior that causes fear and can bring him into forceful contact with other people around him. It often is connected with feelings of frustration and the teenager's need to prove himself at all costs. He may express it against a person or object that is causing him to have feelings of frustration. By so doing, he hopes to overcome the frustration and be able to control the person or handle the object as a non-handicapped boy or girl his age would.
Anxiety	He may have a present or continuing strong desire or drive that misses its goal. This condition is a state of continual fear, either high or low in anxiety. Feelings of being threatened may also accompany it.

Depression	He usually will not respond to any kind of stimulation and has a lowered initiative. He very often has gloomy thoughts. He may be restless, have periods of despair, and have a tendency to condemn himself.
Guilt	He may have a feeling of regret for something he thinks he has or has not done. Guilt is often accompanied by indirect expressions and a poor sense of personal worth. Sometimes it can be an imagined guilt that may be deeply repressed. Parents' attitudes very often can be a contributing factor.
Self-abasement	He is often very submissive and has strong feelings of inferiority. He yields to other people. This trait is often related to the degree of his handicap.
Self-abuse	He misunderstands both his selves, which often results in excessive masturbation and self-degradation.
Self-accusation	He blames himself, usually falsely, and to a serious degree. This often is connected closely with how he regards himself and how his handicap, major or minor, limits him in living a normal life.
Self-deception	He fails to recognize the realistic aspects of his situation and some things that closely concern him.
Self-extinction	He has little sense of his own personality as a self-experiencing, self-directing entity. Very often he will try to live through the lives of those in his immediate environment, seeing himself only as a reflection of them.

SOCIAL AND EMOTIONAL PROBLEMS*

Dislike pity shown by other people

Think others don't know enough about being handicapped

Get annoyed by people wanting to help too much

Get angry when not treated by others as normal

---

*G. N. Wright and H. H. Remmers, *The Handicap Problems Inventory*. Purdue Research Foundation, copyright 1960. Reprinted with permission.

Lack a well-rounded social life

Feeling unsure of what others think about the handicap

Fear of making a blunder in public that points out the handicap

Feeling awkward in meeting people

Not feeling on equal terms with others socially

Trying to hide handicap from others

Seem to be looked upon by people as different

Seem to be treated as a second-class person

Seem to be considered by others as inferior

Need to live where there are people who will help

Have trouble getting along with others

Take advantage of the sympathy of others

PERSONAL PROBLEMS

Want to be normal

Act as if not handicapped

Have concern about security in later years

Worry about personal appearance

Feel more conscious of self (self-conscious)

Prefer not to discuss handicap with others

Feel ashamed to ask for help when needed

Feel lonesome

Have ambitions too high for condition

Need to show ability to do as much as others

Seem unable to admit certain things can't be true

Worry about self

Do not feel proud of self

Feel it important to do work the handicap makes difficult

Feel ill at ease

Fear having other handicaps later

Feel embarrassed by experiences caused by the handicap

Daydream about doing big things or being a hero

Feel unsure of self

Fear not getting anywhere in life

Daydream about things beyond ability

Do not like being center of attraction

Find it hard to take care of personal needs

Feel ashamed of body

Feel like running away from it all

Do not feel like a whole or complete person

Expect medical science to find a complete cure

Lack will power (ability to stick to it)

Tend to feel sorry for self

FAMILY RELATIONSHIPS

Regret not being able to do enough for family

Cannot financially support family

Feel unsure about future home life

Have trouble in sex matters

Feel "babied" by family

Do not feel truly loved

Feel family disappointed about handicap

Think no one wants a husband or wife who is handicapped

Need to live away from family for personal independence

Feel better with family than with others

Fear he may need to depend on loved ones for a living

Fear having little chance for marriage happiness

Do not have good relations with opposite sex

Is told what to do too often by family

Want more love

Lean on family too much

Feel family thinks success is doubtful because of handicap

Feel hurt because family brings attention to handicap

Do not get along with family members

Do not feel satisfied with treatment from father

Lack family praise for doing well

Fear family expects too much success in spite of handicap

Feel treated differently from other members of family

Need more admiration from family members

Do not feel satisfied with treatment from mother

Believe family shows too much sympathy

Need to play up handicap to get things from family

Are All Children Testable?

Not every handicapped child is testable, but it is a rare child who can not be evaluated to some degree. Although a child may be blind, deaf, and have no reaction to pain, heat or cold, and loss of most of his motor ability, he can be tested if modifications, ingenuity, and patience are employed. The same is true of the child who is thought to have some intelligence but who has no speech. He may respond in some manner to indicate yes or no. To identify different colors and objects or to show whether he is happy or sad, he might raise his one hand for yes and the other hand for no. From such gestures some idea of intellectual ability can be determined. In every case the objective should be to find out at what level the child is functioning in different categories. These categories are as follows:

Chronological age—A child's developmental age level judged in comparison to his chronological age is sometimes known as life age level. For example, when a child is six years old, this is known as his chronological or life age level. To be judged normal, other developmental age levels should equal this as nearly as possible.

Mental age—The age level at which a child concentrates, understands, and functions mentally is known as mental age. Some children are found to function mentally below their life age level even though tests show they are not mentally retarded. For example, a boy who is sixteen years old may have the reading and arithmetic ability of a twelve or fourteen year old. He may read and understand only the most basic books. However, without the guidance of a psychologist, his parents might easily conclude that he is mentally retarded. A retarded mental age does not always mean that a child lacks the potential to learn.

Social age—The age level at which a child dresses himself, feeds himself, communicates, entertains himself, directs himself and moves about and socializes, make up his social age. When a child's handicap is so severe that it prevents him from doing these things his social age level may be lower than his life and mental age levels.

This difference may be improved through home training. An example is if a boy can put on his socks by himself but it's done for him to save time. This contributes to developing a low social age. Putting on and taking off one's own socks is one of the skills required on a social maturity scale often used with the handicapped child. If the child has slow or unintelligible speech but everyone speaks for him rather than encouraging him to speak, he will score a minus on the social scale that measures communication age levels.

By establishing a child's social age, the psychologist can provide the parents with a training guide. On the basis of the child's physical condition and mental age, he can indicate what self-help skills the youngster is capable of acquiring to reach his maximum social age, and suggest how this might be done in the home.

Physical age—A child's physical age depends upon the impairment he has. A case in point is ten-year-old cerebral palsied Karen who cannot sit up by herself or walk or talk. Because of this, she has the physical ability of a child under one year of age. This makes Karen physically retarded although her mental age and social age is at the ten-year-old level or better.

Emotional age—This category refers to a child's ability to cope with the world around him. It determines how he faces disappointments, frustrations, and responds to the world's challenges. It is quite possible for a handicapped child with normal intelligence to have an emotional age so low that he does not function at his top mental capacity.

When a child displays emotional immaturity, it is important to find out why. The way the family treats him, handles him, reacts to him, is frequently the way he will regard himself and react to his environment. The emotional health of the handicapped boy or girl with dull, average, or superior intelligence must take precedence over his physical condition. Emotionally he must adjust himself to his handicap before he will make worthwhile progress in performing simple physical skills. If he has never walked and is finally taught to on crutches, it will be small gain if he refuses to walk in public on his crutches. He must be helped to understand that regardless of the crutches, *he is* able to get around by himself and is not dependent on someone else to take him everywhere.

Educational age—This category is defined as the level at which a child can read, spell, and otherwise learn. It is another way for the psychologist to measure his mental ability. From the results of achievement tests, it is possible to learn whether the child would benefit from attending a regular or special school.

Knowledge of a child's educational ability can be put to good use every day in the home. A case in point might be twelve-year-old Carol who has had little schooling. Her test results show that she has a reading age of an eight-year-old, but a potential in reading skills and comprehension of a twelve-year-old. Certainly it would be worthwhile to encourage this girl to continue learning to read to her maximum potential. This might be done by visual aids, on a tutoring basis, or as a member of a school group of slow readers.

Just because a disabled child has not been able to attend school full time is no reason for him to remain ignorant the rest of his life. He can be taught many things if those around him know at what age level he is presently functioning. It is my practice to tell them this piece of information. Having this knowledge at hand makes it possible to help him make maximum use of the learning abilities he possesses.

11

School for the Younger Child

What is the best school for the handicapped child? There are few private schools for the orthopedically handicapped and/or brain damaged child, who has average or better intelligence. This is not to minimize the work done in special education classes in the public school systems throughout the country. It is to suggest that a child may need an educational program tailored to his specific learning and social needs. Following is a proposed school which I have devised and recommend for such children.

The School's Basic Philosophy

The schools should be psychologically oriented, and give the child an opportunity to become master of himself, discover who he is, and learn what he can do within his limitations. He should learn to function at his intellectual, emotional, and social maximum. He should be psychologically tested before being accepted for enrollment, and the most up-to-date educational and psychological techniques should be used.

Philosophy of Staff Policy

Members of the professional staff, including teachers' aides, should be selected on three personal qualities:
1. Emotional maturity and commendable personality traits.
2. The ability to integrate himself well with his co-workers.
3. Professional qualifications

If these criteria are not met, not only would the staff suffer, but each child he came into contact with would suffer as well. This proposal keeps in mind that a child with a physical, emotional, behavioral, or social problem is particularly sensitive to personality problems in the adults around him.

Admitting Requirements

I. *Age Range:* Between five years and eight years
II. *Examinations Necessary Prior to Enrollment:*
   1. Psychological diagnostic work-up.
   2. Physical examination by a pediatrician, including vaccination for small pox, inoculation for infantile paralysis, the Shick test for diphtheria, and the Dick test for scarlet fever.
   3. Examination by optometrist.
   4. Dental examination.
   5. Orthopedic examination outlining the best way the child should be handled in the classroom.
   6. Neurological examination.
III. *Personal Requirements*
   The child should be toilet-trained and able to perform basic self-help skills (e.g. feed self fairly well, put on and take off clothing with assistance).
IV. *Physical Requirements*
   Child should be ambulatory. (Children in braces, on crutches, or in wheelchairs would be considered according to their ability to manipulate themselves.)
V. *Intellectual Requirements:*
   A psychological evaluation would determine the child's *mental age, emotional age, social age, chronological age, verbal performance,* and *perceptual quotients.*

For example, if Bobby's IQ were between 80–89 (dull, normal intellectual category) but he showed learning potential, he would be considered for admission to the school as readily as the child with an IQ between 90–100 (average intellectual category). These IQ classifications are based on the intelligence classifications established by David Wechsler, Chief Psychologist, Bellevue Psychiatric Hospital, New York City, in his tests, Wechsler Intelligence Scale for Children and Wechsler Preschool and Primary Scale of Intelligence.

Parents

A child cannot make significant development unless he has parents behind him who are interested in his improvement. This school would recognize that it *is* difficult for some parents to project such interests toward a child who is handicapped. The parents should not be forgotten people. Their problems in raising their handicapped youngster would be considered. Counseling sessions for parents would be available either in group sessions or on an individual basis.

Teaching Aids

Teachers at the school would be trained to know how essential it is to adapt teaching materials to meet the physical limitations for the handicapped child. He should anticipate that a child with poor coordination who is learning to read may have trouble holding a book and turning pages. Though a parent might hold the book for the child at home, the teacher would know it is better for him to hold it himself. This can be done in several ways. He can set up a reading rack with wire holders to keep the pages of the book open, or he can put plastic tabs on each page so that the child can grasp them easily and turn the pages himself.

If a child has difficulty in controlling his neck muscles, making his head wobble, it may be hard for him to focus his eyes on a book or paper on his desk. The teacher would then adapt the educational materials to help the child cope with this problem. For example, in a first grade geography class the teacher would select a book with large print which he could place on a reading rack before his student. The position of the book would help the child focus his eyes on the pages better. Later the child might respond better to visual presentations, so the teacher could follow up with visual aids related to the subject. In this case, the child should not have to concern himself with page turning, writing, or other activities that require physical coordination. In the darkened room where the movie is shown, the child can relax and is therefore highly receptive to the structured learning environment.

Furniture in the classroom should be adapted to the needs of the various children's handicaps. Toy shelves and bookshelves would be securely fastened to the wall and a bar placed in front of the bookshelves allowing the child with poor walking and standing balance to hold on while he makes his own selections. Seating a group of children at a round table can help to minimize feelings of insecurity. No child is alone, not even the one with poor sitting balance who might feel uneasy. Each child is seated so that he can observe the actions, reactions, and facial expressions of his classmates as he performs certain skills. This provides him with proof of being accepted by the group.

The round table arrangement allows the teacher to hold the group's attention more easily. With five or six children around him, he can touch each child and establish personal contact with him. Seated close together, one might expect a certain amount of giggling and horseplay, but a teacher who is consistent in his demands and requires each child to pay attention to what he is saying or doing can maintain discipline. Not every child participates in group activity. If a child's behavior is too distressing to the group, he would be separated from the group.

Special Education Techniques

1. Attribute games: In all areas of learning the ability to think clearly, to reason, and to approach problems in an organized and logical manner is essential. Attribute games provide an enjoyable and motivating way to develop this ability in each child. Special blocks could introduce the child to shape, color, size and thickness. Since no two blocks are alike, these would teach the child to sort and classify, to put into sequence, and to handle class relationships.

2. Foundations for mathematics: This aids the child in acquiring basic arithmetic principles, concepts, and skills from which later arithmetic ability and facility with numbers develops. The program provides a base for satisfactory performance in elementary school mathematics. It could be divided into four units which could be used as a complete program, or individually, to introduce and develop specific concepts at the kindergarten, first, or second grade levels.

3. Perceptual skills development: Recognizing shapes and forms, the ability to determine sameness and difference by comparing properties, orientation or quantity, and the ability to classify or group together things that are alike, are among the basic skills which each child must develop. This includes sets of cards and books. Each set varies in difficulty from very simple recognition of property or attributes—shape, size, or color—to discrimination of minor differences in figuration, quantity, orientation, sequence, or relationships of parts to the whole.

4. Visual-motor integration: Blocks, beads, parquetry and pegboards are among the simplest teaching aids to help children understand, through concrete experience, the concepts they will later need to apply to such skills as reading, spelling, writing, and working with numbers. Although they are not an end in themselves, they are an important part of learning.

5. Auditory discrimination in depth: This teaches pupils of any age the basic auditory perceptual skills they must have in order to read and spell correctly. The program is structured for use both developmentally and remedially. It covers:

a. Preschool and Kindergarten—Awareness of the sound structure of our language to students.
b. Beginning readers—Base for auditory perceptual judgement upon which a reading program can be built.
c. Slow learners, or students with learning disabilities—Special help in establishing basic concepts and a variety of reinforcement material at a high interest level.
d. Remedial approach—The students' reading and spelling performance is developed in relation to his level of oral language.

6. Eye-hand coordination: This program gives practical experience in developing visual discrimination, coordination or arm, hand, and eye dexterity, and controlled rhythmic movement goals. Body awareness and relationships in working in a confined space at a restricted or designed activity; control of both hands together in aligning the worksheet with one hand while the other works; scanning a page rapidly and changing focus of attention from one group of words to another are some of the learning skills emphasized.

Pre-vocational training

As early as second grade, pre-vocational training should be introduced. This is a new theory I have developed to introduce him at an early age to preparing for job placement as a handicapped adult. This is an essential concern for the child's future life. Many young people sixteen years and older are totally unprepared for any type of employment. Some are too immature to be trained and placed on a job, others are too environmentally immature to benefit from vocational training and placement. Had they been introduced to early vocational training they would be better able to handle themselves.

The teacher realistically considers the child's various limitations and capabilities and directs his efforts and interests into channels that may lead to purposeful work in skilled, unskilled, or professional careers. He aims to help the child realize that the world owes him nothing because he is physically handicapped, but teaches him that he must contribute to society what he is capable of giving within his particular physical capability.

The school would offer pre-vocational programs to young children.

They would be given simple office jobs such as filing envelopes by color to determine eye-hand coordination ability. Blocks of various sizes could be placed in a formboard to teach them different object categories. Tasks should be assigned that require cooperative effort. The teacher might assume the role of an employer and hire a child for a specific job in the classroom. As the child works, the teacher would observe his performance and decide what other skills the child might possess. This training program aims to help the child form healthy habits in relation to himself and to the "workers" around him.

12

Therapeutic Value of Playtime

Play and exercise can be joined together.

A child can make noticeable improvements in his walking, use of his hands, in his speech, and his ability to generally care for himself, if he is given plenty of time to practice such skills. However, this usually adds up to many hours each day if he is really to practice and accomplish doing them.

He may have many tasks. He may have to develop hand-eye coordination, learn to reach out, or learn to grasp and release. If he has tense fisted hands, he must learn to try to relax them so he can perhaps button or be able to hold different shaped objects. If his hands move involuntarily, then he must try to control them. If he can get about in any manner by himself, his legs may need strengthening, and he may need to develop agility. If he is to learn to feed himself, he may first have to learn to raise his hands up over his head or bend an arm at the elbow to bring the spoon to his mouth.

With planning and good programming, many of these skills can be incorporated into his playtime hours in such a way that he sees the activities only as a time of play despite the fact that their primary objective is therapy. The advantages to the rehabilitation team as a whole are many. Instead of badgering and drilling him to learn and practice certain skills, games that require him to wave his arms, or use his fingers may be helpful. In fact, to do all sorts of things requiring the use of his body can be of help. Furthermore, there is a minimum of fuss and rebellion on the child's part. The child who plays store, or house, or doctor or cowboy is a happy and relaxed child.

What is the Value of Playtime?

If a child is palsied, dystrophied, or otherwise brain damaged, it may be that he cannot walk, does not speak clearly, or cannot endure long periods of physical activity and general play in which most children indulge. However, he should not only watch and wish he could do what he sees other neighborhood children doing. Play is an important part of every child's life. It has been said that play is a child's work. The handicapped child's need for play is as great as any other child's. It is essential to introduce him to kinds of activities he can enjoy. In play he can learn the feeling of things—how hard they are, how soft, how big and heavy, or whether they are round, square or pointed. From his playtime he comes to see whether his ball or truck or crayon is red, blue or yellow.

All at once he discovers he can roll the ball, maybe push the truck with his hand or foot, make a mark on paper with a crayon. Play now is giving him the opportunity to test his ideas and feelings and put them into action. He will find that with one toy he can do this and with another toy he can do something different.

Case Histories of the Therapeutic Value of Toys

Six-year-old Jenny had poor speech, seemed depressed, and played by herself all the time. She shunned her four- and eight-year-old sisters' invitations to play with them. For Christmas she was given a furnished doll house with which she began to play enthusiastically, chattering away as she never had before. Soon her sisters joined her and were welcomed. Jenny was encouraged by their enthusiasm and soon all three played together. Her parents observed that for the first time this handicapped child was playing cooperatively with other children.

Jenny's reaction was understandable. When the doll house arrived, she was told that it was her very own, that without her permission no one else could play with it, touch it, or change its furniture around. When her sisters eyed her new toy wistfully and asked what was inside, Jenny happily and importantly told them about the tiny furniture and the kitchen and bathroom fixtures. Words poured forth from her and for the first time she knew the unique experience of sharing fun with others.

Four-year-old Robert was afraid to sit by himself. When the doctor learned that the boy could not sit on a chair without being tied to it or lie on a cot without guardrails, he was surprised. His evaluation of the child showed him capable of the balance required. To prove this to his parents, the doctor took Robert into a clinic playroom and as his mother watched from an observation window, sat the boy on an attractive rocking horse. Holding him securely the doctor gave Robert several rides, and then as the boy gained confidence in his ability to sit astride the horse, he gradually loosened his hold and finally withdrew it. Despite the surprise and concern of his mother, the child did not fall, and in fact begged for more rides.

It was suggested to Robert's parents that they buy him a rocking horse, which they did. He became more confident, his feelings of physical insecurity lessened as day after day he rode his horse, Trigger, and spent hours playing Roy Rogers and the Lone Ranger. His performance convinced his parents that he was able to do more than they had allowed him to do, and they gained new confidence in him.

Alice was five years old and had lost a leg in an automobile accident. When her new artificial leg was put on, she refused to try using it. "It isn't like my other leg, the one the doctor took," she wailed. "It can't hold me up. I'll fall down. Please let me sit here," she begged.

Alice's parents were advised to make her want to walk. To motivate her, they bought her a set of housekeeping utensils, some new dolls and a doll carriage. Alice kept house every day, and raised her family of dolls. Her new carpet sweeper was intriguing, and before long she was pulling herself up on her feet to push it. When her mother went to the market for groceries, Alice went along because it was time for her doll's afternoon carriage ride. Together, she and her mother walked to the store. In the market, the doll carriage was parked for a bit and Alice helped her mother push the grocery cart around the store. It took about six months of this routine to put Alice at ease, but by then she began going about her home by herself, holding on to pieces of furniture. Eight months later she had learned to go to the bathroom herself instead of asking her mother to take her. She loved her newly discovered independence and soon gave little thought to the fact that one of her legs was artificial.

How to Select Toys for Your Child
1. Observe your child.
Play with him. Watch to see what he can do with his hands, arms, and fingers. Can he walk? Can he get about by himself? Is most of his

time spent sitting in a wheelchair? Does he understand directions? What seems to hold his interest?

2. Determine your child's play stage.

Your child may be at a single stage of mobility where he can simply grab an object or he may be at several stages where he can grab an object, transfer it from one place to another, put one thing down and grab a new object in place of it in the same hand. He may be in a transitional stage where he can only grab an object but is trying hard to develop the next step of transferring it from one hand to the other.

3. Select toys that serve several purposes.

To save storage space and also save money, concentrate on toys with multiple uses. For example, any doll would please a child, but a doll that can be dressed and undressed, buttoned and unbuttoned, fed and changed, can improve hand-eye coordination. And it is likely to improve speech as the child talks to it lovingly or admonishingly. A wobbly clown will make him laugh, and if the game is to blow him down, a child can get fine practice in the good lip and breath control required as preparation for intelligible speech.

4. Don't be guided by chronological age if your child is severely handicapped.

A toy suitable for a younger or older child may be just right for your child in light of his physical limitations. For the same reason, he may continue to play with a toy long past the time a child his age normally would, because he can manage it well and adapt it for himself. In choosing toys, don't be limited by the suggested age. Select them with their developmental purpose in mind.

5. Choose toys that are sturdy and durable.

All children are dismayed when their toys break. The handicapped child is perhaps even more disturbed, concluding that it may have been his fault. Buy toys that are sturdy and will not shatter if dropped accidentally. If they are on wheels, be sure that they do not tip over easily. If the toy flys apart the minute your child touches it or hits it involuntarily with a flailing arm, he may become discouraged and lose his incentive to play with it.

6. Pick attractive toys that motivate your child and create a desire to play.

Color is a part of the magic of toys, and bright colors do much to stimulate a child's interest. A child who is reluctant to make the effort to exert himself, use his arms and hands and legs and entertain himself, will often respond to the allure of a bright toy. Keep this in mind when you make your choice.

7. Use toys to encourage your child to develop his best muscular skill ability.

Resist the temptation to insist that your child play with a toy as it was meant to be played with. When he grows familiar with it and finds he can manage it, he may be encouraged to handle it in a variety of ways. This can improve his muscular skill ability.

8. Let toys help stimulate your child to express his feelings.

If your child has a severe speech handicap, this is important. Toys that he can hammer on, clay he can knead, and dolls he can talk to can serve as an outlet for him. A toy train, for instance, is often used by a child to express his feelings. As he "choo-choo-choo's" away, the sound gives him welcomed emotional release.

9. Take advantage of the opportunity toys give your child to socialize.

Give normal children who are strangers to each other toys to play with and they are soon friends, busily engaged in the activity before them. Handicapped children have far fewer opportunities to have social experiences with other children. Be sure that your child has a few toys he can occasionally share with two or three other children in his playroom. His playmates will stimulate him to participate more than he might otherwise, and he will have the pleasurable experience of relaxing with friends.

The toys suggested on the following pages should serve as a helpful guide in making selections for your child and in suggesting gifts other people may want to get him. Don't be afraid to improvise and don't feel that you must get exactly the toy listed. You may find something along the same lines that suits your child's need and interests better.

Toys for the Child Who Has Difficulty Using His Arms and Hands

THERAPEUTIC AIM OF TOY	TYPE OF TOY
1. Reach, grasp, release	
To encourage and stimulate him to want to reach out.	Toys that dangle, move, are large, bright and desirable. Any kind of toy that will move your child to want to reach out. Keys on a chain, bright cars, trucks, trains, balls, a shiny musical horn.

THERAPEUTIC AIM OF TOY	TYPE OF TOY
To encourage him to hold on to a toy if it is put in his hands	Bright toys. Long, thin toys that have a pliable or hard handle section. Any object small enough to fit into the palm of the hand. Rattles, bells on handles, that can be held in the palm of the hand, loosely stuffed flexible animals.
To encourage him to reach out for and touch a toy even though he may not be ready to grasp it.	Throwable toys, toys that require slight manipulation, toys your child can grasp easily, hold and then let go. A spoon, stuffed dog, empty thread spool, blocks.
To develop his ability to open his hand and close it precisely.	Toys that can be squeezed, thrown, taken apart or stacked, any kind of toy that requires the child to grasp and then release a toy repeatedly. Toys that require him to open and close his hand. A soft rubber doll or animal that squeaks when squeezed; such games as toy bowling that require rolling a ball.

2. Thumb and Finger Grasp

To encourage him to use fingertips to lift his toys rather than grasp them with the palm of his hand.	Large toys he can stack, take apart, push. Lightweight objects or parts of objects that must be picked up with thumb and forefinger because of their particular size and shape. Blocks to stack on a wooden spindle, hand puppets, a harmonica, wooden take-apart toys, trains, or trucks.
To encourage him to use only a few fingers and his thumb.	Small stacking toys he can manipulate creatively. Crayons, wooden ABC blocks, a painting set and brush, games using checkers, minute doll furniture, pieces of colored ribbon or strips of colored art paper to be stuck on a felt board.
To make it necessary for him to use his thumb and index finger only	Creative toys with very small parts he can take apart. Chinese checkers, large buttons to pick up and put in a cup or box.

To develop the fine use of thumb and index finger	Toys and games he must hold, wind, construct or assemble. Toys with tiny parts. Toys that require that he make precise use of the tips of his thumb and index finger. Jack-in-the-box, winding toys, turning the pages of books, a pinball game; working with the zipper on a bag, picking up match sticks or tiny beads.

3. Finger Use

To encourage him to use his fingers freely.	Toys, games, and activities that are messy, creative, manipulative. Activities that motivate finger flexing, pressing, unrestricted movement of the fingers. A counting frame of colored beads, sand and water, flour and water mixture, finger paints, clay, finger games.
To improve the use of his individual fingers, particularly his index finger.	Toys, games and activities that require a lot of finger action. Any toy that needs precise use of a finger or placing, pressing or circulating motions. A toy dial telephone, a gun, puppets on a string.
To develop strength in his thumb so that eventually he can do activities requiring a fine dexterity.	Thumb toys requiring thumb action, thumb manipulation or any exact use of or pressing from the thumb. Button puppets, pasting pictures on a large cardboard, doll snap clothespins, marbles, tiddlywinks, a toy cash register.
To stimulate the coordinated use of his fingers and to improve general dexterity in his whole hand.	Any activity using the hand in which fine finger coordination is required. Any activity that requires that all fingers move exactly at the same time. Activities that call for synchronized use of both hand and fingers. A stencil book, sewing colored yarn onto a square of cardboard, a tool chest, typewriter, toy piano, knitting toy.

THERAPEUTIC AIM OF TOY	TYPE OF TOY
4. Using the Arms Together	
To encourage him to use both arms naturally, and to minimize any tightness in his arms, particularly at his shoulders and elbows.	Large, wide-area reaching toys, toys he must use his arms to reach for, throw or move in different directions. Toys to punch; a water and scrub board, swing, games using both hands and arms, a tricycle, boxing gloves.
To encourage him to use both arms, not just the one that is handicapped.	Large holding toys that are lightweight and long, requiring a wide stretching motion of his arms, even if one arm is used more than the other. Two pot covers, a rolling pin, toy lawn mower, mixing bowl, and spoon to stir flour and water batter, etc.
To help him develop the dominant (right or left) use of one hand only—but only if he is ready to do so.	Toys that are manipulative but also simple for him to use. Toys that are creative, constructive, dramatic. Toys he must hold in one hand while he makes them work with his other hand. Stringing beads, toys that hook together, a garden set, toy mailbox, housekeeping tools such as a mop or carpet sweeper, tinker toys.
To help him learn to use both hands, leading hand and helping hand, in natural situations.	Fine-skilled manipulative toys that are creative and dramatic and require a precise use of both hands. Any activity with his hands that calls for screwing, placing, matching or alternating motions. Paste paper, scissors, doll feeding equipment, hammer and nails, games requiring two people, washing doll clothes.
5. Hand and Eye Coordination	
To help him develop gross arm control.	Toys that are non-restrictive. Games that do not have to be held by a hand, but do need to be

	placed by a hand. Activities that offer some reward for success and no concern for failure. Toys that bob in bath water, a punch bag, finger paints, plastic balls suspended from the ceiling to be batted back and forth; simple painting of planks of lumber; rocking of doll cradle or baby carriage.
To help him develop the ability to use his arm and hand to place objects, even if he does so crudely and awkwardly.	Toys and games that require that he throw objects within a large area, a ball field, a play court, a given circle or square marked on the floor, beanbags into a bucket or wastebasket; coloring between drawn lines.
To develop maximum control in his arm.	Toys that he can readily tinker with, that interlock, that he can take apart; activities and toy skills in which the eye guides the hand to put a part in place. A toy construction set, puzzles, trains, cars or trucks that can be disassembled, kitchen pans and cups to stack.
To train the exact control and placement of his arm.	Any fine-skill toys that need placement or that he can construct. Any skill in which he has to exercise fine use of his hand, place things exactly, utilize fine hand-to-eye coordination. Simple pegboards, lacing a weighted high top shoe, jigsaw puzzles, a record player with a simple record arm, any household object that fits.

Play Equipment for the Child Who Is Immobile

Just because a child is confined to a wheelchair or must be tied into a standard chair, or bolstered up by pillows is no reason to think he is not interested in having activities around him he can do or watch being done. He can still enjoy the fun of playing. He can still be a part of what goes on around him and live usefully with other people. Although he might not be able to move about by himself, planning can make it possible for him to explore, investigate, experiment, and discover.

By bringing play to the child, by setting up a play environment that makes it possible for him to feel free to exercise his childhood wants and desires, all this can take place. It means that the rehabilitation team must provide the child with play equipment that gives him a surface to work on, room to operate with his things, materials he can handle easily and which are acceptable to him. Following are some suggestions for equipment that will make this possible for the child to enjoy.

Therapeutic chair	Your doctor will prescribe this.
Work table	Either attached to the child's chair or designed so his wheelchair can be pushed up to it and his knees tucked under it.
Beaverboard or corkboard	Drawing paper can be thumbtacked to it if the child has a lot of involuntary motion in arms and hands.
Metal reading rack	Used to rest an open book on. Helpful to the child who cannot easily hold a book in his lap or in front of him.
Sand and water play table	This can be raised 35″ or 38″ off the floor to accommodate a wheelchair or other therapeutic chair pushed up to it.
Enlarged play materials	It is fairly simple to obtain over-sized crayons, blocks, puzzles, cans of finger paints (which you might fasten to the table) and a large picture to color.
Armchair seat	A useful accessory you can use in many ways. Attach it to one end of a teeter-totter, place it on the bottom of a wading pool for your child to sit in. Perhaps your child will be able to slide down a slide in it if you fasten him in it securely.
Doll carriage	Weight this with sandbags to prevent it from tipping over easily.
Toy shelves	Install them in the playroom or bedroom in places where your child in a wheelchair has ready access to them and can help himself to what he wants.
Sandbags	Have an assortment of all shapes, weights and sizes, to stabilize play equipment when needed.

Tip-top table	Drawing paper can be tacked to it and then it can be set up in front of your child for drawing or painting on.
Table clamps	Excellent for clamping down equipment such as an easel, drawing board, reading rack, etc.
Large wooden box	One about 6″ deep serves well for crayons, pencils and chalk. Child can reach in, grasp or release an object.

Toys are a very important part of a child's world. If, however, he cannot manipulate them as he wishes, they become a source of frustration to him.

13

The Rehabilitation Team

The therapeutic aspect of the rehabilitation team is to make a contribution to the handicapped individual's growth and development. They put their heads together and think of techniques for the handicapped person to use. There are cases where ordinary rehabilitation techniques have to be used and cannot be altered in any way. But in many cases the stigma of being different can be minimized if the therapist and the doctors treating the individual gives the idea a little thought.

The Role of the Doctor

The doctor meets the parent's need for a satisfying relationship when their child's physical handicap is questioned. Parents often come to the medical specialist with feelings that are reflections of past experiences with other doctors they have consulted. These feelings can range from distrust to complete trust, not only in the specialist but in the "miracle worker" they think him to be. Their one hope often is that he in some way will "unhandicap" their child, particularly if the handicap occurred at birth.

Most parents bring to the doctor a need for reassurance. If they must hear that something is wrong, they would like to hear that time or various treatments by doctors and others will erase their child's condition. Whether these feelings are spoken in words and recognized by the parents or not, the hope is inevitable.

The doctor is often put on the spot by parents. He often walks a tightrope during the first visit by the parents and child to his office. The parents are wondering what the doctor will tell them about their child's condition, and the doctor is concerned whether the parents will accept what he has to tell them. He hopes they will develop trust in him so that they will carry out the treatment he prescribes.

It is not uncommon for some parents to wander from one doctor to another looking for *the* one that they hope will cure their child. I have known such families who could ill afford to do this. The more practical thing parents can do is to inquire around in their community for the best doctor to treat their child's particular need, try to place their trust in him, and stick with him.

One of the most important things the doctor can do for the parents is to tell them what type of handicap the child has, how it occurred and, if possible, how it may develop in the future. This knowledge in itself, for some parents, lessens their concern over the child's condition. When parents know what a child has, how it happened, if they did or did not have a part in causing it, this in itself can be reassuring for them. Sometimes parents want to know all the facts about their child's condition. Frequently parents have not been told enough about the condition. This can make parents hard to handle, rejective of their child, or totally despondent over the whole situation. But this situation need not exist. If parents will ask their doctor direct questions about their child's condition, chances are they will be given answers.

For instance, if the child has muscle spasms, parents might ask the doctor for medication that would bring about physical relaxation. Most times he will prescribe it if he feels the child can benefit from it. He may not realize that a child sleeps with tense muscles during the night unless the parents tell him.

Parents' concern about a child walking over on the heels of his shoes may prompt a doctor to recommend special shoes that will prevent not only wearing the heels down but improve the child's walking gait. Parents should remember that doctors are not mind readers!

Need for Medical Follow-up

Most doctors want to keep a follow-up on the child's progress. This is particularly true if the child is under the age of four years. As he grows older some new handicaps may develop, or some of the handicaps he had when he was younger may disappear. The doctor needs to be kept well informed.

Parents who live considerable distances from metropolitan areas often are not fortunate in having all the specialists nearby, and their child may be deprived of the services of many different specialists. Those parents who do live in good sized metropolitan areas are more fortunate. Their communities usually have one or two agencies that provide rehabilitation services for the child. Such agencies are usually made up of several doctors who have specialized in various fields of physical medicine.

The Medical Team in a Rehabilitation Center

This team should be made up of doctors who have specialized in various fields of medicine. It might be helpful to know some of these medical specialists, their specific fields, and how they can benefit one individual and yet not be necessary for another. Listed below are some of the specialists that can be consultants to a rehabilitation team.

Dentist:
One who deals with the prevention of tooth disease, especially as it relates to the health of the body as a whole.

Neurologist:
A physician specializing in organic diseases of the nervous system.

Neurosurgeon:
A physician specializing in the surgery of nerve tissue, and surgery of the central and peripheral nervous system.

Optometrist:
One engaging in increasing the efficiency of visual perception. He may prescribe visual training, corrective exercises, and glasses, but may not use surgery or internal medicine.

Orthopedist:
A physician specializing in the correction or cure of deformities or diseases of the spine, bones, joints, muscles, or any parts of the skeletal system in children or persons of any age.

Pediatrician:
A physician specializing in the health and diseases of children.

Psychiatrist:
A person licensed to practice medicine, who is engaged professionally in the prevention, diagnosis, treatment, and care of mental problems.

Treating the child's condition medically, however, is only half the job. There are other aspects of his development that must be handled as well. If the doctor is to make any medical progress it is helpful to have the child psychologically evaluated, to know how he is doing in school (if he is of school age) and to know something about his home environment. In addition to this, the doctor should have already set up a treatment program with a physical therapist, and a speech and/or occupational therapist if he feels they are needed. If braces and crutches are in order, he should recommend to the parents where these can be obtained. But all of this can mean nothing unless the parents are willing to follow up the suggestions made to them by the doctor.

Psychological Requirements of the Therapeutic Team

The disabled individual is unknown to the therapist until they have had time to work together, and even this time may not provide all he needs to know about his patient. Therefore, he must rely on the family to tell him pertinent facts so that he can better establish rapport. For instance, in the case of a child, the physical therapist might ask the parent to show him how he holds the child up to walk. If the child operates a wheelchair by himself, it is important that the therapist know how the child does this. The therapist should know if the child is afraid to lie on a bed or therapy table without someone nearby. Or, is he less afraid if there are sides on the bed or treatment table? Many therapists are not aware that a handicapped child who cannot move around by himself is afraid of falling off a narrow treatment table or rolling stretcher. As an example, a child lying on a table may suddenly realize that there is no one nearby to protect him from falling. He gets frightened, cries and moves around on the table anxiously. In the process, he may wiggle himself to the edge of the table and fall off.

Personality Assets Needed in Therapists

Therapists should have a stable personality and be able to separate their own emotional problems from their work. The relationship between patient and therapist is often a continuously intimate one over a period of years. It demands concentration, patience, and discipline on the part of the therapist. To the child, the therapist may be like a parent. Therefore, he may turn to the therapist for answers, guidance, and encouragement as he progresses in therapy. This necessitates being able to give affection and understanding to each patient. This is essential if the child is to have respect for the therapist and cooperate with him.

If the therapist is gentle and shows respect for the child's body during therapy sessions, then regardless of the handicap the child will develop respect for his physical self more easily. If the therapist handles his body in an impersonal way, he may make him feel unimportant to himself. Even the therapist's tone of voice, manner, and actions make it evident that he either accepts the patient as a person or considers him just part of his job. When the therapist makes the child aware of his good qualities, he helps him adjust more easily to his handicap.

Eliminating Therapeutic Stigmas

If the child is to integrate himself into society, there are a few adaptations which should be heeded. For example, if eight- or ten-year-old Debbie needs some type of walker to get about by herself, perhaps she could use instead a doll carriage that has been weighted down by sandbags so that she could not easily tip it over. As she grows older she might be able to own a market basket such as is found in the supermarket. These two items will not turn as many public eyes on her when she is out walking. Everybody is used to seeing a little girl push a doll carriage, and everyone has seen people push a market basket from the supermarket back home after a shopping spree.

Of course Carl should not be asked to push a doll carriage. However, there is nothing wrong in taking the top of the doll carriage off and perhaps building some type of boat or truck with all the trimmings of horns and whistles on it. As he grows older there would still be nothing unusual about him also pushing a supermarket basket around the neighborhood.

If leg exercises can be best acquired from riding a bicycle, and if the girl or boy cannot balance a two-wheeled bicycle when they are ten or twelve years old, a senior citizen bicycle is the answer for them. This machine has two big wheels in the back separated by a basket in which books from the library or groceries from the store can be carried. It can also be brought inside the house in the winter and mounted on a sunporch or a back porch so that a handicapped individual can continue his leg exercise during the cold months.

Adaptations for the needs of the child/adult can be made in the recreation rooms of many homes. This does not mean that the room should be outfitted for the handicapped member of the family alone. One corner of the room, for example, could have parallel bars, a treatment table, pulleys hanging from the ceiling, and any other apparatus from which the growing child might benefit. By placing these things in such a logical place there is no stigma on the handicapped boy or girl. There are few non-handicapped boys and girls who would pass up a chance to pull on pulleys or to jump around on a trampoline, let alone swing back and forth on parallel bars.

It is a rare child who remains unmotivated in a group situation. For example, Robby may benefit in speech therapy if he is a member of a group of children his own age. Children can be copycats. The speech therapist may see both vocal and psychological development taking place before his eyes if he works out a program where three to six children are taking their therapy in a group. The stimulation that one child can give another child sometimes is phenomenal. One child will hear another one say the word "Dick", and when he hears it said he may be motivated to try to say the same word. Psychologically, there is much to be gained in this approach. Not only is a child being motivated to speak, but he is also learning to overcome self-consciousness. The therapist plays a big role in how successful the group approach can be and how much it can benefit the child. If he has a story to read them and tells them before he starts that they are to listen carefully and tell him what he read after they have heard the story, there is a better chance that they will make the effort to keep alert to see if one can outshine the other in telling what he has remembered.

Requirements Therapists Should Meet

Parents should familiarize themselves with the background of any therapist working with their child. Parents of a non-handicapped youngster attend PTA meetings to make sure he is receiving proper education. It is just as important that parents of the handicapped child familiarize themselves with the qualifications of the persons administering any type of therapy to their child.

Following are basic qualifications for the three major rehabilitative therapies, (physical, occupational and speech):

Physical Therapy

Physical therapy is a health care profession whose practitioners work in hospitals, clinics, nursing homes, and private practice. Physical therapy practitioners work with patients who are disabled by illness or accident, or who were born with a handicap. They evaluate neuromuscular, musculoskeletal, sensorimotor, and related cardiovascular and respiratory functions of the patient. Evaluation includes performing and interpreting tests to assist in diagnosis, and to determine the degree of impairment of relevant aspects, such as muscle strength, motor development, functional capacity, or respiratory and circulatory efficiency.

Evaluation provides the basis for the selection of appropriate therapeutic procedures and the evaluation of the results of treatment. Physical therapy practitioners plan and implement initial and subsequent treatment programs on the basis of test findings, and within the referral of the licensed physician with whom they maintain contact regarding the care of the patient. The treatments given by physical therapists and physical therapist assistants include exercises for increasing strength, endurance, coordination, and range of motion; stimuli to facilitate motor activity and learning; instruction in activities of daily living and the use of assistive devices; and the application of physical agents such as heat and cold, sound and water to relieve pain or alter physiological status. In addition, they try to motivate and instruct the patient, his family, and others who might help him through his treatment and convalescent period.

Licensure or registration—In the fifty states, the District of Columbia, and the Commonwealth of Puerto Rico, the practice of physical therapy on the professional level is regulated by law. "Licensure" or "registration" is the legal qualification to practice. State examinations are given at least once a year, and physical therapists must comply with the legal requirements and procedures of the state in which they practice. Specific information regarding licensure requirements may be obtained from the Board of Medical Examination of the state in question.

Advancement—Qualified physical therapists who continue to grow professionally move into a variety of advanced positions. They can choose among consultative, administrative, teaching and research positions in clinical centers, universities and other private and public institutions.

Education for professional qualifications in physical therapy—Currently there are several patterns of education leading to professional qualifications in physical therapy. All programs include the equivalent of two or three years of college to fulfill general requirements of the college or university; and one or two years of professional education which include the basic health sciences, the clinical sciences, and supervised administration of evaluative and therapeutic procedures to patients in hospitals and treatment centers.

The certificate program requires a bachelor's degree in a major other than physical therapy and fulfillment of certain science requirements for admission. It usually takes twelve to sixteen months to complete the training. Upon completion of the program, a certificate is awarded.

Graduates of certificate programs are considered equally as graduates of bachelor's degree programs. There is no distinction between the baccalaureate and certificate graduates in terms of adequacy of preparation, hiring practices, or salary schedules.*

Occupational Therapy

The American Occupational Therapy Association has published a statement to clarify the responsibility of the therapist to the patient for occupational therapy service. It also outlines the therapist's responsibility to the medical management plan of the patients treated.

This statement covers the qualified occupational therapist and the qualified occupational therapy assistant: one having satisfactorily completed the formal academic and clinical preparation requisite to his level, professional or assistant, and successfully entered into and held current the registration or certification which signifies his level and identifies him as a registered occupational therapist (O.T.R.) or a certified occupational therapy assistant (C.O.T.A.).

Occupational therapists share with the physician a dedication to the treatment of patients and protection of their welfare. They maintain a close relationship to medicine, and continually strengthen it as ever increasing professional skills enable them to provide more competent service.

Occupational therapy also shares with the medical profession a concern for individual and community health and therefore extends its contribution beyond restorative measures and acute treatment concerns to the maintenance of health and prevention of disease and disability.

Relationship with the Physician

The registered occupational therapist (O.T.R.) and the certified occupational therapy assistant (C.O.T.A.) respond to a request for service from many sources. The O.T.R. enters a case at his own professional discretion; the C.O.T.A. enters as authorized by his supervising O.T.R. and each:

A. recognizes that the physician, duly licensed by the appropriate body to practice medicine and surgery, is the person who holds full responsibility for the medical management of a patient; and
B. practices within the limits of competency and the supervisory pat-

---

*Careers in Physical Therapy, (American Physical Therapy Association).

tern commensurate with his level of qualification, professional or assistant; and

C. implements occupational therapy's concepts and provides judgment and skill in the evaluation of a *patient* and formulation of his comprehensive, continuing medical management and care plan;

D. refers a case which, in his judgment, appears to be a medical one to a qualified physician for medical management; and

E. treats, within the patient management plan, collaboratively with all others who care for the patient, and apprises the physician and appropriate supportive personnel of his findings and actions, all of which he documents in the legal medical record; and

F. implements occupational therapy's concepts and provides judgment and skill in the evaluation of a *client,* and the formulation of a *health program* directed toward the maintenance of his health and freedom from disease, disability, or dependency;

G. refers a client who, in his judgment, appears to be in need of social, vocational, or other specialized management to one professionally qualified to provide it; and

H. guides the client in the utilization of the concepts of occupational therapy where applicable to the improvement of his general welfare; apprises collaborating personnel of occupational therapy's findings and actions, and documents same in the client's record.*

Qualifications: To be eligible for Registered Occupational Therapist membership, an individual must have met the educational and qualifying standards set by the Delegate Assembly for a registered occupational therapist. To be eligible for Student Occupational Therapist membership, an individual must be enrolled in an accredited occupational therapy curriculum. To be eligible for Certified Occupational Therapy Assistant membership, an individual must have met the educational and qualifying standards set by the Delegate Assembly for a certified occupational therapy assistant.

The Registry of Occupational Therapists

1. The Association shall maintain a registry of occupational therapists qualified with respect to basic professional preparation.
2. Persons shall be newly admitted to this registry by successful completion of the national registration examination and by payment of

---

*Statement of Occupational Therapy Referral, (The American Occupational Therapy Association, Inc.).

annual membership dues. Criteria for eligibility to write the registration examination shall be established by the Delegate Assembly upon the recommendation of the Council on Standards.

Ethics and Discipline

1. The members of the Association may accept referrals from qualified physicians and from others seeking occupational therapy service in both medical settings and in the broader health care community. They shall collaborate with duly licensed physicians in those instances where medical management is active or indicated.

2. Advertising by occupational therapists under their professional title shall be in accordance with propriety and precedent on medically associated professions.*

Speech Therapy

The American Speech and Hearing Association issues its Certificate of Clinical Competence to individuals who provide satisfactory evidence of ability to work independently, and without supervision, with those having disorders of speech, hearing, and language. The designation of Speech Pathologist or Audiologist indicates the field of major interest, training and experience.

The requirements for the Certificate emphasize competence that results from specialized training and experience. Those who apply for the Certificate should have secured a broad general education to serve as a base for the professional training and experience gained at upperclass and graduate levels.

To qualify for the Certificate of Clinical Competence, an individual must:

1. be a member of the American Speech and Hearing Association
2. submit transcripts from one or more accredited colleges or universities. They must also provide evidence that they have completed 60 semester hours of a well-integrated program that includes 18 semester hours in courses that provide both fundamental and supplementary information about speech, hearing, and language disorders.
3. submit evidence of the completion of 275 clock hours of supervised, direct clinical experience with individuals presenting a vari-

---

*Bylaws of The American Occupational Therapy Association, Inc., (The American Occupational Therapy Association, Inc.).

ety of disorders of communication, this experience should be obtained within the training institution or in one of its cooperating programs.

4. present written evidence from his supervisors of nine months of full-time professional employment pertinent to the Certificate being sought. This experience is known as the Clinical Fellowship Year (CFY) and must follow the completion of requirements 1, 2, and 3.

5. pass a written examination that evaluates the candidate's knowledge in specified areas.

6. be approved by the American Board of Examiners in Speech Pathology and Audiology (ABESPA) on recommendation of the Clinical Certification Board.*

---

*Requirements for the Certificate of Clinical Competence 1972, (Clinical Certification Board, American Speech and Hearing Association).

14

Case Histories Tell a Lot

The following case histories will show psychological profiles at certain age levels, and what I have recommended to doctors and other professionals for long term improvement in development.

Case I

CATHY—3 months

Physical / Social developmental age:
Between 1 and 3 months

Tests Administered:
1. Gessell Developmental Schedule
    Score: Between 4 and 16 week level with most deficiencies in the adaptive area of development
2. Bayley Scales of the Infant Development
3. Cattell Infant Intelligence Scale
4. Vineland Social Maturity Scale
    (This is considerably below the three month age level.)

This child was given a series of infant developmental scales to determine her general growth progress. Her crib was used as the examining table and I was assisted by a licensed practical nurse.

One of the noticeable things about this infant's development was that she appeared to have poor vision. Whether it was partial or total blindness had to be determined. The child responded to a light shone in her eyes. However, when objects were moved across her eyes and up and down in front of them, she gave no indication of seeing them!

Her overall physical behavior appeared to be that of a partially sighted child. For instance, on the Gessell Development Schedule, she did show brief eye following but tended to stare at her surroundings. On the Cattell Infant Intelligence Scale, she failed to follow a ring which was moved vertically and horizontally in front of her eyes while in a supine position. The same vision difficulty was observed when using the Bayley Scales of Infant Development—Motor Scale Record Form. A child with no vision trouble would be able to do this in the second month of life. On the Vineland Social Maturity Scale, she had a social age below the three month level. When the baby was brought to my office, the mother was counseled on how best to motivate the child to a higher social level which would better compare to her birth age.

Upon further examination, it was discovered that this child had webbed toes on both feet (second and third toes). It was also observed that she was apparently right handed. It might be noted that in some cases webbed toes and poor vision go together.

She seemed to have occasional periods when she able to hold her head fairly steady. It was noted that the child had a hearing impairment. There were times during the testing session when she could hear a bell rung near her ear and other times she could not.

Conclusions and Recommendations:

1. This child seemed to be developmentally functioning between the first and second month of life at the time she was evaluated.

2. It was suggested that both her sight and hearing be examined for some degree of impairment.

3. To get a thorough picture of this child's overall condition, it was recommended that she have a complete neurological examination, including an EEG.

4. It would be helpful to have the parent or parents of this child counseled.

Case II

MARK—1 year 8 months

Physical / Social developmental age:
Between birth level and 1 year

Tests Administered:
1. Gessell Developmental Schedules
2. Vineland Social Maturity Scale
3. Verbal Language Developmental Scale

This child was physically and socially retarded in development. On the Gessell Development Schedule he rated accordingly:

A. Motor Area—28 week level
B. Adaptive Area—16 week level
C. Language Area—28 week level
D. Personal-Social Area—16 week level

On the Vineland Social Maturity Scale, he secured an approximate social age level between birth and one year. His motor deficiencies fell primarily in the self-help categories. I counseled his mother regarding things she might encourage the child to do in the home that could raise his social maturity age level.

On the Verbal Language Development Scale, this little boy again rated only between birth and 1 year level. It could be estimated that he fell between the four and six month level.

Conclusions and Recommendations:

This was a child that should be kept under close medical/psychological/social observation. I recommended seeing this little boy every six months until he reached the age of three and a half or four years. This was the only way that some estimation could be made regarding his future intellectual, educational, and social functioning ability. In any event he would obviously be slow in developing in these areas. It was felt that it was much too early and the child was much too young to determine whether he was, or would be, mentally retarded per se. Chances were he would probably be at least a slow learner as he began to reach the educational age level. The mother was counseled accordingly, and seemed to accept the advice and guidance given.

Case III

BOBBY—2 years

Mental age: Between 5 and 9 months
Social age: Between birth and 14 months
Language age: 6 month level

Tests Administered:
1. Infant Intelligence Scale (Cattell)
2. Vineland Social Maturity Scale
3. Verbal Language Development Scale (M. J. Mecham)

This child cried during much of the time he was being tested. However, it was possible to secure a measurement of his approximate psycho-intelligence, social age developments.

On the Cattell Scale, he had a ceiling rating of five months and a basal rating of nine months (both of which might be significantly different in a different testing environment—the child seemed to show a great deal of fear of his surroundings). His deficiencies fell in the following categories:

6 months

1. Could not secure block when given him.
2. When block was hidden under cup, made no attempt to find it.
3. Showed no recognition of self when asked to look at self in mirror.
4. Showed no persistent reaching out for items or people.

7 months

1. Unable to put pellet in bottle or cup.
2. No recognition when shown self in mirror.
3. Did not take two blocks when offered.
4. Paid no attention to exploring pieces of paper in any way.

8 months

1. Unable to say "Da, da," etc.
2. Would not manipulate in any way a piece of string.
3. Made no effort to secure pellet.
4. Was not interested in examining ball in detail.

On the Vineland Social Maturity Scale he scored between the birth level and the fourteen months level. Most of his assets (social) were in the self-help general category, locomotion (his own means of) and in communications (he cried incessantly). Regarding communications, he did not measure up to the age equivalent common to his peers in that he did not speak at all. He was *unable* to follow simple directions, mark with crayons, or fetch and carry familiar objects. However, he may be able to be trained to locate objects when he is older.

His Verbal Language Development Level was below the first year. He did not:

1. respond to name or "no, no."
2. would not echo words and sounds (such as "ma-ma", etc.)
3. He did not seem to comprehend "bye-bye."

One test item he *did* respond to was pointing to a doll's face, hands, head, eyes, mouth, and hair. However, when asked, he did not transfer such identification to his personal self—he wouldn't point to his own hair, etc.

Conclusions:

While this child is mentally retarded, he did show some potential for being classified as trainable. To do him justice it was imperative that he be re-evaluated at the age of 42 months (3½ years). At the time of evaluation, it appeared unlikely that this child could cooperate well on a post-operative rehabilitation program. Any such training following surgery (e.g. walking in braces, etc.), would have to be taught him via the "habitual" method rather than his responding mentally to rehabilitation.

Case IV

KEVIN—3 years 6 months

Mental age: Falls between fifth month and one year level

Tests Administered:
1. Vineland Social Maturity Scale
2. Verbal Language Development Scale
3. Bayley Scale of Infant Development
4. Infant Intelligence Scale (Cattell)
5. Gessell Developmental Schedules (preliminary behavior inventory)

This young man was quite obviously intellectually functioning between one and a half and two years below his chronological age of three years six months. Due to this, it was quite impossible to give him any intelligence scale geared to a child his physical age. Therefore, I had to resort to the tests listed above.

On the Vineland Social Maturity Scale, the child's age equivalent was about six months below the first year level. His successes were scattered—falling into the self-help and locomotion categories. His failures were in the categories of occupation and communication.

On the Verbal Language Development Scale, he rated at the one year level and below. He did not imitate sounds, did not follow simple instructions, and would not echo words, or sounds such as "da-da" and "ma-ma."

Recommendations:

It was recommended that when he was returned to his home from the hospital, and the clinic in his home town, that the parents be encouraged to enter him into a nursery training program for the mentally retarded. The sooner this young man is given an opportunity to develop to his maximum potential—which will be low—the better the chances are that he may perform quite well in the trainable categories as he grows older.

Case V

JON—4 years 6 months

Mental age: 3 years 5 months

Test Administered:
1. Infant Intelligence Scale (Cattell)
2. Stanford-Binet Intelligence Scale

This was a hostile, emotional child. During the testing session it was difficult to establish good rapport with him. He was easily distracted, needed a great deal of urging to perform the test items and seemed to distrust his own ability to perform. He gave up easily and was withdrawn throughout the whole session. It was difficult to establish a positive relationship with this child. He cried when not given his own way, and "some of his language is not fit to print!"

On the Cattell scale, his basal intellectual ability was at the third year, first quarter category. His ceiling level of ability (items that he failed the most) was at the fourth year, second half. He was able to do the following things on both the Cattell Scale and The Stanford-Binet Intelligence Scale.

1. String beads
2. Demonstrate a test vocabulary of 16 words
     (equal to a four-year-old level.)
3. Build a tower of eight blocks
4. Block building; a bridge
5. Repeat six digits after the examiner
6. Follow simple commands fairly well
7. Was able to identify objects by use

8. Was able to repeat a six word sentence from memory
9. Fold paper very well after watching me do it

His deficiencies fell in the area of eye-hand coordination (was unable to draw a man, a reasonably good circle, square or triangle), and he showed evidence of a short attention span and an inability to comprehend detailed directions or conversation.

Recommendations:

I hesitated to classify this young man as mentally retarded. He fell between the mild and borderline intelligence classification. Whether this will rise or fall as he grows older can only be determined by periodic psychological re-evaluations. I noted an abnormalcy in this child's facial expression and shape of head. It appeared to me to show slight characteristics of dwarfism or microcephalic characteristics.

Case VI

CHRIS—6 years 5 months

Tests Administered:
1. Peabody Picture Vocabulary Test
   Vocabulary Mental Age: 3 years 4 months
   Vocabulary IQ: Approximately 55
2. Cattell Infant Intelligence Scale
   (To be explained in following report)

One outstanding impression was that this young man was babied at home. This would naturally retard emotional/psycho-learning abilities. It could also have a significant effect on his physical rehabilitation.

During the testing session, he cried off and on. However, he was able to make a tower of six blocks successfully and identify eyes, nose, mouth, two ears, hair, fingers, arm, neck, and tongue. He could say two digits—one, two.

This child showed considerable perceptual problems which would indicate that he was nearly certain to have some degree of learning disability when he entered school. When given vocabulary cards at random, he was able to identify clock, house, lamp, tree, chairs, tables, grandfather clock, and school house. When he was asked to say anything, however, he would immediately start to cry. The aides and nurses at the hospital reported that he had begun to participate in group play. This would again bear out that when he was encouraged to work with his age group, he had the potential to do so—despite his being treated as a baby in the home.

On the Cattell Infant Intelligence Scale at the third year, first quarter level, he was unable to repeat two digits. At the third year, second quarter level he was unable to repeat three digits. At the fourth year level, he was able to follow simple commands, identify fifteen vocabulary words by pointing to them, discriminate between a short and long stick, identify objects in pictures and their use. At the fourth year second half, he was unable to complete the drawing of a man, comprehend adequately or repeat sentences from memory.

Conclusions:

How much rehabilitation ability this child may have is questionable. Since he was babied a lot in the home, it appeared to be quite low. In counseling sessions with the parents, I put emphasis on entering this child in some school environment in his home community. I pointed out the importance of encouraging him to develop as many self-skills as possible to make him independent and to improve his seemingly uncontrollably emotional behavior. The child seemed to be able to feed himself and do some minor self-help skills, such as pull a shirt over his head, pull his pants up and down, and perhaps put on his socks.

It was indeed unfortunate at this time that we did not have facilities in this area to place this young man for one year and concentrate on maturing him in the physical, emotional, social, and educational areas. I suggested to his parents that he be admitted to some special education class as soon as possible.

Case VII

KIMMY—8 years 11 months

Mental age: 9 years 9 months
Verbal IQ: 126
Performance IQ: 114
Perceptual Quotient: 83—between the 10th and 20th percentile

Tests Administered:

1. Wechsler Intelligence Scale for Children
2. The Development Test of Visual Perception

This young lady presented rather a complex picture. An orthopedic problem was only secondary to her permanent handicap—a perceptual disturbance probably due to brain damage. Children with this specific difficulty are not mentally retarded. However, as in the case of this child, they usually do have a high Verbal IQ and a low Performance IQ. This often manifests itself in behavior problems. In this girl's case, her orthopedic problem served to emphasize behavior difficulties.

Her test ages in the various categories on the Wechsler Intelligence Scale for Children were as follows:

INFORMATION: 15 years plus
COMPREHENSION: 10 years 2 months
ARITHMETIC: 7 years 2 months
SIMILARITIES: 12 years 2 months
VOCABULARY: 9 years 6 months
DIGIT SPAN: 6 years 6 months
PICTURE COMPLETION: 10 years 2 months
BLOCK DESIGN: 10 years 2 months
OBJECT ASSEMBLY: 10 years 6 months
CODING: 7 years 10 months
MAZES: 9 years 2 months

Note that with one or two exceptions, she was a superior child in the various areas of learning. However, her so-called learning problem centered itself in the ability to read and do math. Since she was of general superior intelligence, she was very aware of these retardations in her ability to learn. This was frustrating to her and now that she temporarily was unable to walk and "get out and play with the girls," as she put it, the frustration grew.

Her various age levels in developmental visual perception were as follows:

I. EYE-MOTOR COORDINATION   A test of eye-hand coordination involving the drawing of continuous straight, curved, or angled lines between boundaries of various widths, or from point to point without guide lines.   9 years 6 months

II. FIGURE-GROUND   A test involving shifts in perception of figures against increasingly complex grounds. Intersecting and "hidden" geometric forms are used.   4 years 6 months

III. CONSTANCY OF SHAPE   A test involving the recognition of certain geometric figures presented in a variety of sizes, shadings, tex-

tures, and positions in space, and their discrimination from similar geometric figures. Circles, squares, rectangles, ellipses, and parallelograms are used.   5 years 0 months
IV. POSITION IN SPACE   A test involving the discrimination of reversals and rotations of figures presented in series. Schematic drawings representing common objects are used.   8 years 9 months
V. SPATIAL RELATIONSHIPS   A test involving the analysis of simple forms and patterns. These consist of lines of various lengths and angles which the child is required to copy, using dots as guidepoints.
6 years 6 months

It will be noted that for her age, this girl had particular difficulty in the area of perception of figures against complex backgrounds, recognizing geometric figures in a variety of sizes, colors, and positions, and in spatial relationships.

While these perception deficiencies may not have a direct effect on her physical rehabilitation, the frustration that they cause her may aggravate her dislike of wearing braces and other therapeutic necessities to get her back on her feet.

However, these facts should not deter anyone from making every effort to get this young lady mobile again. In fact, it is imperative that this be done, if we take into consideration her fundamental handicap of visual perception.

I spoke with this girl about the importance of her cooperating if she wanted to get up out of a wheelchair and be able to get about by herself again. (Incidentally, children with a visual perception problem like this may be hyperactive and find it difficult to be confined to one place. Everyone handling this young lady should understand what pressure she is under from being confined to a wheelchair.)

Recommendations:

1. That this young lady be given plenty of activities to do while she is confined to a wheelchair. It might be helpful if her family engage her in some activities to help her.

2. That the physician having the most contact with her try to develop some rapport and assure the girl that if she does what she is told by her doctor, she will soon be able to get about more and more by herself.

3. That firm, but kind discipline be used with this young lady throughout her rehabilitation period. Chances are that if the people

treating her—doctors, therapists, etc.—note her high intelligence and speak to her on this level, she will be cooperative.

4. That those in contact with her daily help her to look positively on the prospect of overcoming her orthopedic problem.

Case VIII

BILL—12 years 4 months

Test Administered:
Wechsler Intelligence Scale for Children

This young man was tested while in the hospital and in traction. Since he was flat on his back, it was quite impossible to give him any test but a verbal one. Thus, he was administered the WISC (the verbal scale of this intelligence test). The results were as follows:

Verbal IQ: 97 (this places the child in the category of average intelligence—verbally. The only performance test he could easily take was picture completion. On this, he received a mean test age of 15 years 2 months.)

His mean test age in the various categories on the verbal scale are as follows:

INFORMATION: 9 years, 2 months
COMPREHENSION: 9 years 6 months
ARITHMETIC: 10 years 6 months
SIMILARITIES: 10 years 10 months
VOCABULARY: 10 years 6 months
DIGIT SPAN: 14 years 2 months

Conclusions:

It was felt that this child would have scored higher on this test had he not been in traction flat on his back. It was suggested that when he was able to sit up in an orthopedic chair, he should be administered the full scale of this test. This would give a full scale IQ rather than just the verbal section.

When this young man's physical rehabilitation begins (after he is out of traction), he should be expected to understand exactly what is requested of him. He does have the intelligence, and therefore should not be trained on a habitual basis, but be urged to do everything he is asked to improve his physical ability. If this approach is used, I see no reason, from a psycho-social viewpoint, why this young man should not make significant progress and eventually become quite independent.

Case IX

KAREN—14 years 3 months

Mental age: 11 years 9 months
Verbal scale IQ: 87
Abilities involving analogies, permutations, discrimination of design and alterations of pattern as well as other logical relations—rate in the below average IQ category.

Tests Administered:
1. Wechsler Intelligence Scale for Children
2. Coloured Progressive Matrices (Sets AA, AB, B)

This young lady was tested while lying flat on her back. It therefore was impossible to give her any performance tests that involved block design, completing puzzles, etc. However, she was able to take an oral IQ test on which she received a verbal IQ of 87.

Her test age profile in the verbal test categories area is as follows:

INFORMATION: 9 years 10 months
COMPREHENSION: 11 years 2 months
ARITHMETIC: 11 years 2 months
SIMILARITIES: 10 years 10 months
VOCABULARY: 9 years 10 months
DIGIT SPAN: 11 years 2 months

This gives her an equivalent mental age of eleven years eight months.

The Coloured Progressive Matrices test is designed primarily to measure the relations within abstract material. It consists of abstract designs in which a part has been removed and the subject chooses the missing insert from six or eight alternatives. On this test, her score was at the 25th percentile, which classifies her below average in intellectual capacity. However, this must not be interpreted to mean that she is acutely mentally retarded. In all probability once she is sitting up in an orthopedic chair and can be given a performance test that requires her to put puzzles together or make block designs, her ability in abstract thinking might be at a higher level.

Conclusions:

It is felt that this young lady may not be working at her fullest intellectual capacity. She does have the intelligence to cooperate noticeably in her future physical rehabilitation training. It is not recommended that she be taught on a habitual basis, but that she be made to intellectually understand what is being asked of her and why she is being asked to do certain exercises to improve her physical condition.

This girl seems to be quite a normal thinking youngster. There is considerable emotional immaturity present in her overall personality profile. This can well account for her low test ages, low intellectual age, and thus, a low IQ. In an effort to improve these so-called retardations, her parents had a conference with me prior to her dismissal from the hospital. It was my opinion that this young lady was babied too much in the home and that if the parents had some guidance in helping her mature in all areas of development, she would benefit.

Case X
TERRY—16 years 11 months

Tests Administered:
1. Wechsler Adult Intelligence Scale
2. Wide Range Achievement Test
3. Handicap Problems Inventory

I began seeing this young lady in an effort to improve her obvious emotional and social immaturity. This was done by means of individual counseling sessions, but little significant progress was made.

Terry attended an exceptional children's center in her community when she was between the ages of two and seven. While there, she was classified as mentally retarded. She admittedly suspects she is still retarded when the fact is discussed with her today. The test results state otherwise. It is felt that the time spent at the center during her early years did significant damage to her total personality development and is a contributing factor to her apparent social and emotional immaturity today. The mother states that she is more comfortable playing with children between the ages of twelve and fifteen years of age. She also reports significant behavior in the home that can be attributed to a child between the ages of twelve and fifteen years.

On the Wechsler Adult Intelligence Scale, this young lady scored a Verbal IQ of 95, a Performance IQ of 91 and a Full Scale IQ of 93. When she was doing the object assembly test, she showed particular perseverance when trying to put the hand puzzle together. She insisted that it was some kind of animal.

On the Wide Range Achievement Test she received the following:

READING GRADE LEVEL	9.6
SPELLING GRADE LEVEL	9.6
ARITHMETIC GRADE LEVEL	6.7

Due to her advanced chronological age of sixteen years eleven months, this placed her below the 50th percentile level as compared to others her age.

Some of Terry's feelings regarding herself, her family, and her place in society were significant. These were revealed during fifteen sessions of counseling.

Feelings Toward Self	Feelings Toward Family and Others
Feels discouraged easily.	Feels left out of family.
Doesn't like being around other handicapped people.	Does not get along with family members.
Feels embarassed by others.	Feels she is not treated normally by her family.
Finds trouble in adjusting to handicap.	Feels she is treated as an inferior by her family.
Feels she lacks a well-rounded social life.	Fears losing loved ones.
Envies people who do not have handicaps.	Gets upset because family watches everything she does.
Doesn't want to discuss handicap.	Feels treated differently from brothers and sisters in family.
Doesn't feel on equal terms with others physically.	Resents being told what to do so much by her family.
Feels she is a second class person.	

Recommendations:

It is felt that this young lady should be given a full battery of projective tests in an effort to determine whether her present emotional and social immaturity is due to a neurological or perhaps an environmental or personality cause. Results from such a battery of tests would be most helpful in determining future planning for Terry.

Suggested Case History Forms

The prime objective of any rehabilitation team or school staff is to gather as much data as possible concerning each child or adult. Every member of the rehabilitation team or teaching staff can then become familiar with every aspect of each person's developmental profile.

Following are four types of case history forms that I have found useful in my thirty years of experience on rehabilitation teams. Some of the forms provide space for doctor and psychologist, as well as social worker.

If "Case History I" is filled out in its entirety, it gives a complete picture of a child's or adult's medical, therapeutic, psychological, emotional, social, and educational history from childhood to adulthood. It can also be of help in determining the fee the family should be charged for various treatments in centers.

Once the child has passed the adolescent stages of development and is ready for vocational training and placement, the form labeled "Referral for Vocational Evaluation" may be used. This can be used when the person has just graduated from high school or vocational school, or before he goes to or graduates from college. It gives a comprehensive picture of what the individual can do and what he is capable of being trained to do. The form helps prevent disabled young people from training to do what they wish and yet are physically unable to do. It presents a realistic picture of the future vocational pursuits according to an individual's physical capabilities.

CASE HISTORY I

Present Date_____
day-month-year

A. PATIENT

    Circle one: * CHILD   ** ADOLESCENT   *** ADULT

    Name _____ Age_____ Birthdate_____
day-month-year

    Home Address _____

                           City   State   Zip   Phone

* CHILD: Between the ages of birth and twelve years of age.
** ADOLESCENT: Between the ages of twelve years and twenty-one years of age.
*** ADULT: From twenty-one years of age and up.

Type of handicap _____

Is this patient cared for by:

Orderly_____ Nurse_____ Maid_____ Governess_____ Mother_____

Father_____ Grandparent_____ Aunt_____ Brother or Sister_____

Himself_____ Institution_____ Other_____

B. RECOMMENDED BY _____

Circle one: Teacher Doctor Social Worker Psychologist Minister

Professional Address _____

C. PURPOSE OF CONSULTATION:

1. Psychological testing? _____

2. Counseling for child (i.e. play therapy, etc.)? _____

_____

3. Counseling and testing for child _____

4. Counseling for parents _____

5. Counseling for child and parents_____

6. Vocational counseling for adolescent or young adult (counseling, testing, etc.)

_____

7. Complete and detailed psycho-social-mental-emotional evaluation of child_____

8. Single consultation only_____

D. MOTHER

Name _____ Age_____ General Health_____

Education: High School_____ Graduated (yes or no)_____

College_____ Graduated (yes or no)_____ Other training_____

Marital status: Married_____ How long_____ Widowed_____ How long_____

Divorced_____ Separated_____ Legally (yes or no)_____

Remarried_____

Vocation_____ Part-time_____ Full-time_____

(other than housewife)

Business Address _____ Phone_____

E. FATHER

Name _____ Age_____ General Health_____

Education: High School_____ Graduated (yes or no)_____

College_____ Graduated (yes or no)_____ Other training _____

Marital Status: Married_____ How long_____ Widower_____ How long_____

Divorced_____ Separated_____ Legally (yes or no)_____

Remarried_____

Type of business & address _____

Type of position held_____ Phone_____

How long have you been at present job? _____

What are your daily business hours?_____ Weekends_____

Does your work require out-of-town travel or home entertaining?_____

How often?_____

Does your wife sometimes accompany you? _____

Do you do any of your business at home?_____

Do you take a yearly vacation?_____ How many weeks? _____

Do you go on family vacations?_____ Do you take your handicapped child on

vacation with you?_____

F. SIBLINGS (brothers and sisters)
Number of brothers _____ Ages___/___/___/___/___/___/___/
Number of sisters_____ Ages___/___/___/___/___/___/___/
General health of each:
Boys _____
Girls _____
Are there any siblings with physical or mental handicaps?_____
Indicate type of handicap _____
How many are in school now? _____
Do they attend public or private school? _____
College _____

G. MEDICAL HISTORY:
1. Who has been the attending neurologist? _____
    Address _____
    Diagnosis_____
    Last examination_____
2. Who has been the attending orthopedist? _____
    Address _____
    Diagnosis_____
    Last examination_____
3. Who has been the attending pediatrician?_____
    Address _____
    Diagnosis_____
    Last examination_____
4. Who is the attending dentist?_____
    Address _____
    Last examination_____
5. Other medical specialists in attendance_____
    Name_____ Specialty_____
    Address _____
    Diagnosis_____
    Name_____ Specialty_____
    Address _____
    Diagnosis_____
    Name_____ Specialty_____
    Address _____
    Diagnosis_____
6. How old was your son or daughter when you first noticed he was
    handicapped?_____ What abnormality did you first notice?_____
    _____
7. Does he use or require any orthopedic aids such as braces, crutches, special
    shoes, specially built chair and table, wheelchair?_____
    Which one(s)_____
8. Is he on any medication?_____ Kind _____
    What for _____ When: day_____ night_____
    mealtime_____
9. Does he have convulsions? _____ Kind: (grand mal

or petit mal) _____ When: day_____ night_____

How often? _____ Are they controlled?_____

How old was he when the first convulsion occurred? _____

10. Does he wear glasses?_____ When were his eyes last examined? _____

    Can he read?_____ Well_____ With difficulty_____

11. Does he sleep well at night? _____

    Does he wet the bed?_____ Every night_____

    Has he his own bedroom?_____ Does he sleep in a parent's room? _____

12. Was the mother in good health when she was carrying this child?_____

    Was this pregnancy your 1st_____ 2nd_____ 3rd_____ other _____

    Had you had any miscarriages before this pregnancy? _____

    How many?_____ Stillbirths_____ How many?_____

    Was this birth full term?_____ If not, how many months?_____

    How long were you in labor? Hours_____ Days_____ Was child

    delivered by instruments?_____

    Was the Rh Factor involved?_____

    Was child a "blue baby" at birth? _____

    Describe any other unusual characteristics about his birth_____

    _____

    Were you anesthetized at his birth?_____

H. THERAPY

At which rehabilitation or other type center has, or does, your son or daughter

receive therapy?_____

Address_____

Executive Director _____

Medical Director _____

Check the following forms of treatment he receives, or has received in the past:

1. Physical therapy_____ Times/wk._____
2. Occupational therapy_____ Times/wk._____
3. Speech therapy_____ Times/wk._____
4. Vocational guidance_____ Times/wk._____
5. Psychological therapy_____ Times/wk._____
6. Does he attend summer camp?_____ No. of weeks_____ Where?_____

   Does he enjoy camp?_____ Do the non-handicapped sisters and brothers go

   to camp also? _____

I. PARENTS

1. Do you belong to:

   A parents' group_____

   A psychological group therapy? _____

2. Have you ever had any individual counseling with a social worker, psychologist,

   doctor, etc.? _____

When?_____ Where?_____

J. PSYCHO-EMOTIONAL-SOCIAL

1. Is your son or daughter a behavior problem? _____

   Is he: Happy?_____ Friendly?_____ Moody?_____ Hostile?_____

   Does he cry a lot?_____ Is he aggressive?_____ Is he afraid of

   strangers?_____ Is he emotionally dependent on you?_____

2. Is he toilet trained?_____ At what age?_____ Day_____ Night_____
Does he have occasional accidents? _____
Can he care for his own toiletting? _____

3. Does he exhibit sex problems? Yes_____ No_____ Some _____
Describe _____
Has he asked any questions about sex? Yes_____ No_____
Has he been given any sex education by a parent? Yes_____ No_____

4. Has he ever been psychologically tested? Yes_____ No_____
Where? _____ Date_____
Were you told the test results? Yes_____ No_____ If so, what were you
told?_____
Have you ever been told your child was mentally retarded? Yes_____
No_____ When_____
Has he ever been in a school for the mentally retarded? Yes_____ No_____
When_____ Where_____ Address_____
How long was he in school? _____
Has he ever been a resident student at a school for the physically handicapped?
Yes_____ No_____ If so, where?_____
For how long?_____ Why?_____ Explain _____

5. Does he associate easily with children and/or people his own age?
Yes_____ No_____
Handicapped only_____ Non-handicapped_____ Both evenly_____
Does he participate well in a group?_____ Is his social life exclusively with the
handicapped?_____ Is he a member of any non-handicapped groups in his
community (brownies, cub scouts, scouts, church clubs)? _____
_____
Does he stay around home a lot? _____
Does he entertain friends in his home?_____

K. EDUCATION

1. Does the boy or girl attend school?_____
Name of School _____
Address _____
Principal's name _____
Teachers' names _____
_____

2. Kind of school: Private_____ Public_____ Nursery_____ Trade_____
Vocational_____ High School_____ Junior College_____
Four-year College_____ Homebound school program_____
How many times a week? _____

3. How old was he when he started school?_____
What grade is he presently in? _____
Is he presently in an ungraded class? _____

4. Is he given any type of therapy at school?_____
Physical_____ Occupational_____ Speech_____ Psychological
guidance_____ Vocational guidance and training _____

5. What are the school's comments regarding his behavior adjustment,
and progress, in school?_____
_____

6. Has he been given any achievement tests recently?_____
   (reading, arithmetic, general knowledge)
   State kind _____
   Were you told the results?_____ If so, what were you told? Explain _____
   _____
   _____

L. PHYSICAL SKILLS
   Which of the following skills can the child do fairly well?
   1. *Speech:* Can he indicate "yes" and/or "no"?_____
      Can he speak fairly clearly in sentences? _____
      Does he communicate via gestures (waving hand, blinking eyes, etc.)?
      Explain _____
      _____

   2. *Use of hands:* Can he pick up objects?_____ Can he grasp a pencil or
      crayon?_____ Can he write his name?_____ draw a line?_____ mark on
      paper with pencil or crayon? _____
      Can he dress himself?_____ Tie his shoes?_____ Button his clothing?_____
      Feed himself?_____ Wash his hands and/or face_____ Comb his hair?_____
      Brush his teeth?_____ Take his own bath?_____
      Can he drink from a glass?_____ With a soda straw?_____ Assisted by
      adult?_____ If a child, can he open and suck a lollipop by himself?_____
   3. *Body skills:* Can he sit unsupported?_____ Can he sit in a standard child's play-
      chair?_____ Must chair have arms?_____ Can he sit in a highchair?_____
      Does he do best in an orthopedic chair?_____ Must he sit in a high-back
      chair?_____ Has he control of his head and neck?_____ Does he need a
      headrest on the chair to balance his head?_____ Can he walk unassisted?_____
      With crutches? _____
      Is he in a wheelchair most of the time? _____

M. YOUNG ADULT
   1. Is he in college?_____ Year _____
      What is he training for: (teacher, doctor, business, etc.)_____
      _____
      Is he away from home?_____ Is he a day student in a hometown
      college?_____ Does he carry as many subjects per semester as every other
      student? _____
   2. Has he dated a member of the opposite sex?_____ Handicapped_____
      Non-handicapped_____
   3. Can he drive a car?_____
   4. Is he sociable? (telephones, entertains at home, enjoys socializing with the non-
      handicapped)_____
      Feels at ease with the non-handicapped? _____
      Feels uneasy with the non-handicapped? _____
      Seeks out the handicapped rather than the non-handicapped?_____
      Does not socialize?_____ Clings to mother or other member of family?
      _____ Goes nowhere without her or them? _____
   5. Has he ever earned any money? _____
      Doing what? _____
      Has he a job? _____ What kind?_____

Where? _____._____

Salary?_____

How does he get to it? By himself ?_____ Parents?_____

Other? _____

Has he his own checking account?_____ Savings account?_____

Does he handle his own finances?_____ If not, who does?_____

Has he a private income equal to a living wage?_____ Is his future financially provided for by his family?_____ Does he receive any kind of financial aid or income from a State or Federal source, (e.g. Social Security Disability, etc.)?
_____

D. REFERRAL FOR VOCATIONAL EVALUATION *

FROM: _____ DATE:_____

TO: _____

IDENTIFICATION:

Name of Client _____

Social Security No. _____

Address _____

Sex_____ Age_____ Race_____ Marital Status_____

No. of Dependents _____

SOCIAL-VOCATIONAL-MEDICAL:

Economic Stratum _____

Family Environment_____

Formal Education _____

Usual Occupation _____

Vocational Success_____

Leisure Activities _____

Physical or Mental Impairments _____

General Health _____

BEHAVIORAL OBSERVATIONS:

General observations (appearance, mannerisms, communications, attitude, motivation):
_____
_____
_____

REASON FOR REFERRAL:

Statement of Problem: _____
_____

Specific Questions _____
_____

Enclosures_____
_____

*Gandy, J.: The Psychological-Vocational Referral in Vocational Rehabilitation. Unpublished Master's Thesis, University of South Carolina, 1968.

APPENDIX I

National Headquarters of Agencies Servicing the Handicapped

Foundation for Child Development
345 East 46th Street
New York, N.Y. 10017

The Genetics Foundation
9 West 57th Street
New York, N.Y. 10019

The March of Dimes
1275 Mamaroneck Avenue
White Plains, N.Y. 10605

Muscular Distrophy Association of
America
810 Seventh Avenue
New York, N.Y. 10019

Myasthenia Gravis Foundation
230 Park Avenue
New York, N.Y. 10017

National Association for Retarded
Citizens
2709 Avenue E East
Arlington, Texas 76011

National Multiple Sclerosis Society
205 East 42nd Street
New York, N.Y. 10017

National Society for Crippled
Children and Adults
2023 West Ogden Avenue
Chicago, Ill. 60612

United Cerebral Palsy Association
66 East 34th Street
New York, N.Y. 10016

APPENDIX II

Federal Agencies Servicing the Handicapped

Department of Health, Education and Welfare (Washington, D.C. 20201)

Office of Education
  Education for Exceptional Children
  Bureau of Education for the Handi-
    capped

Office of Vocational Rehabilitation

Public Health Service
  National Institutes of Health
  National Cancer Institute
  National Heart Institute
  National Institute of Arthritis and
    Metabolic Diseases
  National Institute of Mental Health

National Institute of Neurological Diseases and Blindness

Bureau of Medical Services

Bureau of State Services

Social Security Administration Bureau of
  Family Services

Division of Welfare Services

Children's Bureau
  Division of Health Services
  Division of Social Services

141

APPENDIX III

Agencies Interested in Rehabilitation of Handicapped Adults

American Insurance Association
85 John Street
New York, N.Y. 10038

American Legion, National
  Rehabilitation Commission
1608 K Street, N.W.
Washington, D.C. 20006

American Rehabilitation Committee
28 East 21st Street
New York, N.Y. 10010

Committee for the Handicapped of the
  People-to-People Program
1028 Connecticut Avenue, N.W.
Washington, D.C. 20036

Goodwill Industries of America
1217 K Street, N.W.
Washington, D.C. 20005

International Society for Rehabilitation
  of the Disabled
432 Park Avenue South
New York, N.Y. 10010

National Rehabilitation Counseling
  Association
1522 K Street, N.W.
Washington, D.C. 20005

Veterans of Foreign Wars, National
  Rehabilitation Service
200 Maryland Avenue, N.E.
Washington, D.C. 20002

APPENDIX IV

Sources for Making Day-by-Day Living Easier for the Handicapped

Abilities Incorporated
Willets Road
Albertson, N.Y.

American Home Economics
  Association
2010 Massachusetts Avenue, N.W.
Washington, D.C. 20036

American Institute of Architects
1735 New York Avenue, N.W.
Washington, D.C. 20036

American Physical Therapy Association
935 Franklin Avenue
Garden City, N.Y. 11530

Clothing and Research Development
  Foundation, Inc.
1 Rockefeller Plaza
New York, N.Y. 10020

Department of Occupational Therapy
College of Home Economics
Colorado State University
Fort Collins, Colorado

Consumers Power Company
212 West Michigan Avenue
Jackson, Michigan 49201

Housing Research Center
College of Home Economics
Cornell University
Ithaca, N.Y.

Home Economics Extension Division
U.S. Department of Agriculture
Washington, D.C.   20505

Institute of Physical Medicine and
  Rehabilitation
New York University Bellevue Medical
  Center
400 East 34th Street
New York, N.Y.   10016

Pennsylvania State University
College of Home Economics
University Park, Penna.

President's Committee on Employment of
  the Handicapped
Washington, D.C.   20201

Public Housing Administration
Housing and Home Finance Agency
Washington, D.C.   20413

Social Security Administration
U.S. Department of Health, Education
  and Welfare
Washington, D.C.   20201

University of Connecticut
School of Home Economics
Storrs, Connecticut   06268

University of Illinois
Department of Home Economics
Urbana, Illinois   61803

University of Illinois
Small Homes Council
Urbana, Illinois   61803

University of Michigan
Home Economics Extension Service
East Lansing, Michigan

University of Rhode Island
College of Home Economics
Kingston, Rhode Island

University of Vermont
Department of Home Economics
Burlington, Vermont

U.S. Department of Agriculture
Agriculture Research Service
Clothing and Housing Research Division
Beltsville, Maryland   20705

Virginia Polytechnic Institute
School of Home Economics
Blacksburg, Virginia

Wayne State University
Department of Home Economics
Detroit, Michigan

Women's Bureau
U.S. Department of Labor
Washington, D.C.   20210

APPENDIX V

National Directories Listing Agencies or Professional Personnel That May Provide Services for the Handicapped

The Library
National Easter Seal Society for Crippled Children and Adults
Revised March, 1975

The more than 1400 Easter Seal societies in the 50 states, District of Columbia, and Puerto Rico support a wide variety of services for physically handicapped children and adults. Requests for information on Easter Seal services in a specific state should be addressed to the state society concerned. A directory of state societies affiliated with the National Easter Seal Society for Crippled Children and Adults, will be found in Appendices VII and VIII. Easter Seal programs and facilities are also described in some of the published directories listed below. This last has been compiled to help persons and agencies acquire copies of directories useful to them and to identify ones they may want to consult in the reference collection of a library.

American Academy for Cerebral Palsy
   Membership roster, committee appointments and by-laws. Issued annually. Apply: Executive Office, 1255 New Hampshire Ave., N.W., Washington, D.C. 20036.
   Members are listed alphabetically, geographically, and by specialty.

American Annals of the Deaf. Directory issue (April or May of each year) $5.00.
   Order from: Conference of Executives of American School for the Deaf, 5034 Wisconsin Ave., N.W., Washington, D.C. 20016.
   Lists speech and hearing facilities serving the deaf, including public day schools and classes, denominational and private schools in the U.S., and schools and classes in Canada. Membership list of American Instructors of the Deaf, information on teacher training centers, and much miscellaneous information on programs and services for the deaf are included.

American Association of Homes for the Aging
   Directory of non-profit homes and facilities. Paperbound. $3.00. Order from: American Association of Homes for the Aging, 1050 17th Street, N.W., Washington, D.C. 20036.
   A state-by-state, city-by-city, alphabetical listing of nonprofit voluntary and governmental homes, with information on bed capacity, name of administrator, and sponsor or affiliating agency. Also listed are homes in Canada, Puerto Rico, and the Virgin Islands.

American Association on Mental Deficiency
   Directory of residential facilities for the mentally retarded. 1968. 116 p. Paperbound. $4.50. Order from: American Association on Mental Deficiency, 5201 Connecticut Ave., N.W., Washington, D.C. 20015
   A national directory of public and private residential facilities (schools, hospitals, homes) in the United States and Canada. Also includes a list of state authorities for licensing private residential facilities and an index of administrative officers of residential facilities. Each entry gives location, director of the facility, admission policies, characteristics of the resident population, age levels accepted, program, personnel, residential units and residents per room, and fees charged.

American Association on Mental Deficiency
   Directory of members. Biannual. $5.00. Order from: American Association on Mental Deficiency, 5201 Connecticut Ave., N.W., Washington, D.C. 20015.
   An alphabetical listing of AAMD members, including academic degree, address, and divisional classification. Names are also indexed by state and city.

American Board for Certification in Orthotics and Prosthetics
   Registry of certified facilities and individuals in orthotics and prosthetics. Issued annually. Apply to: American Orthotic and Prosthetic Association, 1440 N St., N.W., Washington, D.C. 20005.
   A state-by-state listing of prosthetic and orthopedic appliance facilities. The list of persons is alphabetical by last name, showing type of certification and residence address.

American Foundation for the Blind
  Directory of agencies serving the visually handicapped in the United States. (18th ed.) 1973. 364 p. Paperbound. $10.00. Order from: American Foundation for the Blind, 15 W. 16th St., New York, N.Y. 10011.

  A state-by-state listing of services on the state and local level with supplementary lists of specialized agencies and organizations (of professional workers and councils of agencies for the blind, federal agencies, guide dog schools, medical research organizations, national consultative voluntary organizations, resources for reading and educational materials), useful directories, and organizations with an interest in the blind.

American Hospital Association
  Guide to the health care field. Annual. $14.50 plus postage. Order from: American Hospital Association, 840 Lake Shore Drive, Chicago, Ill. 60611.

  The annual listing of hospitals and inpatient care institutions other than hospitals that have met the standards set up by U.S. and Canada accreditation bodies (osteopathic hospitals are included). Also gives information on health organizations, agencies, schools, hospital statistics, a guide for hospital buyers, and a list of AHA institutional members.

American Medical Association
  Directory of national voluntary health organizations. (7th revision) 1971. 122 p. $2.50. Order from: Council on Voluntary Health Agencies, American Medical Association, 535 N. Dearborn St., Chicago, Ill. 60610.

  Describes the purpose, organizational pattern, financing and programs of national voluntary health agencies and several other health organizations of medical interest. The introduction contains major AMA policy actions concerning such agencies.

American Medical Association
  Survey of state medical association committees concerned with rehabilitation. Revised annually. Apply to: Committee on Rehabilitation, American Medical Association, 535 N. Dearborn St., Chicago, Ill. 60610.

  Lists state medical associations, those having rehabilitation committees (with name of chairman included), as well as the availability of 23 state and 15 county or community rehabilitation services directories. The directories, most of which have not been compiled by medical societies, are listed as useful sources of information.

American Occupational Therapy Foundation, Inc.
American Occupational Therapy Association
  6000 Executive Boulevard, Rockville, Maryland 20852.

American Personnel and Guidance Association (American Board on Counseling Services)
  Directory of approved counseling agencies; 1973 ed., $3.00.) Order from: American Personnel and Guidance Association, Publication Sales, 1607 New Hampshire Ave., N.W., Washington, D.C. 20009.

  Counseling services of 190 agencies in the U.S., Puerto Rico, and Canada that have been investigated and approved by the American Board on Counseling Services, Inc. are listed for the aid of school counselors, college guidance offices, and social service agencies.

American Physical Therapy Association
  Membership directory. 1966. 132 p. Paperbound. $5.75. Order from: American Physical Therapy Association, 1156 15th St., Washington, D.C. 20005.

An alphabetical listing of active, inactive, and life members of the Association, graduates of physical therapy courses or schools approved by the Council of Medical Education and Hospitals of the American Medical Association (since 1936) and the American Physical Therapy Association (prior to 1936).

American Psychological Association

Membership register. Apply to: American Psychological Association, 1200 17th St., N.W., Washington, D.C. 20036.

The register is a printout of the names and address of members as they appear on the dues and subscription statement.

American Public Health Association

Membership directory; members and fellows, affiliated societies and regional branches, agency members, sustaining members. 1967. 327 p. $7.00, soft cover; $10.00, hard cover (price to nonmembers; less for members). Order from: American Public Health Association, 1015 18th St., N.W., Washington, D.C. 20036.

Information is included on degrees, class of membership, section affiliation, and present position of members.

American Public Welfare Association

Public welfare directory. Published annually. $15.00. Order from: American Public Welfare Association, 1155 16th St., N.W., Suite 201, Washington, D.C. 20036.

Lists federal agencies and their regional personnel; state public welfare departments and other state agencies supervising or coordinating related programs; state district offices; county welfare directors; and local agencies serving cities of over 30,000 population. Appendixes contain additional information on disclosure of information to public assistance agencies, VA policy on release of information, residence requirements, international social service and agencies, supplementary directories, and a section on Canadian public welfare agencies.

American Registry of Physical Therapists

Directory (1936–1971). 1972. $5.00. American Registry of Physical Therapists, 30 N. Michigan Ave., Chicago, Ill. 60602.

This last issue of the now defunct Registry is a listing of physical therapists registered with the organization. Addresses of therapists are included.

American Speech and Hearing Association

Directory. Published annually. $20.00. Hard Cover. (Price to nonmembers and organizations; less to members.) Order from: American Speech and Hearing Association, 10801 Rockville Pike, Rockville, Maryland 20852.

Alphabetical and geographical listings of members, fellows, and life members of the organization, as well as information on accredited training programs, clinical service programs, certification requirements, professional ethics, state associations, and minimum requirements of hearing programs offering guidance in selection of hearing aids.

Association for Children with Learning Disabilities

Directory of educational facilities for the learning disabled. 5th ed. 1973. 48 p. Academic Therapy Publications, 1539 Fourth St., San Rafael, Ca. 94901.

An update of the 1971 directory, this publication includes information on the type of facility, size, sex and age of children served, and fees.

Council for Exceptional Children
   Directory of federal programs for the handicapped. $1.00. Order from: Council for Exceptional Children, 1920 Association Drive, Reston, Va. 22091.
   This review of federal programs for the handicapped was reprinted from the Congressional Record.

Council of Organizations Serving the Deaf
   Council membership directory, 1969. 1969. 42 p. Paperbound. Apply to: Council of Organizations Serving the Deaf, 4201 Connecticut Ave., N.W., Washington, D.C. 20008.
   The Council, organized in 1967, embraces 18 national member agencies working in the various areas of work with the deaf. The purposes, functions, structure, and activities of each are briefly described.

Ellingson, Careth
   Directory of facilities for the learning disabled and handicapped. by Careth Ellingson and James Cass. 1972. 624 p. $20.00. Order from: Harper & Row Publishers, 10 E. 53rd St., New York, N.Y. 10022.
   This directory includes analytical descriptions of diagnostic facilities, as well as descriptions of remedial, therapeutic, and developmental programs.

Health Insurance Institute
   Inventory of state and areawide health planning agencies and related organizations. March, 1970. n.p. Mimeo. Looseleaf. Health Insurance Institute, 277 Park Ave., New York, N.Y. 10017.
   Organized by states, this directory identifies the following in each state: state comprehensive health planning agency, HiCHAP coordinator, regional office of U.S.P.H.S, state health department, state mental health authority, hospital and medical facilities construction agency, regional medical program, community health planning agencies, and model cities program.

International Association of Laryngectomees
   Directory. Issued annually. Apply to: International Association of Laryngectomees, 219 E. 42nd St., New York, N.Y. 10017.
   A listing of Association officers, directors, committees, affiliated clubs, their officers, meeting dates, places and times, and facilities for speech instruction, as well as miscellaneous information on sources of supply of items of benefit to laryngectomees. Also available is the folder: **The I.A.L. registry; laryngectomized instructors of post-laryngectomy voice (esophageal voice).** A state-by-state, city-by-city listing of laryngectomized instructors who have applied for and been accepted for listing. The Association has no certification program but has verified the success achieved by the instructors.

International Association of Rehabilitation Facilities
   1974 membership directory. 1974. 28 p. Mimeo. Order from: International Association of Rehabilitation Facilities, 5530 Wisconsin Ave., Suite 955, Washington, D.C. 20015. $5.00.
   The first such directory of members since the merger of the Association of Rehabili-

tation Centers and the National Association of Sheltered Workshops and Homebound Programs. (See also reference above under Association of Rehabilitation Centers.)

Massachusetts Council of Organizations of the Handicapped
A directory of organizations of the handicapped in the United States. 1974. 474 p. $5.00. Order from: Massachusetts Council of Organizations of the Handicapped, 41 Woodglen Rd., Hyde Park, Mass. 02136.

A geographically arranged listing of self help organizations of the physically and mentally handicapped throughout the country.

National Assembly of National Voluntary Health & Social Welfare Organizations, Inc.
Service Directory of national organizations, voluntary and governmental. Issued biennially. $8.00. Order from: The National Assembly of National Voluntary Health & Social Welfare Organizations, 345 E. 46th St., New York, N.Y. 10017.

National Association for Mental Health
Mental health programs for pre-school children. 1974. $7.00. Order from: NAMH Publications Dept., 1800 N. Kent St., Arlington, Va. 22209.

A joint information service publication of NAMH and the American Psychiatric Association.

National Association of Social Workers
Directory of agencies: U.S. voluntary, international voluntary, and intergovernmental. 1973. 96 p. Order from: National Association of Social Workers, 1425 H St., N. W., Washington, D.C. 20005.

Information on membership, purposes, and programs of more than 300 agencies is provided.

National Association of Social Workers
Directory of professional social workers. 1973. Paperbound. $25.00. (Nonmembers) Order from: National Association of Social Workers, 1425 H St., N.W., Washington, D.C. 20005.

Lists full members, and student members.

National Association of Social Workers
Encyclopedia of social work (successor to the **Social Work Yearbook**). (16th issue) 1971. 1060 p. $22.50. Order from: National Association of Social Workers, 1425 H St., N.W., Washington, D.C. 20005.

In addition to 71 subject articles and 94 biographies of outstanding social work and welfare leaders of the past, the book contains a Directory of Agencies section, listing international agencies (voluntary and intergovernmental); national governmental and voluntary agencies (U.S.); and Canadian governmental and voluntary agencies. Each agency entry provides information on purpose and activities and gives address and name of its chief executive. Publications of agencies are also noted.

National Congress of Organizations of the Physically Handicapped
Roster of organization of the physically handicapped and their chapters. 2d. ed.

1970. 28 p. Mimeo. $4.00. Order from: National Congress of Organizations of the Physically Handicapped, 1405 Yale Pl., Minneapolis, Minn. 55403.

Available also is the mimeographed **COPH Roster of Publications,** 1969 edition, listing periodicals for and by the physically handicapped. $2.00.

National Council for Homemaker-Home Health Aid Services, Inc.

Directory of homemaker-home health aide services, 1966–1967. 1967. 181 p. Paperbound. $3.00. Order from: National Council for Homemaker Services, Inc. 1740 Broadway, New York, N.Y. 10019.

Representing more than a 150% growth in the field since publication of the 1963 directory, this listing contains in its mail section all known agencies providing direct service in the United States. Arrangement is alphabetical, by state and city, with notations of groups served by each agency. Canadian agencies are listed in a separate section.

National Council on the Aging

A national directory of housing for older people. 1969. 362 p. Paperbound. $5.50. Order from: National Council on the Aging, 1828 L St., N.W., Washington, D.C. 20036.

An alphabetical listing of about 600 housing facilities under nonprofit or private sponsorship, already in existence or under construction; information is arranged state-by-state; community and type of facility provided are indicated. A careful distinction is made between housing and institutional facilities; this is not a directory of nursing homes or homes for the aged.

National Council on the Aging

National directory of voluntary agencies. 1971. 90 p. Paperbound. Free on request. Order from: National Council on the Aging, 1828 L St., N.W., Washington, D.C. 20036.

Prepared for the Office of Economic Opportunity, this pamphlet lists about 300 organizations with peripheral or specific interest in the field of aging.

National Easter Seal Society for Crippled Children and Adults

The Easter Seal directory of resident camps for persons with special health needs. 9th ed. 1975. Mimeo. $1.50. Order from: National Easter Seal Society for Crippled Children and Adults, 2023 W. Ogden Ave., Chicago, Ill. 60612.

A list of 250 resident camps by state, with an alphabetical index by name. Camps are identified as to physical, mental, social and emotional disabilities served.

National Foundation

International directory of genetic services, compiled by Henry T. Lynch, M.D. 4th ed., March, 1974. The National Foundation, P.O. Box 2000, White Plains, N.Y. 10602.

The directory is divided into 2 sections: genetic services and amniocentesis. Over 300 genetic centers are listed in the U.S. alone.

National Health Council

National voluntary health agencies; profiles of 19 member agencies of the National Health Council. Rev. 1969. Paperbound. Apply to: National Health Council, 1740 Broadway, New York, N.Y. 10019.

This directory was designed for limited distribution to business and professional leaders to inform them of the goals, accomplishments, and procedures of the major national voluntary health agencies supported by the American public.

National Research Council—National Academy of Sciences. Division of Medical Sciences. Committee on Prosthetic-Orthotic Education

Amputee clinics in the United States and Canada. Revised annually. Mimeo. Paperbound. Apply to: Committee on Prosthetic-Orthotic Education, Division of Medical Sciences, National Research Council, 2101 Constitution Ave., Washington, D.C. 20418.

This roster was developed primarily to serve as a mailing list for the distribution of prosthetic educational materials. It has also proved useful as a source of information for patient referral. Types of services available and medical director are included in each listing.

National Society for Autistic Children

U.S. facilities and programs for children with severe mental illnesses—a directory, compiled by the National Society for Autistic Children for the National Institute of Mental Health. 1974. 448 p. Order from: The National Institute of Mental Health, 5600 Fishers Lane, Rockville, Md. 20852.

Facilities and programs are listed alphabetically by state. Information given includes: capacity of the program, fees, physical makeup of the facility, staff, and admission criteria.

People-to-People Program. Committee for the Handicapped

Directory of organizations interested in the handicapped. 1974. 44 p. Order from: People-to-People Program, Suite 610, La Salle Bldg., Conn. Ave. and L St., Washington, D.C. 20036.

An expansion and revision of the first edition, published in 1960. Contains descriptions of the organization and programs of more than 60 governmental and private agencies, as well as information on the utilization of volunteer workers and international programs. Intended mainly for distribution abroad, to promote the exchange of information on technics and procedures for rehabilitation and employment of the handicapped.

Porter Sargent, Publisher

Directory for exceptional children. (7th ed.) 1972. 1150 p. $14.00. Order from: Porter Sargent, Publisher, 11 Beacon St., Boston, Mass. 02108.

Concise descriptions of more than 3600 schools, homes, hospitals, treatment and training centers, and psychiatric and guidance clinics include information on: services offered, admission policies, costs, and specialized instruction and care for the retarded, maladjusted or physically handicapped. Classified facilities by special needs they serve.

President's Committee on Mental Retardation

In service to the mentally retarded. 1970. 28 p. Apply to: The President's Committee on Mental Retardation, Washington, D.C. 20201. A listing of 65 voluntary agencies, identifying briefly for each their particular interest in the mentally retarded.

Rehabilitation International

Compendium on the activities of world organizations interested in the handicapped, published for the Council of World Organizations Interested in the Handicapped. 1974. Request from: Rehabilitation International, 432 Park Avenue South, New York, N.Y. 10016.

Included are statements prepared by the member organizations describing the nature of their interest and activity, and descriptions of the activities in the United States.

U.S. Administration on Aging

National directory of senior centers. 1966. 260 p. $2.00. Paperbound. Order from: Superintendent of Documents, U.S. Government Printing Office, Washington, D.C. 20402.

Senior centers are listed alphabetically by state and city, giving address and information on services offered in each. Single-service centers are mainly organized for recreational or educational purposes. Multi-service centers offer a variety, such as health maintenance, personal, psychiatric and/or health counseling, recreation and adult education, community services, camping, food services, and programs for employment or income maintenance.

U.S. Department of Health, Education, and Welfare

Catalog of HEW assistance providing financial support and service to: states, communities, organizations, individuals. August, 1969; revised Nov., 1970. Mimeo. Looseleaf. 1969 edition, $5.50; Nov., 1970, revision pages, $1.75. Order from Superintendent of Documents, U.S. Government Printing Office, Washington, D.C. 20402.

Federal aid programs are briefly described, including information on: authorizing statute, type of program activity, eligibility, available assistance and restrictions, federal appropriations supporting the program.

U.S. Department of Health, Education, and Welfare. Secretary's Committee on Mental Retardation

Directory of state and local resources for the mentally retarded. Dec., 1969. 121 p. Mimeo. Looseleaf. Apply to: Secretary's Committee on Mental Retardation, U.S. Department of Health, Education, and Welfare, Washington, D.C. 20201.

U.S. National Institute of Mental Health

Mental health directory, 1973. 445 p. Paperbound. $4.00. (National Clearinghouse for Mental Health Information, pubn. no. 1005) Order from: Superintendent of Documents, U.S. Government Printing Office, Washington, D.C. 20402.

Covers the National Institute of Mental Health, state departments dealing with mental health and mental retardation, state hospitals for the mentally ill and mentally retarded, over 3000 outpatient clinics and day-night services, mental health associations, and other sources of mental health information. Compiled annually by the National Clearinghouse for Mental Health Information.

U.S. Office of Education. Bureau of Education for the Handicapped

Selected career education programs for the handicapped. 1973. (73-05501). Office of Education, Washington, D.C. 20202.

Short summaries of over 100 vocational education projects to encourage national replication in each State.

U.S. Public Health Service

Directory of state and territorial health authorities. Issued annually. (Public Health Serv. publ. no. 75) 50 cents. Order from: Superintendent of Documents, U.S. Government Printing Office, Washington, D.C. 20402.

A state-by-state listing of health officers and the organizational unit or service they direct. Listed separately are all state health department directors and state agencies other than health departments designated to administer grant programs of the Public Health Service and the Children's Bureau program of crippled children's services. Regional offices of the U.S. Public Health Service are included.

U.S. Rehabilitation Services Administration
Directory of state division of vocational rehabilitation. Revised annually. Mimeo. Apply to: Rehabilitation Services Administration, U.S. Social and Rehabilitation Service, Washington, D.C. 20201.

A listing by state of the professional personnel in state divisions of vocational rehabilitation. A similar list is available of state agencies for the blind **(Directory of State Agencies for the Blind).**

U.S. Social Security Administration. Office of Research and Statistics
Social security programs in the U.S. 1973. (1770-00218). Order from: Superintendent of Documents, U.S. Government Printing Office, Washington, D.C. 20402. $1.20.

Brings together information on the historical development and present status of old-age, survivors, disability, and health insurance.

United Way of America
Directory. Issued annually. $10.00 (non-members; less to members.) Order from: United Way of America, 801 N. Fairfax St., Alexandria, Va. 22314.

Lists staff, officers and directors of the national organization, as well as member state and local united funds, community chests, and community health and welfare councils in the U.S. and Canada, and in several other foreign countries. An index of campaign data and tabulation of the total funds raised since 1920 are also included.

Wasserman, Paul
Health organizations of the United States, Canada, and internationally; a directory of voluntary associations, professional societies and other groups concerned with the health and related fields, by Paul Wasserman and Joan Giesecke. (3rd ed.) 1974. 249 p. Order from: McGrath Publishing Co., 821 Fifteenth St., N.W., Washington, D.C. 20005.

Gives information on location, officials, purpose and objectives, programs and activities of more than 1,300 organizations, societies, foundations, associations and other non-governmental bodies. Included is a classified listing of the national, regional and international organizations arranged under the subject which relates to their activities and functions.

APPENDIX VI

Directory of State Cerebral Palsy Agencies

Alabama
Pres. UCP of Cullman Area, Ala.
Mr. Robert C. Grant
1604 Catoma Dr., N.W.
Cullman, Ala. 35055

Pres. UCP of East Central Ala.
Mr. Jerry Morrison
P.O. Box 1228
Anniston, Ala. 36201

Pres. UCP of Gadsden & Northeast Ala.
Mr. Earl Garrett
Rt. 7, Box 75
Gadsden, Ala. 35903

Pres. UCP of Grtr. Birmingham
Mr. Bryan Hassler
2151 Highland Ave., Suite 214
Birmingham, Ala. 35205

Pres. UCPA of Huntsville & Tenn.
   Valley, Inc.
Mrs. Dana Thomas
119 Drake Ave., S.W.
Huntsville, Ala. 35801

Pres. UCP of Mobile
Mrs. George J. Waldron, III
1054 Locarno St.
Mobile, Ala. 36608

Pres. UCP of Montgomery Spastic Ch.
   Assoc.
Mr. Phil Richardson
P.O. Box 11000
Montgomery, Ala. 36111

Pres. UCPA of Northwest Ala.
Mr. E. B. Hamner, Jr.
P.O. Box 2388
Muscle Shoals, Ala. 35660

Pres. UCPA of North Central Ala.
Mr. Jerry West
P.O. Box 511
Athens, Ala. 35611

Pres. UCP of Tuscaloosa & West Ala.
Mr. Kenneth M. Vassar
17-D Northwood Lake
Northport, Ala. 35476

Arizona
UCP of Arizona
No Pres.

Pres. UCPA of Central Arizona
Mr. Ronald G. Wilson
Valley Nat'l. Bank
P.O. Box 625
Phoenix, Ariz. 85001

Arkansas
Pres. UCP of Arkansas
Mr. James David Brown
816 Ouashita Circle
Little Rock, Ark. 72205

Pres. UCP of Central Ark.
Mr. John W. Norman
1102 So. Arthur Dr.
Little Rock, Ark. 72204

Pres. UCP of Northeast Ark.
Mrs. Mary K. Townsend
1329 Madison, Apt. 1C
Jonesboro, Ark. 72401

Pres. UCP of South Arkansas
Mrs. Judy Pendleton
1627 Park Lane
El Dorado, Ark. 71730

Pres. UCP of Washington Cty.
Mrs. Mildred Clarkson
805 North Mill
Springdale, Ark. 72764

California
Pres. UCPA of California
Mr. Walter J. Jackson
3551 S. Silver Springs Rd.
Lafayette, Calif. 94549

Pres. UCPA of Alameda-Contra Costa
   Ctys.
James Burchell, Esq.
Hanna & Brophy
436 14th St., Suite 1316
Oakland, Ca. 94612

Pres. UCP of Central Calif.
Mrs. Edward C. Sturgeon
1540 E. Shaw Ave., Suite 107
Fresno, Calif. 93710

Pres. UCPA of Los Angeles
Mr. Kenneth R. Bettencourt
Vice Pres.-Security Pacific Nat'l. Bank
333 South Hope
Los Angeles, Ca. 90017

Pres. UCPA of Marin Cty.
Mr. Leon B. Nelson
Bank of Marin
P.O. Box 600
San Rafael, Calif.   94902

Pres. UCPA of Orange Cty.
Mr. Don Nickerson
State Farm Insurance
16111 Bolsa Chica, Suite C
Huntington Beach, Cal.   92648

Pres. UCPA of Sacramento-Yolo Ctys.
   Inc.
Ms. Marilyn E. Park
1081 38th St.
Sacramento, Calif.   95816

Pres. UCPA of San Diego Cty.
Mrs. Richard G. Schneider
7136 Vista Del Mar
La Jolla, Calif.   92037

Pres. UCP of San Francisco
Mr. Jules Dundes
UCP of San Francisco
1511 Clement Street
San Francisco, Calif.   94118

Pres. UCPA of San Joaquin Cty.
Mrs. Loren Powell
2033 W. Monterey
Stockton, Cal.   95204

Pres. UCPA of Santa Clara & San Mateo
   Ctys.
Mr. Glen R. Eckols
15021 Fruitvale Ave.
Saratoga, Cal.   95070

Pres. UCPA of Sonoma Cty.
Mr. Terry L. Hollandsworth
4497 Bennett View Drive
Santa Rosa, Calif.   95405

Colorado
Pres. UCPA of Colorado Springs
Mrs. Lawrence Gorab
2469 Virgo Dr.
Colorado Springs, Colo.   80906

Pres. UCPA of Denver
Mr. James B. Reed
4103 S. Olive St.
Denver, Colo.   80237

Connecticut
Pres. UCPA of Connecticut
Mr. Vincent J. Lupinacci, Jr.
20 Henry St.
Darien, Conn.   06820

Pres. UCP of Bristol Cty.
Mrs. Tillie Grzymkowski

4 Chidsey Terrace
Terryville, Conn.   06786

Pres. UCP of Fairfield Cty.
Mr. Frank Luciani
1965 Dixwell Ave.
Hamden, Conn.   06514

Pres. UCP of Grtr. Hartford
Dr. Philip Morse
560 So. Main St.
West Hartford, Conn.   06107

Pres. UCP of the Grtr. Waterbury Area,
   Inc.
Mr. Raymond J. Crane
Green Hill
Middlebury, Conn.   06762

Pres. UCP of New Britain
Mrs. Thomas Holleran
45 Bliss Road
New Britain, Conn.   06053

Pres. UCPA of New London
Mr. John E. Palmer
4 Fullmore Drive
Waterford, Conn.   06385

Pres. UCPA of Plainville Cty.
Mr. John J. Gregory
9 Fox Road
Plainville, Conn.   06062

Delaware
Pres. UCP of Delaware, Inc.
Miss Elizabeth R. Schantz
344 N. Dillwyn Rd.
Windy Hills
Newark, Dela.   19711

District of Columbia
Pres. UCP of Washington, D.C.
Mr. Herbert H. Wright
4223 - 38th Street, N.W.
Washington, D.C.   20016

Florida
Pres. UCP of Florida
Mr. Thomas E. Blayney
255 Crown Oaks Way
Longwood, Fla.   32750

Pres. UCP of the Big Bend Area
Mr. Wayne Blanton
Lewis State Bank Bldg., Suite 604
215 S. Monroe
Tallahassee, Fla.   32301

Pres. UCP of Broward Cty.
Mr. James Darst
10670 S.W. 27th Street
Davie, Fla.   33328

Pres. UCP of Central Fla.
Miss Faye Dorman
P.O. Box 190
Cocoa, Fla.   32922

Pres. UCP of Miami
Mr. A. Anthony Noboa
Miami Beach First Nat'l. Bank
1111 Lincoln Rd. Mall
Miami Beach, Fla.   33139

Pres. UCP of Northwest Fla.
Mr. Charles P. Ponitz
3724 Pompano Dr.
Pensacola, Fla.   32504

Pres. UCP of Panama City
Mr. James Heisner
P.O. Box 1039
Panama City, Fla.   32401

Pres. UCP of Polk Cty.
Mrs. Clyde E. Asbury
9 Loma Verde
Lakeland, Fla.   33803

Pres. UCP of Tampa
Mrs. Nancy Ford
First Nat'l. Bank of Tampa
P.O. Box 1810
Tampa, Fla.   33601

Georgia
Pres. UCP of Georgia
Mrs. William F. Sartain
15 Forrest Place, N.W.
Atlanta, Ga.   30328

Pres. UCP of Grtr. Atlanta
Col. Harold Dye
1837 N. Rock Springs Road
Atlanta, Ga.   30324

Pres. UCP of Macon & Middle Ga.
Mrs. Gloria W. Neal
C&S National Bank
487 Cherry St.
Macon, Ga.   31201

Pres. UCP of Muscogee Cty.
Mr. J. Randall Braswell
4205 17th Ave.
Columbus, Ga.   31904

Pres. UCP of Rome & Northwest Ga.
Mrs. Ben Tompkins
408 Cave Spring Rd.
Rome, Ga.   30161

Hawaii
Pres. UCPA of Hawaii
Mr. Norman Brand
1210 Auahi St., Suite 222
Honolulu, Hawaii   96814

Idaho
Pres. UCP of Idaho
Mr. Verne S. Ward
503 10th Ave., South
Nampa, Idaho   83651

Illinois
Pres. UCP of Illinois
Mrs. Joan C. Wolfson
703 Phelps Ave.
Rockford, Ill.   61108

Pres. UCP of the Blackhawk Region
Mr. Steven Stromberg
6255 Porter Rd.
Rockford, Ill.   61103

Pres. UCP of the Five Rivers Area
Mrs. Judith Yeager
508 W. John
Champaign, Ill.   61820

Pres. UCP of Grtr. Chicago
Mr. John T. Trutter
Ill. Bell Telephone Co., Floor 28 A
225 West Randolph Street
Chicago, Ill.   60606

Pres. UCP Land of Lincoln
Mr. Robert Leach
1724-B South Main
Jacksonville, Ill.   62650

Pres. UCP of Northeastern Ill.
Mr. Edward L. Minarich
520 Knox Place
Joliet, Ill.   60435

Pres. UCP of Northwestern Ill.
Mr. Richard A. Kohrs
Route 1, Box 37-A
Lynn Center, Ill.   61262

Pres. UCP of Southern Ill.
Mrs. Bonnie Lewis
P.O. Box 397
Centralia, Ill.   62801

Indiana
Pres. UCP of Indiana
Mr. Robert B. Quinn
Guide Div., General Motors Corp.
2915 Pendleton Ave.
Anderson, Ind.   46011

Pres. UCP of Central Indiana
Mr. Julian D. Coleman, Jr.
115 West 44th St.
Indianapolis, Ind.   46208

Pres. UCP of Delaware Cty.
Mr. William T. Clark
C/O Muncie Federal Savings & Loans
P.O. Box 1192
Muncie, Ind.   47305

Pres. UCP of Grtr. Lafayette
Mr. Harold Young
2809 Meadow Dr.
Lafayette, Ind.   47905

Pres. UCP of Howard Cty.
Mr. Junior A. Milam
1005 N. Wabash Ave.
Kokomo, Ind.   46901

Pres. UCP of Madison Cty.
Mr. Craig R. Dunkin
4208 Alpine Dr.
Anderson, Ind.   46014

Pres. UCP of Shelby Cty.
Ms. Nancy Coers
R.R. 6
Shelbyville, Ind.   46176

Pres. UCP of the Wabash Valley
Mr. Stanley V. Hart
Terre Haute First Nat'l. Bank
523 Wabash Ave., P.O. Box 540
Terre Haute, Ind.   47808

Pres. UCP of Wayne Cty.
Mr. Wesley M. Robison
718 W. Main St.
Richmond, Ind.   47374

Pres. UCP of Whitley Cty.
Mr. James Fleck
Box 405
Columbia City, Ind.   46725

Iowa
Pres. UCP of Iowa
Mr. Robert J. Brighi
Taylor School & Rehab. Center
720 7th Ave. S.W.
Cedar Rapids, Iowa   52404

Pres. UCP of Central Iowa
Mr. Darrell Lundien
1536 S.E. Linn
Boone, Iowa   50035

Pres. UCP of Dubuque
Mr. Gary Hoxmeier
2243 Chippewa Dr.
Dubuque, Iowa   52001

Pres. UCP of Grtr. Cedar Rapids
Mr. David A. Bey
2517 Blue Ridge Drive N.E.
Cedar Rapids, Iowa   52402

Pres. UCP of the Northeast Iowa
Mr. Stanley Lauterbach
1551 W. 11th
Waterloo, Iowa   50702

Pres. UCP of Northern Iowa
Mrs. Paul C. Miller

100 7th Ave.
Charles City, Iowa   50616

Pres. UCP of Northwest Iowa
Mr. Thomas Brennan
P.O. Box 1716
Sioux City, Iowa   51102

Pres. UCP of Southeast Iowa
Mr. Derrald W. Ware
816 E. Finley Ave.
Ottumwa, Iowa   52501

Pres. UCP of Southwest Iowa
Mr. William E. Campbell
Glenwood State School
Glenwood, Iowa   51534

Kansas
Pres. UCP of Kansas
Mr. Joe L. Childs
Box 1744
Hutchinson, Kans.   67501

Kentucky
Pres. UCP of Kentucky
Donald P. Cross, Ph.D.
Univ. of Ky., Taylor Educ. Bldg.
Lexington, Ky.   40506

Pres. UCP of the Bluegrass
Mr. C. A. Coleman
UCP of the Bluegrass
P.O. Box 8003
Lexington, Ky.   40503

Pres. UCP of Eastern Ky.
Mrs. Paul E. McGraw
1602 Lexington Ave.
Ashland, Ky.   41101

Pres. UCP of Grtr. Louisville
Mr. E. Bruce Blythe, Jr.
318 Kentucky Towers
Louisville, Ky.   40202

Pres. UCP of Northern Ky., Inc.
Mr. William T. Robinson, III
2447 Cecilia
Covington, Ky.   41011

Louisiana
Pres. UCP of Louisiana
Mr. Robert J. Jackson
P.O. Drawer 1412
Monroe, La.   71201

Pres. UCP of Grtr. Baton Rouge
Col. Rollo C. Lawrence, Jr.,/Ret. USAF./
745 North St.
Baton Rouge, La.   70802

Pres. UCP of Grtr. New Orleans, Inc.
Mr. J. Mason Webster

Director of Placement
Tulane University
New Orleans, La.   70118

Pres. UCPA of Northeast La.
Mrs. Faye H. Jackson
817 K Street
Monroe, La.   71201

Pres. UCP of Southwest La.
Mrs. Wanda Courmier
1603 Broadmoor St.
Lake Charles, La.   70601

Maine
Pres. Mid-State UCP
Mrs. Marian Mac Donald
RFD
Winthrop, Maine   04364

Pres. UCP of Northeastern Maine
Mr. L. Philip Baron
142 Hammond St., Apt. 10
Bangor, Maine   04401

Maryland
Pres. UCP of Maryland
Mrs. Claudia E. Lukes
3524 Woodbine St.
Chevy Chase, Md.   20015

Pres. UCP of Central Maryland
Mr. Horace F. Burgee, Jr.
3631 Falls Rd.
Baltimore, Md.   21211

Pres. UCP of Prince Georges Cty.
Mr. William I. Buck
Buck Distributing Co.
Upper Marlboro, Md.   20870

Massachusetts
Pres. UCPA of Berkshire Cty.
Mr. Ralph Levine
98 Nancy Ave.
Pittsfield, Mass.   01201

Pres. UCPA of Metropolitan Boston
Mr. Joseph Thompson
95 Bryant St.
West Bridgewater, Mass.   02379

Pres. UCPA of the North Shore
Mr. Samuel A. Vitali
Lt. Governor's Office
State House   Room 259
Boston, Mass.   02133

Pres. UCP of Western Mass.
Mr. William R. Congo
UCP of Western Mass.
152 Sumner Ave.
Springfield, Mass.   01108

Michigan
Pres. UCPA of Michigan
Glen V. Borre, Esq.
330 Frey Bldg.
Grand Rapids, Mich.   49502

Pres. UCP of Bay County
Mr. William O. Ittner
2291 East Hotchkiss Rd.
Bay City, Mich.   48706

Pres. UCP of Berrien Cty.
Mrs. Eunice French
Rt. 1
Singer Lake
Baroda, Mich.   49101

Pres. UCP of Calhoun Cty., Inc.
Miss Susan Darling
277 South Keathley Dr.
Battle Creek, Mich.   49017

Pres. UCP of Cheboygan
Mr. Charles M. Morrison
208 S. Benton St.
Cheboygan, Mich.   49721

Pres. UCP of Dearborn Cty.
Mrs. Shirley Popkey
3528 Monroe
Dearborn, Mich.   48124

Pres. UCP of Muskegon Cty.
Mr. John Poort, Jr.
426 W. Western Ave.
Muskegon, Mich.   49440

Pres. UCP of North Central
Mr. Russell Peterson
Route 1
Cadillac, Mich.   49601

Pres. UCP of Ottawa-Allegan Ctys.
Mr. Roger Bramer
9945 South M-52
St. Charles, Mich.   48655

Pres. UCP of Palmyra Cty.
Mr. Emil Iott
269 Elm St.
Deerfield, Mich.   49238

Pres. UCP of Pontiac
Mr. William G. Wright
2007 E. Hammond Lake Dr.
Pontiac, Mich.   48053

Pres. UCP of Saginaw Cty.
Mr. Eugene B. Webb
12 Franconian Ct.
Frankenmuth, Mich.   48734

Pres. UCP of Sault Ste. Marie
Mr. Richard Y. Burnett
1307 Park Ave.
Sault Ste. Marie, Mich.   49783

Pres. UCP of Washtenaw Cty.
Mr. Richard E. Spencer
625 Hidden Valley Dr., Apt. 202
Ann Arbor, Mich. 48104

Pres. UCPA of Detroit
Mr. Donald Curtis
Touche, Ross, Bailey & Smart
1380 First Nat'l. Bank Bldg.
Detroit, Mich. 48226

Pres. UCP of Genesee Cty.
Mr. Jerry O'Boyle
G-9050 Webster Rd.
Clio, Mich. 48420

Pres. UCP of Grand Rapids & Kent Cty.
Mr. Henry M. Douglas
Douglas Bros., Inc.
106 S. Division
Grand Rapids, Mich. 49502

Pres. UCP of Jackson Cty.
Mrs. Forrest V. Patch
P.O. Box 785
Jackson, Mich. 49204

Pres. UCP of Lansing
Mrs. Ruth Karslake
933 Lantern Hill Dr.
East Lansing, Mich. 48823

Pres. UCP of Marquette Cty.
Mr. John A. Vargo
230 Harlow Block
Marquette, Mich. 49855

Pres. UCP of Midland Cty.
Mrs. Edward Elliott
2007 Wyllys
Midland, Mich. 48640

Minnesota
Pres. UCP of Minnesota
Mr. Edwin O. Opheim
Office of Human Services
444 Lafayette
St. Paul, Minn. 55101

Pres. UCP of Central Minnesota
Mr. Gerald Carlson
St. Cloud Hospital
1406 6th Ave. North
St. Cloud, Minn. 56301

Pres. UCP of Duluth Area
Mr. Ronald P. Cottrell
600 East 2nd St.
Duluth, Minn. 55805

Pres. UCP of Grtr. Minneapolis, Inc.
Mrs. Keith P. Caswell, Jr.
14086 Rice Lake Circle
Osseo, Minn. 55369

Pres. UCP of Grtr. St. Paul
Mr. Fred Putzier
771 Fairmont Ave.
St. Paul, Minn. 55105

Pres. UCP of Mower Cty.
Mrs. Robert Butler
R.R. 1, Box 221
Austin, Minn. 55912

Pres. UCP of the Red River Valley
Mr. Jay Kiefer
1325 South River Drive
Moorhead, Minn. 56560

Mississippi
Pres. UCP of Mississippi
Mr. Walter F. Fisher
Box 186
Taylorsville, Miss. 39168

Pres. UCP of Columbus Cty.
Dr. Charles E. Ambrose
1125 Seventh St. North
Columbus, Miss. 39701

Pres. UCPA of Miss. Gulf Coast
Mr. James B. Rouse, Vice Pres.
Hancock Bank
14th Street
Gulfport, Miss. 39501

Pres. UCP of Natchez Area
Mr. Bert Haydel
101 Gracetown Shopping Center
Natchez, Miss. 39120

Missouri
Pres. UCPA of Missouri
Mr. C. B. Boeckman
1722 Oak Street
Kansas City, Mo. 64108

Pres. UCP of Big Springs Area
Mr. Clyde M. McCrea
1920 Barron Rd.
Poplar Bluff, Mo. 63901

Pres. UCP of Boone Cty.
Dr. Robert A. Mc Quilkin
108 Westwood Ave.
Columbia, Mo. 65201

Pres. UCP of Bootheel, Mo.
Mrs. Sharon Wilson
705 Michael
Kennett, Mo. 63857

Pres. UCP of Buchanan Cty.
Mr. Eugene G. Felling
2507 Meadow Trail
St. Joseph, Mo. 64503

Pres. UCP of Cape Girardeau
Mr. Lloyd G. Estes

1437 Kingsway Drive
Cape Girardeau, Mo.   63701

Pres. UCPA of Grtr. Kansas City, Mo.
Mrs. Virginia D. Gill
700 W. 112th St.
Kansas City, Mo.   64114

Pres. UCP of Mark Twain Area
Mrs. Nancy Walterscheid
27 Lettlers Trail
Hannibal, Mo.   63401

Pres. UCP of Mineral Area
Mr. Harvey Collar
404 Low St.
Flat River, Mo.   63601

Pres. UCP of North Central Mo.
Mr. Richard Ellis
P.O. Box 556
Kirksville, Mo.   63501

Pres. UCPA of Grtr. St. Louis
Mr. Tim King
Ins. Consultants Inc.
1010 Collingwood Dr.
St. Louis, Mo.   63132

Pres. UCP of Sac Osage
Mr. Eldon Steward
Route 2
Box 57
El Dorado Springs, Mo.   64744

Pres. UCP of Scott-Mississippi
Mrs. Lyman Bollinger
Route 1, Box 138
Illmo, Mo.   63754

Pres. UCP of Southwest Mo.
Mr. Garry Adams
2315 Ingram Mill Road South
Springfield, Mo.   65804

Pres. UCP of Tri-Cty.
Mr. Richard Guppy
Box 542
Neosho, Mo.   64850

Pres. UCP of Southwestern Ill.
Ms. Mary Lou Bedient
3811 Shaw Ave., 1st Fl. Apt.
St. Louis, Mo.   63110

Pres. UCP of West Central Mo.
Mrs. J. Gregory Connor
2503 Anderson Ave.
Sedalia, Mo.   65301

Montana
Pres. UCP of Montana
Mrs. Clifford Lillemon
900 4th Ave., N.W.
Great Falls, Montana   59404

Nebraska
Pres. UCP of Nebraska
Dr. Edward L. La Crosse
4927 Ruggles
Omaha, Neb.   68111

New Hampshire
Pres. UCPA of New Hampshire
Mr. J. Philip Boucher
35 Currier Avenue
Peterborough, N.H.   03458

New Jersey
Pres. UCP of Monmouth & Ocean Ctys.
Mr. Robert C. Manfredi
289 Broadway
Long Branch, N.J.   07740

Pres. UCP of North Jersey
Mr. Jay Trien
One Old Mill Road
North Caldwell, N.J.   07006

Pres. UCP League of Union Cty.
Julius R. Pollatschek, Esq.
1000 Stuyvesant Ave.
Union, N.J.   07083

Pres. UCPA of Middlesex Cty.
Prof. Milton H. Cowan
Rutgers Univ., Cook Coll.
7 Elm Row
New Brunswick, N.J.   08901

Pres. UCP of Hudson Cty, N.J.
Mr. James A. McGeady
Reynolds Securities Inc.
120 Broadway
New York, N.Y.   10005

Pres. UCPA of New Jersey
Mr. John L. Davis
61 B Rhus Plaza
Cranbury, N.J.   08512

Pres. UCP of Cumberland Cty.
Mr. Robert E. Moynihan
Woodlawn Ave.
Newfield, N.J.   08344

Pres. UCP of Gloucester & Salem Ctys.
Dr. Dominic W. Flamini
23 Middleton Rd.
Moorestown, N.J.   08057

New Mexico
Pres. UCPA of New Mexico
Mrs. Patricia A. Penrose
1509-6th NW
Albuquerque, N.M.   87102

New York
Pres. UCPA of New York State

Mr. J. Kevin Meneilly, Esq.
6 Bondsburry Lane
Mellville, N.Y.   11746

Pres. UCPA of the Capital District, Inc.
Mr. Kevin G. Langan
Colonie Motors, Inc.
2242 Central Ave.
Schenectady, N.Y.   12304

Pres. UCP of Cayuga Cty.
Mr. Albert T. DeRoose
Box 389
Weedsport, N.Y.   13166

Pres. Central Mohawk Valley CPA.
Mr. Gary J. Pope
Holland Gardens, Apt. L9
Amsterdam, N.Y.   12010

Pres. Finger Lakes UCPA
Mr. William J. Kane
37 Exchange St.
Geneva, N.Y.   14456

Pres. UCP of New York City
Mr. Leo Hausman
Belding Hausman Fabrics, Inc.
6 East 32nd St.
New York, N.Y.   10016

Pres. UCPA of Niagara Cty., Inc.
Mr. Ralph S. De Rosa
622 Pine Ave.
Niagara Falls, N.Y.   14301

Pres. UCP of Orange Cty.
Mrs. Anne S. Deane
34 Dogwood Hills Rd.
Newburgh, N.Y.   12550

Pres. UCP of Queens, Inc.
Jack M. Weinstein, Esq.
108-18 Queens Blvd.
Forest Hills, N.Y.   11375

Pres. UCPA of the Rochester Area, Inc.
Mrs. John Wolbert
808 Phelps Road
Honeoye Falls, N.Y.   14472

Pres. UCPA of Rockland Cty.
Mrs. Patrick Rocchio
75 Hall St.
New City, N.Y.   10956

Pres. UCPA of Schenectady Cty., Inc.
Mr. Robert Treat, Jr.
1525 Barclay Place
Schenectady, N.Y.   12309

Pres. The Special Children's Center
Ithaca Area
Mr. Gustav Landen
1650 Slaterville Road
Ithaca, N.Y.   14850

Pres. UCPA of Suffolk Cty.
Mr. John Del Mastro
977 Jericho Turnpike
Smithtown, N.Y.   11787

Pres. UCPA of Sullivan Cty.
Mrs. Elizabeth L. Berman
40 Yaun Ave.
Liberty, N.Y.   12754

Pres. UCP & Handicapped Children's
   Assn. of Syracuse
Dr. Marian Z. Beauchamp
107 Century Drive
Syracuse, N.Y.   13209

Pres. UCPA of Tri Ctys.
Mrs. Hugh Ross
23 Parkview Place
Glens Falls, N.Y.   12801

Pres. UCPA of Tri-Villages
Mrs. Harold Snell
P.O. Box 31
Ft. Hunter, N.Y.   12069

Pres. UCP of Ulster Cty.
Mrs. Martin Oberkirch, Jr.
Box 165
Ulster Park, N.Y.   12487

Pres. UCP of the Utica Area
Mr. Walter J. Gossin
28 Hughes Street
Whitesboro, N.Y.   13492

Pres. UCP of Westchester Cty.
Mr. Simon B. Siegel
72 Lake Shore Drive
Eastchester, N.Y.   10709

Pres. UCP of Western N.Y.
Mr. Walter Brock
17 Court St.
Buffalo, N.Y.

Pres. UCPA of Nassau Cty.
Mr. Joseph Warantz
3267 Benjamin Rd.
Oceanside, N.Y.   11572

North Carolina
Pres. UCP of North Carolina
Mr. William M. Law
4217 Rowan St.
Raleigh, N.C.   27609

Ohio
Pres. UCPA of Ohio
Mr. Seymour S. Zipper
865 Sunnyside Ave.
Akron, Ohio   44303

Chrmn. of the Board of Trustees
UCP of Akron & Summit Cty.

Mr. John M. Jacobson, Jr.
863 Wallwood Drive
Akron, Ohio 44321

Pres. UCP of Butler Cty. & Vicinity
Paul J. Malott, Ph.D.
707 Oak Street
Oxford, Ohio 45056

Pres. UCP of Cincinnati
Mrs. William H. Hopple, Jr.
3685 Traskwood Circle
Cincinnati, Ohio 45208

Pres. UCP of Columbiana Cty.
Mr. Richard Brian
324 Vine St.
E. Liverpool, Ohio 43920

Pres. UCP of Columbus & Franklin Cty.
Mrs. Russell Rogers
2330 Fenton St.
Columbus, Ohio 43224

Pres. UCPA of Cuyahoga Cty., Inc.
Mr. Myron E. Jackson
1460 Union Commerce Bldg.
Cleveland, Ohio 44115

Pres. UCPA of East Central Ohio
Mr. Larry H. De Camp
1010 25th St., N.E.
Canton, Ohio 44714

Pres. UCP of Fremont & Sandusky Cty.
    & Vicinity
Mrs. Ralph Laney
865 N. Main St.
Clyde, Ohio 43410

Pres. UCP of Lancaster, Fairfield Cty., &
    Vic.
Mr. Clark McGhee
410 Marietta St.
Bremen, Ohio 43107

Pres. UCP of Lima & Allen Ctys.
Rev. William Fells
199 E. Blue Lick Road
Lima, Ohio 45801

Pres. UCP of Metropolitan Dayton
Glenn E. Mumpower, Esq.
111 W. First St., Suite 500
Dayton, Ohio 45402

Pres. UCP of Northwest Ohio
Mr. Harold Vaillant
Pres. Mid-Am Tool Co.
6061 Telegraph Rd.
Toledo, Ohio 43612

Oklahoma
Pres. UCP of Oklahoma
Mr. Harper V. Orth

P.O. Box CC
Norman, Okla. 73069

Pres. UCP of Cleveland Cty.
Mr. William R. Upthegrove
Dean, Engineering Coll., Okla. Univ.
202 W. Boyd St.
Norman, Okla. 73069

Pres. UCPA of Comanche Cty.
Mrs. Joyce Hennesee
1709 B Ave.
Lawton, Okla. 73501

Pres. UCP of Grtr. Oklahoma City
Mr. Maurice G. Woods
6420 N. Hillcrest
Oklahoma City, Okla. 73116

Oregon
Pres. UCP of Oregon
Mr. Norman Crawford
Northwest Natural Gas
123 N.W. Flanders St.
Portland, Oregon 97209

Pres. UCP of Northwest Oregon
Mr. Norman Crawford
Northwest Natural Gas
123 N.W. Flanders St.
Portland, Oregon 97209

Pennsylvania
Pres. UCP of Pennsylvania
Joseph L. Cohen, Esq.
Town House Apts.
660 Boas St., Apt. 1515
Harrisburg, Pa. 17102

Pres. UCP of Beaver, Butler & Lawrence
    Ctys.
Mr. Peter Grittie
1732 Atkinson St.
New Castle, Pa. 16101

Pres. UCP of the Capital Area
Dr. Gerald D. Kaspar
4740 Del Brook Rd.
Mechanicsburg, Pa. 17055

Pres. UCP of Central Penn.
Mr. Jerry Boyer
Juniata Valley Office M.H./M.R.
400 Highland Ave.
Lewiston, Pa. 17044

Pres. UCP of Columbia & Montour Ctys.
Mr. Joseph Mc Glinn
Editor—Danville News
Ferry St.
Danville, Pa. 17821

Pres. UCP of Crawford, Venango,
    Clarion & Mercer Ctys.

Mr. P. C. Murray
R.D. 2—Dunham Rd.
Meadville, Pa.   16335

Pres. UCP of Delaware Cty.
Mr. Spencer A. Manthorpe
101 Rose Tree Road
Media, Pa.   19063

Pres. UCP of Lackawanna Cty.
Mr. Louis V. Russoniello
521 Wyoming Ave.
Scranton, Pa.   18509

Pres. UCP of Lancaster Cty.
Emmett Lehman, Esq.
53 N. Duke St.
Lancaster, Pa.   17602

Pres. UCP of Lebanon Cty.
Mr. David G. Gittleman
328 E. Pershing Ave.
Lebanon, Pa.   17042

Pres. UCP of Lehigh Valley
Mr. Robert Sadler, III
471 So. Cedarbrook Rd.
Allentown, Pa.   18104

Pres. UCP of North Central Pa.
Mr. Harry F. Keller
6 Scott St.
Sykesville, Pa.   15865

Pres. UCP of Northwestern Pa.
Mr. Norbert Rydzewski
4217 Wayne St.
Erie, Pa.   16504

Pres. UCPA of Philadelphia & Vic.
Michael J. Pepe, Jr., Esq.
2603 Orthodox St.
Philadelphia, Pa.   19137

Pres. UCPA of the Pittsburgh Dist.
George H. Bentz, D.D.S.
130 Abington Drive
Pittsburgh, Pa.   15216

Pres. UCP of Reading & Berks Cty.
Mr. Lewis R. Hertzog, Jr.
P.O. Box 4083
Mt. Penn, Pa.   19606

Pres. UCP of Schuylkill, Carbon &
    Northumberland Ctys.
Mr. Charles E. Wernert
Box 346, R.D. 2
Schuylkill Haven, Pa.   17972

Pres. UCP of Southern Alleghenies
    Region
Mr. Moses Spiegel
550 Vine St.
Johnstown, Pa.   15901

Pres. UCP of Southwestern Pa.
Sam Tirimacco, M.D.
250 N. Jefferson Ave.
Canonsburg, Pa.   15317

Pres. UCP of Western Pa.
Jerome Lombardi, Esq.
404 Linden St.
Vandergrift, Pa.   15690

Pres. UCPA of Wyoming Valley
Marshall S. Jacobson, Esq.
Blue Cross Bldg., Suite 1000
15 So. Franklin
Wilkes-Barre, Pa.   18701

Rhode Island
Pres. UCP of Rhode Island
Mrs. Thomas H. Donahue, III
24 Elm Lane
Barrington, R.I.   02890

South Carolina
Pres. UCP of South Carolina
Mr. Ralph D. Proper
5820 Beverly Drive.
Hanahan, S.C.   29406

South Dakota
Pres. UCP of South Dakota
Ms. Helen C. Buchanan
1311 Campbell Dr.
Huron, S.D.   57350

Pres. UCP of Central So. Dakota
Mrs. Pat Douglas
417 Utah S.E.
Huron, South Dakota   57350

Pres. UCP of the Sioux Empire
Mrs. Thomas Clauson
1017 South Menlo Ave.
Sioux Falls, S.D.   57105

Tennessee
Pres. UCP of Grtr. Chattanooga
Mr. Douglas M. Vandergriff
4700 Brentwood Dr.
Chattanooga, Tenn.   37416

Pres. UCP of Memphis & Shelby Cty.
Mr. Herbert Lichterman
Box 6
Memphis, Tenn.   38101

Chrmn. UCP of Middle Tenn.
Mr. Lipscomb Davis, Jr.
C/O Davis Cabinet Co.
901 S. Fifth St.
Nashville, Tenn.   37213

Pres. UCP of Middle-East Tenn.
Mr. W. Carroll Logan

3509 Kesterwood Dr.
Knoxville, Tenn.   37918

Texas
Pres. UCPA of Texas
Mrs. Ann R. Dunn
3005 Hanover
Dallas, Tex   75225

Pres. UCP of the Alamo Area
Mr. Tom Streeter
2634 Friar Tuck
San Antonio, Texas   78209

Pres. UCP of the Coastal Bend Area
Senator Ronald W. Bridges
6402 Weber Rd. R-4
Corpus Christi, Texas   78415

Pres. UCPA of Dallas Cty.
Mr. Richard K. Marks
5115 McKinney
Dallas, Texas   75205

Pres. UCP of El Paso, Inc.
Mr. Richard Du Bois
3313 Dublin
El Paso, Texas   79925

Pres. UCP of the Lower Rio Grande
Valley
Mr. Norman L. Richard
2304 Shidler Dr., Apt. 35
Brownsville, Tex.   78521

Pres. UCP of Tarrant Cty.
Mr. J. Robert Hester, Jr.
801 E. Abram
Arlington, Tex.   76010

Pres. UCP of Texas Gulf Coast, Inc.
Mr. Clyde Hanks, III
4311 W. Alabama
Houston, Tex.   77027

Utah
Pres. UCPA of Utah
Mr. Arthur L. Monson
Rm. 105 City & County Bldg.
Salt Lake City, Utah   84111

Vermont
Pres. UCP of Vermont, Inc.
Mrs. Mary Beard
R.D. 2
Johnson, Vt.   05656

Virginia
Pres. UCP of Virginia
Mr. Burton L. Joyner
P.O. Box 2129
Roanoke, Va.   24009

UCP of Charlottesville & Albemarle Cty.,
Va.
No President

Pres. UCP of Metro. Hampton Roads
Mr. Jay P. Edwards
4321 Ewell Road
Virginia Beach, Va.   23455

Pres. UCP of Northern Virginia
Mrs. R. B. Clark
505 Hillwood Ave.
Falls Church, Va.   22042

Pres. UCP of Roanoke Valley
Mr. Burton L. Joyner
P.O. Box 2129
Roanoke, Va.   24009

Washington
Pres. UCPA of Washington
Mrs. E. L. Reinhart
712 Randolph Pl.
Seattle, Wash.   98122

Pres. UCP of Benton & Franklin Ctys.
Mr. Roy G. Franklin
Franklin, Mayhan & Co.
P.O. Box 2588
Tri-Cities, Wash.   99302

Pres. UCP of the Inland Empire Unit
Mr. George E. Bordner
4220 N. Bessie Rd.
Spokane, Wash.   99206

Pres. UCP of King & Snohomish Ctys.
Mr. Joseph S. Lemon
Bank of California
P.O. Box 3123
Seattle, Wash.   98114

Pres. UCP of Lower Puget Sound
Mr. Loren Bafus
507 N. Devoe Road
Olympia, Wash.   98501

Pres. UCP of Pierce Cty.
Mrs. Lawrence Howard
6913 44th Ave., East
Tacoma, Wash.   98443

Pres. UCP of Wenatchee Valley
Mr. Morris E. Payton
UCP of Wenatchee Valley
P.O. Box 1
Wenatchee, Wash.   98801

West Virginia
Pres. UCPA of West Virginia
Mr. Edward A. Dickerson
2 Estill Drive
Charleston, W. Va.   25314

Wisconsin
Pres. UCP of Wisconsin
Mrs. Marylin Anderson
635 W. Mac Arthur Ave.
Eau Claire, Wis.   54701

Pres. UCP of the Coulee Region
Ms. Becky Lundquist
2570 Mickel Road
La Crosse, Wis.   54602

Pres. UCP of Grtr. Dane Cty.
Ms. Christine Grannis
28 Paget Road
Madison, Wis.   53704

Pres. UCP of Kenosha Cty.
Mrs. Michael B. Thompson
593 Sheridan Rd.
Racine, Wisc.   53403

Pres. UCP of North Central Wis.
Sister Francine Kosednar
Wausau Hospital North
Maple Hill—Occupational Therapy
Wausau, Wis.   54401

Pres. UCP of Northeastern Wis.
Mr. James A. Kneeland

C/O Lo Cascio Insurance
P.O. Box 1166
Green Bay, Wis.   54305

Pres. UCP of Northwestern Wis.
Mrs. Robert Hanson
2220 Cummings
Superior, Wis.   54880

Pres. UCP of Racine Cty.
Mr. Charles Hartwig
1506 4¼ Mile Rd.
Racine, Wis.   53402

Pres. UCPA of Southeastern Wisc.
Mrs. Dorothy H. Leber
207 E. Hanover Place
Peoria, Ill.   61614

Pres. UCP of West Central Wis.
Ms. Ruth Gullerud
347 Heather Road
Eau Claire, Wis.   54701

Pres. UCP of Winnebagoland
Mr. Safford W. Mc Myler
1382 Lakeshore Dr.
Menasha, Wis.   54952

APPENDIX VII

Directory of State Societies for Crippled Children and Adults

State	Officer	Telephone
Alabama Society for Crippled Children and Adults, Inc. 2125 E. South Boulevard P.O. Box 6130 Montgomery, Alabama 36106	Charles T. Higgins Executive Director	(205) 288-0240
Easter Seal Society for Alaska Crippled Children and Adults 726 E Street P.O. Box 2432 Anchorage, Alaska 99501	Don Clement Executive Director	(907) 277-1324
Easter Seal Society for Crippled Children and Adults of Arizona, Inc. 706 North First Street Phoenix, Arizona 85004	Gene Brantner Executive Director	(602) 252-3426

State	Officer	Telephone
The Easter Seal Society for Crippled Children and Adults of Arkansas, Inc. 2801 Lee Avenue Little Rock, Arkansas 72205	Mrs. Virginia Armistead Executive Director	(501) MO3-8331
Easter Seal Society for Crippled Children and Adults of California 742 Market St., Suite 202 San Francisco, California 94102	William R. Barrett Executive Director	(415) 391-2006
Easter Seal Society for Crippled Children and Adults of Colorado, Inc. 609 W. Littleton Boulevard Littleton, Colorado 80120	Francis Steers Executive Director	(303) 795-2016
Easter Seal Society for Crippled Children and Adults of Connecticut, Inc. P.O. Box 2790 Hartford, Connecticut 06101	Malin Martin Executive Director	(203) 236-3273
Easter Seal Society for Crippled Children and Adults of Delaware, Inc. 2705 Baynard Boulevard Wilmington, Delaware 19802	Guion Miller Executive Director	(302) OL8-6417
District of Columbia Society for Crippled Children, Inc. 2800, 13th Street, N.W. Washington, D.C. 20009	Harold D. Fangboner Executive Director	(202) AD2-2342
Easter Seal Society for Crippled Children and Adults of Florida, Inc. State Road 46 Route 1, Box 350 Sorrento, Florida 32776	L. Paul Murray Executive Director	(904) 383-6186
Georgia Easter Seal Society for Crippled Children & Adults, Inc. 1211 Spring Street, N.W. Atlanta, Georgia 30309	Miss Mary F. Webb Executive Director	(404) TR3-1391
Easter Seal Society for Crippled Children and Adults of Hawaii 1350 Hunakai Street—Room #4 Honolulu, Hawaii 96816	Bill L. Hindman Executive Director	(808) 735-1747
Easter Seal Society for Crippled Children and Adults of Idaho, Inc. 1090 Federal Way Boise, Idaho 83705	Leonard Hopper Executive Director	(208) 343-2529
The Easter Seal Society of Illinois for Crippled Children and Adults, Inc. P.O. Box 1767—2715 S. 4th Street Springfield, Illinois 62705	Jim Gray, RPT Executive Director	(217) 525-0398

State	Officer	Telephone
Indiana Easter Seal Society for Crippled Children and Adults, Inc. 3816 East 96th Street Indianapolis, Indiana 46240	James A. Carter Executive Director	(317) 844-7919
Easter Seal Society for Crippled Children and Adults of Iowa, Inc. P.O. Box 4002 Highland Park Station Des Moines, Iowa 50333	Rolfe B. Karlsson Executive Director	(515) 289-1933
Kansas Chapter National Easter Seal Society for Crippled Children and Adults 214 W. 6th St. Room 201 P.O. Box 1774 Topeka, Kansas 66601	Executive Director	(913) 354-9501
Kentucky Easter Seal Society for Crippled Children and Adults, Inc. P.O. Box 1170 Louisville, Kentucky 40201	William T. Isaac Executive Director	(502) JU4-9781
Louisiana Chapter, National Easter Seal Society for Crippled Children and Adults 3939 Veterans Blvd. Suite 218 Metairie, Louisiana 70002	Daniel H. Underwood Executive Director	(504) 885-9960
Pine Tree Society for Crippled Children and Adults, Inc. 84 Front Street Bath, Maine 04530	William F. Haney Executive Director	(207) 443-3341
Maryland Society for Crippled Children and Adults, Inc. 3700 Fourth Street Baltimore, Maryland 21225	Bruce G. Eberwein Executive Director	(301) 355-7676
Easter Seal Society for Crippled Children and Adults of Massachusetts, Inc. 37 Harvard Street Worcester, Massachusetts 01608	Richard A. LaPierre Executive Director	(617) 757-2756
Easter Seal Society for Crippled Children and Adults, Inc. of Michigan 10601 Puritan Avenue Detroit, Michigan 48238	Mrs. Millah Nikkel Executive Director	(313) DI1-1721-22
The Minnesota Easter Seal Society, Inc. 4815 W. 77th Street (Rm. 120) Minneapolis, Minnesota 55435	G. Paul Scudder Executive Director	(612) 835-5195
Easter Seal Society for Crippled Children and Adults of Mississippi, Inc.	Lee O. Dees Executive Director	(601) 354-5705

State	Officer	Telephone
P.O. Box 4958 733 No. State Street, Suite 1 Jackson, Mississippi 39216		
Easter Seal Society for Crippled Children and Adults of Missouri 8124 Delmar Blvd. St. Louis, Missouri 63130	John H. Kniest Executive Director	(314) 862-3000
Ohio Society for Crippled Children and Adults, Inc. P.O. Box 6728 5 N. Broadleigh Road Columbus, Ohio 43209	Karl P. Reiser Executive Director	(614) 237-7641
Oklahoma Society for Crippled Children, Inc. 2100 Northwest 63rd Street Oklahoma City, Oklahoma 73116	Wallace P. Bonifield Executive Director	(405) 848-7603
Easter Seal Society for Crippled Children and Adults of Oregon 4343 S. W. Corbett Avenue Portland, Oregon 97201	Bruce Whitaker Executive Director	(503) 228-5109
Easter Seal Society for Crippled Children and Adults of Pennsylvania P.O. Box 497, R.D. #1 Fulling Mill Road Middletown, Pennsylvania 17057	William E. Graffius Executive Director	(717) 939-7801
Puerto Rico Chapter National Society for Crippled Children and Adults G.P.O. Box 325 San Juan, Puerto Rico 00936	Mrs. Evangelina S. Farrant Executive Director	(809) 767-6718
Easter Seal Society for Crippled Children and Adults of Rhode Island, Inc. 667 Waterman Ave. East Providence, Rhode Island 02914	Miss Nancy D'Wolf Executive Director	(401) 438-9500
Easter Seal Society for Crippled Children and Adults of South Carolina, Inc. 3020 Farrow Road Columbia, South Carolina 29203	Mrs. T. Jackson Lowe Executive Director	(803) 256-0735
Easter Seal Society for Crippled Children and Adults of South Dakota, Inc. 106 W. Capital P.O. Box 297 Pierre, South Dakota 57501	Mrs. Lillian Myers Executive Director	(605) 224-2605
Easter Seal Society for Crippled Children and Adults of Tennessee, Inc. 2001 Woodmont Boulevard	Mrs. Ellen Geis Interim Exec. Dir.	(615) 298-3386

State	Officer	Telephone
P.O. Box 15832 Nashville, Tennessee 37215		
Easter Seal Society for Crippled 　　　Children and Adults of 　　　Texas, Inc. 4429 North Central Expressway Dallas, Texas 75205	William E. Russell Executive Director	(214) 526-3811
Easter Seal Society for Crippled 　　　Children and Adults of 　　　Utah, Inc. 4868 South State Street Murray, Utah 84107	William Bean Executive Director	(801) 262-6459
The Vermont Achievement Center 88 Park Street Rutland, Vermont 05701	Robert H. Dombro Executive Director	(802) 775-2395
Easter Seal Society for Crippled 　　　Children and Adults of 　　　Virginia, Inc. 4841 Williamson Road P.O. Box 5496 Roanoke, Virginia 24012	F. Robert Knight Executive Director	(703) 362-1656
Easter Seal Society for Crippled 　　　Children and Adults of 　　　Washington, Inc. 521 Second Avenue, West Seattle, Washington 98119	William E. Unti Executive Director	(206) AT4-5707
Easter Seal Society for Crippled 　　　Children and Adults of 　　　West Virginia, Inc. 612 Virginia Street, East Charleston, West Virginia 25301	John C. Stepp Executive Director	(304) DI6-3508
Easter Seal Society for Crippled 　　　Children and Adults of 　　　Wisconsin, Inc. 2702 Monroe Street Madison, Wisconsin 53711	Kenneth L. Svee Executive Director	(608) 231-3411
Easter Seal Society for Crippled 　　　Children and Adults of 　　　Wyoming, Inc. P.O. Box 40 Buffalo, Wyoming 82834	Ivan E. Glandt Executive Director	(307) 684-5101

For Information:

Washington Office:

The National Easter Seal Society 　　　For Crippled Children 　　　and Adults Washington Bldg. 1435 "G" Street, N.W. (Suite 1031–32) Washington, D.C. 20005	Miss Roberta Van 　　Beek	(202) 347-3066

APPENDIX VIII

Directory of Local Affiliates

Alabama

Spain Rehabilitation Center
University of Alabama Medical Center
Birmingham, Alabama   35233

John M. Miller, III, M.D.
Professor and Chairman
Dept. of Rehabilitation
    Medicine
(205) 323-8822

Southeast Alabama Crippled Children's Clinic-
    Rehabilitation Center
P.O. Box 338
Dothan, Alabama   36301

Carlice Flowers
Administrator
(205) 792-0022

Huntsville Rehabilitation Center
316 Longwood Drive, S.W.
Huntsville, Alabama   35801

Carl Shreve
Administrator
(205) 534-6421

Mobile Rehabilitation Association, Inc.
1874 Pleasant Avenue—P.O. Box 7008
Mobile, Alabama   36607

Administrator
(205) 476-3800

Central Alabama Crippled Children's Clinic
    Rehabilitation Center
2125 East South Boulevard
Montgomery, Alabama   36111

Col. LeRoy Priest
Administrator
(205) 288-0240

Northwest Alabama Crippled Children's Clinic
    Rehabilitation Center
P.O. Box 2388
Muscle Shoals, Alabama   35662

E. B. Hamner, Jr.
Administrator
(205) 381-1110

Opportunity Center
217 West 13th Street
Anniston, Alabama   36201

Michael Johns
Director
(205) 237-0381

Occupational Rehab. Center
1616, 6th Avenue, South
Birmingham, Alabama   35233

Roy Forman
Administrator
(205) 933-8090

Tennessee Valley Rehabilitation Center
Calhoun Community College
P.O. Box 1926
Decatur, Alabama   35601

Charles Harvell
Director
(205) 353-2754

Darden Rehabilitation Center
Alabama School of Trades
Gadsden, Alabama   35903

Mrs. Ola Mae Farmer
Administrator
(205) 547-5458

Walker Rehabilitation Center
2002 Commerce Avenue
Jasper, Alabama   35501

(205) 384-9064

Achievement Center
510 West Thomason Circle
Opelika, Alabama   36801

Lamar Odom
Manager
(205) 745-3501

West Central Alabama Rehab. Center
2906 Citizens Parkway
P.O. Box 1347
Selma, Alabama   36701

Larry F. Lewis
Administrator
(205) 872-8422

Alabama Institute for Deaf and Blind
P.O. Drawer 17
Talladega, Alabama   35160

Ray Miller
Manager
(205) 362-9053

West Alabama Rehabilitation Center
1110—6th Avenue, East—P.O. Box 2817
Tuscaloosa, Alabama   35401

Don Hand
Administrator
(205) 759-1211

Alaska
Dr. Philip Moore Chapter of the Easter Seal Society for
    Alaska Crippled Children and Adults, Inc.
P.O. Box 575
Ketchikan, Alaska   99901

Fairbanks Chapter of the Easter Seal Society for
    Alaska Crippled Children and Adults, Inc.
1020 Gillman Way,
Fairbanks, Alaska   99701

Juneau Chapter of the Easter Seal Society for
    Alaska Crippled Children & Adults, Inc.
P.O. Box 971
Juneau, Alaska   99801

Matanuska Valley Chapter of the Easter Seal Society
    for Alaska Crippled Children & Adults, Inc.
Box 696
Wasilla, Alaska   99687

Mrs. Christine Smith

Sitka Chapter of the Easter Seal Society for
    Alaska Crippled Children & Adults, Inc.
P.O. Box 435
Sitka, Alaska   99835

Mrs. Mary Richards

Arizona
Easter Seag Society for Crippled Children
    and Adults of Southern Arizona
920 North Swan Road
Tucson, Arizona   85711

Executive Director
(602) 795-7542

California
Easter Seal Society for Crippled Children
    and Adults of Alameda County
2757 Telegraph Avenue
Oakland, California   94612

Takumi J. (Tak) Taketa
R.P.T.
Executive Director
(415) 835-2131

Easter Seal Society for Crippled Children
    and Adults of Butte County
172 E. 6th Avenue
Chico, California   95926

Wayne Speegle
Executive Director
(916) 342-0202

Easter Seal Society for Crippled Children
    and Adults of Contra Costa County
2363 Boulevard Circle—Room #4
Walnut Creek, California   94596

Mrs. Doris Hazlett
Executive Director
(415) 939-7353

Easter Seal Society for Crippled Children
    and Adults of Fresno County
245 North Calaveras Street
Fresno, California   93701

James C. Cotter
Executive Director
(209) 485-1521

The Easter Seal Society of Humboldt County
507 F. Street, Room #219 FPG
Eureka, California 95901

Mrs. Brenda Cheatham
Executive Director
(707) 442-9345

Kern County Society for Crippled Children
610 Fourth Street
Bakersfield, California 93304

Mrs. Betty J. Huckins
Executive Director
(805) 322-5595

Easter Seal Society of Los Angeles County
1545 Wilshire Blvd., Suite 600
Los Angeles, California 90017

Alan Facter
Executive Director
(213) 483-5692 and
483-5333

Easter Seal Society for Crippled Children
and Adults of Marin, Inc,
1601—2nd Street
San Rafael, California 94901

Mrs. Phyllis
Widdershover
Executive Director
(415) 454-2460

Easter Seal Society of the Monterey Peninsula, Inc.
1340 Munras St. (Suite 201)
Monterey, California 93940

Mrs. Gloria Lockwood
Executive Director
(408) 373-2333

Rehabilitation Institute of Orange County
1800 East La Veta Avenue
Orange, California 92666

Praim S. Singh, M.S.W.
Executive Director
(714) 633-7400 or
541-8822

The Easter Seal Society for Crippled Children
and Adults of Riverside and Imperial Counties
21401 Box Springs Road
Riverside, California 92507

Mike Fawbush
Executive Director
(714) 683-5600

The Easter Seal Society for Crippled Children
and Adults of Sacramento, Inc.
3205 Hurley Way
Sacramento, California 95825

Duane J. Holiday
Executive Director
(916) 483-3211

Easter Seal Society for Crippled Children
and Adults of Salinas Valley
16 West Gabilan Street (Suite B)
Salinas, California 93901

Mrs. Cynthia Stanford
Executive Director
(408) 758-0090

Easter Seal Society for Crippled Children
and Adults of San Bernardino County
241 East 9th Street
San Bernardino, California 92402

Mel Upp
Executive Director
(714) 888-4125

Easter Seal Society for Crippled Children and Adults
of San Diego County
Children's Health Center
8001 Frost Street
San Diego, California 92123

Miss Sandra Schoenkopf
Director
(714) 277-5808

The Easter Seal Society for Crippled Children
and Adults of San Francisco, Inc.
6221 Geary Blvd.
San Francisco, California 94121

Miss Margaret Kearney
Executive Director
(415) 752-4888

Easter Seal Society for Crippled Children
and Adults of San Joaquin/Stanislaus Counties, Inc.
902 North Hunter Street
Stockton, California 95202
    For Information Only (*Do not* send mail or
    packages to this address):
    1700 McHenry Village Way, Unit II
    Modesto, California 95350

Mrs. Athena Moran
Executive Director
(209) 465-0231

(209) 527-1850

Society for Crippled Children and
    Adults of San Mateo County
1764 Marco Polo Way
Burlingame, California 94010

P. Lee Mason
Executive Director
(415) 697-8924

Easter Seal Society for Crippled Children
    and Adults of Santa Barbara County, Inc.
31 East Canon Perdido
Santa Barbara, California 93101

Gordon Shasky
Executive Director
(805) 963-6663

Easter Seals Serving Santa Clara/San Benito Counties
761 Coleman Avenue
San Jose, California 95110

Alfred Mabey
Executive Director
(408) 295-1893

Easter Seal Society for Crippled Children
    and Adults of Santa Cruz County
P.O. Box 626—621 Water St.
Santa Cruz, California 95061

Mrs. Kathryn Parodi
Executive Director
(408) 427-3360

Society for Crippled Children and Adults of
    San Luis Obispo County, Inc.
P.O. Box 795
San Luis Obispo, California 93406
        (For large packages use:
        977 Pismo Street
        San Luis Obispo, California 93401)

Mrs. Jane C. Moore
Executive Secretary
(805) 543-4122

Easter Seal Society for Crippled Children
    and Adults of Solano County
P.O. Box 552
Vallejo, California 94590

Mrs. Ruth M. Hall
Executive Director
(707) 644-2397

Easter Seal Society for Crippled Children
    and Adults of Sonoma County
400 Montgomery Drive
Santa Rosa, California 95405

Mrs. Bebe Stockman
Executive Director
(707) 545-7673

Easter Seal Society for Crippled Children
    of Tulare County
P.O. Box 1447
Visalia, California 93277
        (For large packages, use street address:
        2722 East Wescott Street
        Visalia, California 93277)

J. Christopher Faso
Executive Director
(209) 734-2024

Easter Seal Society for Crippled Children
    and Adults of Ventura County
10730 Henderson Road
Ventura, California 93003

C. T. (Tom) Hashbarger
Executive Director
(805) 647-1141

Colorado
Rocky Mountain Rehabilitation Center
2501 East Yampa Street
Colorado Springs, Colorado 80909

Richard E. Olson
Executive Director
(303) 473-3475

Easter Seal Rehabilitation Center
260 South Kipling Avenue
Lakewood, Colorado 80226

Mrs. Harriette Barter
Clinic Director
(303) 238-6301 ext. 40

Pueblo County Society for Crippled
    Children and Adults, Inc.
P.O. Box 1014
Pueblo, Colorado 81002
        (For large packages, use street address:
        999 Fartino Blvd., West, Space 44
        Pueblo, Colorado 81008)

Mrs. M. Elaine Schober
Executive Director
(303) 544-3562
      545-2568

High Plains Easter Seal Society
Box 592
Sterling, Colorado   80751

James B. Harrigan
Executive Director
(303) 522-5858

Connecticut
The Easter Seal Rehabilitation Center of
    Eastern Fairfield County, Inc.
226 Mill Hill Avenue
Bridgeport, Connecticut   06610

Edmund S. McLaughlin
Executive Director
(203) 366-7551

The Hartford Easter Seal Rehabilitation
    Center, Inc.
80 Coventry Street
Hartford, Connecticut   06112

Miss June Sokolov
Executive Director
(203) 243-9741

The Easter Seal Rehabilitation Center of
    Southeastern Connecticut, Inc.
216 Norwich—New London Turnpike
P.O. Box 393
Uncasville, Connecticut   06382

F. Thomas Ulrich, RPT
Executive Director
(203) 848-9264

Central Connecticut Easter Seal
    Rehabilitation Center, Inc.
181 Cook Ave.
Meriden, Connecticut   06450

Kenneth D. Gertz, RPT
Executive Director
(203) 237-7835

The Easter Seal-Goodwill Industries
    Rehabilitation Center, Inc.
20 Brookside Avenue
New Haven, Connecticut   06515

Carl Puleo
Executive Director
(203) 389-4561

Easter Seal Rehabilitation Center of
    South Western Connecticut, Inc.
26 Palmer's Hill Road
Stamford, Connecticut   06902

James Shearin
Executive Director
(203) 325-1544

Easter Seal Rehabilitation Center
    of Greater Waterbury, Inc.
22 Tompkins Street
Waterbury, Connecticut   06708

Donald L. Wise
Executive Director
(203) 754-5141

Florida
Easter Seal Society for Crippled Children
    and Adults of Volusia County, Inc.
Volusia Easter Seal Center
P.O. Box 9117
Daytona Beach, Florida   32020

Harry M. Singer
Executive Director
(904) 255-4568

The Easter Seal Society for Crippled Children
    and Adults of Broward County, Inc.
Easter Seal Rehabilitation Center
333 S.W. 28th Street
Fort Lauderdale, Florida   33315

James Connor
Executive Director
(305) 523-8516

Easter Seal Society for Crippled Children
    and Adults of Northeast Florida
835 Main Street
Jacksonville, Florida   32202

Mrs. George (Delores)
    Bosse
Executive Director
(904) 355-2631

Easter Seal Society for Crippled
    Children & Adults of Monroe County
Center of Hope
P.O. Box 2097—Flagler Station
Key West, Florida   33040

Mrs. Emily Pine, RPT
Executive Director
(305) 296-2877

Brevard Crippled Children's Association
Melbourne Easter Seal Rehabilitation Center
450 E. Sheridan Road
Melbourne, Florida 32901

Mrs. Melba W. Tedford
Executive Director
(305) 723-4474

Easter Seal Society of Dade County, Inc.
"A Rehabilitation Center for Crippled Children
and Adults"
1475 N.W. 14th Avenue
Miami, Florida 33125

Mrs. Marguerite Kaiser
Executive Director
(305) 325-0470

Central Florida Speech & Hearing Center
710 East Bella Vista Street
Lakeland, Florida 33801

Ms. Gay Ratcliff
Director of Clinical
Services
(813) 686-3189

Easter Seal Society for Crippled Children
& Adults of Southwest Florida
Easter Seal Therapy Center
1542 Carson Street
Ft. Myers, Florida 33901

Mrs. Barbara Szalay
Executive Director
(813) 334-3297

Crippled Children's Society and
Rehabilitation Center for Children
and Adults, Inc.
300 Royal Palm Way
Palm Beach, Florida 33480

Miss Betty McMurchy
Executive Director
(305) 655-7266

Easter Seal Society of West Florida
610 S. Pace Blvd.
Pensacola, Florida 32501

James Hutson
Executive Director
(904) 438-9368

Easter Seal Society for Crippled Children
and Adults of Pinellas County, Inc.—Easter Seal
Rehabilitation Center
7671 U.S. Highway #19
Pinellas Park, Florida 33565

Andrew A. Orsini, RPT
Executive Director
(813) 527-5793

Manatee Easter Seal Society for the Physically
Handicapped, Inc.
Co-sponsors with the Sarasota County Society for
Crippled Children & Adults of *Happiness
House Rehabilitation Center, Inc.*
P.O. Box 25   401 Braden Ave.
Bradenton, Florida 33506   Sarasota, Florida   33580

Mrs. Joan Grayson
Executive Director

Sarasota County Society for Crippled Children
& Adults, Inc.
Co-sponsor with the Manatee Easter Seal Society for
the Physically Handicapped, Inc.
(See listing under *Manatee Easter Seal Society*)

See Listing under
Manatee ESS

Easter Seal Rehabilitation Center—Easter Seal
Society of the Capital Area
910 Myers Park Drive
Tallahassee, Florida 32301

Prentis Wilson
Executive Director
(904) 222-4465

Easter Seal Society for Crippled Children
and Adults of Hillsborough County (A. Pickens
Coles Easter Seal Center)
2401 East Henry Avenue
Tampa, Florida 33610

Leonard H. Gotler
Executive Director
(813) 236-5589

Gulf Coast Easter Seal Rehabilitation Center
628 North Cove Boulevard
Panama City, Florida 32401

Executive Director
(904) 763-8488

North Central Florida Easter Seal Society
4502 S.E. 24th Street
Gainesville, Florida 32601

Mrs. Ruth Schaeffer
Executive Director

Easter Seal Society of Orange, Seminole
& Osceola, Inc.
(Easter Seal Speech & Hearing Center)
231 East Colonial Drive
Orlando, Florida 32801

William F. Monfort
Director
(305) 841-8353

Georgia
Easter Seal Rehabilitation Center
1362 West Peachtree Street
Atlanta, Georgia 30309

Lee Baker
Director
(404) 873-2886

Southwest Georgia Easter Seal Rehabilitation
Center
1906 Palmyra Road
Albany, Georgia 31705

Robert E. Jordan
Director
(912) 439-7061

Easter Seal Rehabilitation Center
1505—15th Street
P.O. Box 3523
Augusta, Georgia 30904

Avys D. Billue
Director
(404) 733-4401

Easter Seal Speech & Hearing Center
1803 Gloucester Street—Suite 108
Brunswick, Georgia 31520

Richard D. Wright
Executive Director
(912) 264-3141

Hawaii
Easter Seal Society for Crippled Children
and Adults of Hawaii County
P.O. Box 715—49 Kaiulani Street
Hilo, Hawaii 96820

Mrs. Peggy Jaeger
Executive Secretary
(808) 935-6310

Easter Seal Society for Crippled Children
& Adults of Kauai
P.O. Box 667
Lihue, Hawaii 96766

Shayne Horita
Executive Secretary
(808) 245-6983

Easter Seal Society of Maui-County for Crippled
Children & Adults
95 Mahalani Street
Wailuku, Hawaii 96793

Jackie Sarner
Executive Director
(808) 244-9517

Easter Seal Society for Crippled Children
and Adults of Oahu
1350 Hunakai Street—Room #4
Honolulu, Hawaii 96816

Bill L. Hindman
Executive Director
(808) 735-1747

Illinois
Easter Seal Society of Southwestern Illinois
for Crippled Children and Adults, Inc.
(Serving Madison, St. Clair, Monroe, Washington,
Bond, Clinton and Jersey Counties)
410 E. Broadway
Alton, Illinois 62002

Tom H. Pryce
Executive Director
(618) 462-8897

Easter Seal Society for Crippled Children
and Adults
(Serving Southern Kane & Kendall Counties)
412 Hankes Avenue
Aurora, Illinois 60505

Richard Merz
Executive Director
(312) 896-1961

Easter Seal Society for Crippled Children and
    Adults of Southern Illinois, Inc.
P. O. Box 3249—801 South Oakland Street
Carbondale, Illinois   62901

Mrs. Mildred L. Holland
Executive Director
(618) 457-3333

Easter Seal Society of Metropolitan Chicago, Inc.
220 South State Street
Chicago, Illinois   60604

Louis Lamer
Executive Director
(312) 939-5115

Easter Seal Society of Central Illinois, Inc.
243 West Cerro Gordo
Decatur, Illinois   62522

Miss Shirley Freshman
Director
(217) 429-1052

Easter Seal Society for Crippled Children
    & Adults of Southeastern Illinois
P.O. Box 279—711 Monroe Ave.
Charleston, Illinois   61920

Robert M. Gray
Executive Director
(217) 345-9421

Easter Seal Association for the Crippled, Inc.
799 S. McLean Boulevard
Elgin, Illinois   60120

Mrs. Margaret (Peggy)
    Muetterties, ST
Executive Director
(312) 742-3264

Easter Seal Society for Crippled Children and
    Adults of Will County, Inc.
316 North Bluff
Joilet, Illinois   60435

Timothy Madden
Director
(815) 727-5457

Easter Seal Society, Mid-Eastern Illinois
895 S. Washington Street
Kankakee, Illinois   60901

Fred Trevarthan, ST
Executive Director
(815) 932-0623

Lake County Easter Seal Society
4611 West Grand Avenue
Gurnee, Illinois   60031

Mrs. Myrtle Cunningham
Director
(312) ON2-2112

Easter Seal Society for Crippled Children
    and Adults of Lasalle County, Inc.
1013 Adams Street
Ottawa, Illinois   61350

Mrs. Marcia S. Esche,
    RPT
Executive Director
(815) 434-0857

Crippled Children's Center
(Serving Peoria, Tazewell, Woodford & Fulton Counties)
320 East Armstrong
P.O. Box 1137
Peoria, Illinois   61603

John Murphy
Executive Director
(309) 672-6330

Tri-County Association for the Crippled, Inc.
201 South Fifth Street
Quincy, Illinois   62301

Mrs. Mary Rittenberg
(217) 222-5489

Foundation for Crippled Children and
    Adults of Rock Island County, Inc.
3808 Eighth Avenue
Rock Island, Illinois   61201

Donald C. Davis, Ph.D.
Foundation Director
(309) 786-2434

Du Page Easter Seal Treatment Center, Inc.
706 East Park Boulevard
Villa Park, Illinois   60181

Vladimir Josifek
President
(312) 832-2270

Easter Seal Society for McHenry County
708 Washington Street—P.O. Box 326
Woodstock, Illinois   60098

Mrs. Dolly Sterling
President
(815) 338-1707

Indiana

The Vanderburgh County Society for Crippled
    Children and Adults, Inc.   Executive Director
3701 Bellemeade Avenue   (812) 479-1411
Evansville, Indiana   47715

Allen County Society for Crippled   Percy Talati
    Children and Adults, Inc.   Executive Director
2722 Fairfield Avenue   (219) 744-1238
Fort Wayne, Indiana 46807

Trade Winds Rehabilitation Center—   Franklin M. Rosenbaum
    Lake County Chapter of Indiana Society   Executive Director
    for Crippled Children and Adults   (219) 949-4000
5901 West 7th Avenue
Gary, Indiana 46406

Marion County Easter Seal Society for Crippled Col. John J. Christy,
    Children and Adults   U.S.A. (Ret.)
3242 Sutherland Avenue   Executive Director
Indianapolis, Indiana 46205   (317) 924-3251

Clark County Easter Seal Society for Crippled Alva R. Willis
    Children and Adults   Executive Director
145 Forest Drive, Oak Park   (812) 283-7908
Jeffersonville, Indiana 47130

La Porte County Society for Crippled Children Mrs. Robert Goers
    and Adults   Executive Secretary
507 Fourth Street   (219) 362-9854
LaPorte, Indiana 46350

Delaware County Easter Seal Society for Crippled William H. Hickman
    Children and Adults, Inc.   Executive Director
R.R. #6—Box 195   (317) 288-1073
Muncie, Indiana 47302

Wayne County Easter Seal Society for Crippled Children Mrs. David (Pat) Bowers
    and Adults, Inc.   Executive Secretary
3431 College Corner Road
Richmond, Indiana 47374

St. Joseph County Society for Crippled Children Mrs. Anne F. Kovas
    and Adults, Inc.   Acting Executive Director
521 West Colfax Avenue   (219) 233-4366
South Bend, Indiana 46601

Iowa

Easter Seal Society for Crippled Children Walter Tomenga
    and Adults of Polk County, Inc.   Executive Director
2920 Thirtieth Street   (515) 274-1529
Des Moines, Iowa 50310

Easter Seal Society for Crippled Children and Glen R. Zeigler
    Adults of Siouxland, Inc.   Executive Director
406 29th Street   (712) 258-5523
Sioux City, Iowa 51104

Kentucky

Eastern Kentucky Area—Kentucky Society James E. Draughn
    for Crippled Children   Eastern Kentucky
2050 Versailles Rd.   Director
Cardinal Hill Hospital   (606) 24-5701
Lexington, Kentucky 40504

Cardinal Hill Hospital
2050 Versailles Road
Lexington, Kentucky   40504

Robert A. Silvanik
Executive Director
(606) 254-5701

West Kentucky Center for Handicapped Children
2229 Mildred Street
Paducah, Kentucky   42001

Jerald Ellington
Executive Director
(502) 444-9687

Northern Kentucky Easter Seal Center for
    Crippled Children and Adults
212 Levassor Avenue
Covington, Kentucky   41012

Philip Andriot
Northern Kentucky
    Director
(606) 491-1171

Maryland
Allegany League for Crippled Children
City Hall Plaza—P.O. Box 267
Cumberland, Maryland   21502

Mrs. Dorothy V.
    Emerson, R.N.
Executive Secretary
(301) 722-1840

Western Maryland Council
Maryland Society for Crippled Children and Adults
901 Dewey Ave.
Hagerstown, Maryland   21740

Coordinator

Easter Seal Rehabilitation Center
6510 Laurel Bowie Rd.
Bowie, Maryland   20715

Mrs. Barbara Shimanuki
Coordinator
(301) 577-7222

Easter Seal Treatment Center
1000 Twinbrook Parkway
Rockville, Maryland   20851

R. Adm. John W.
    Crumpacker, USN
    (Ret.)
Executive Director
(301) 424-5200

Michigan
Bay County Society for Crippled Children
5871 West Side Saginaw Road
Bay City, Michigan   48706

Mrs. Margaret Bennett
Executive Secretary
(517) 686-0850

The Easter Seal Society for Crippled
    Children and Adults of the Thumb Area
1000 Pine Grove Ave.
Pt. Huron, Michigan   48060

Peter P. Tyler
Executive Director
(313) 985-8818

The Easter Seal Society for Crippled Children
    & Adults of Genesee County, Inc.
1420 West 3rd Avenue
Flint, Michigan   48504

Mrs. Peggy McWhirter
Executive Director
(313) CE 8-0475

Easter Seal Society for Crippled Children
    and Adults of Grand Valley, Inc.
217 Division S.
Grand Rapids, Michigan   49506

Miss Anne Macqueen
Executive Director
(616) 458-1494

Easter Seal Society for Crippled Children
    & Adults, Inc. of Wayne County
P.O. Box 101
Inkster, Michigan   48141

David Daugherty
Executive Director
(313) PA 2-3055
    or   3056

Jackson County Society for Crippled Children
1218 Greenwood Avenue
Jackson, Michigan   49203

Mrs. Irwin S. (Ruth)
    Gourlay
Executive Secretary
(517) 782-6054

Kalamazoo Society for Crippled Children, Inc.
301 W. Cedar
Kalamazoo, Michigan   49006

Mrs. Jacoba Walker
Executive Secretary
(616) 345-6532

Mid-Michigan Easter Seal Society
2901 Wabash Road
Lansing, Michigan   48901

John B. Farnham
Executive Director
(517) 882-0211

Macomb County Society for Crippled Children
39093 Harper
Mount Clemens, Michigan   48043

Richard A. Meade
Executive Director
(313) 468-0700

Muskegon County Society for Crippled Children
220 Midtown Building
Houston and 3rd Streets
Muskegon, Michigan   49440

Mrs. Verna Nekola, R.N.
Executive Secretary
(616) PA 2-6397

Oakland County Society for Crippled
    Children and Adults, Inc.
1105 North Telegraph Road
Pontiac, Michigan   48053

Mrs. Kit McDonnell
Executive Director
(313) 338-9626

The Easter Seal Society for Crippled Children
    and Adults, Inc. of Berrien County
2015 Lakeview Avenue
St. Joseph, Michigan   49085

Mrs. Nellie Miller, R.N.
Executive Director
(616) 983-3981

Easter Seal Society for Crippled Children
    and Adults of Michigan—Southwest Area
301 West Cedar Street
Kalamazoo, Michigan   49006

Jim Magyar,
Field Representative
(616) 345-1490

Easter Seal Society for Crippled Children
    and Adults of Michigan—Upper Peninsula
220 Harlow Building
Marquette. Mivmigan   49855

James Wealton
Field Representative
(906) 226-7434

Easter Seal Society for Crippled Children
    and Adults of Michigan
Post Office Box 87
Mesick, Michigan   49668

Ellis Griner
Field Representative

Easter Seal Society Field Office
69 Enterprise
Ann Arbor, Michigan   48103

Bill Ross
Field Representative

Mississippi

Easter Seal Rehabilitation Center
P.O. Box 363   and 401 East Beach Boulevard
Biloxi, Mississippi   39533   Biloxi, Mississippi   39530

Mrs. Nancy Breeland
Director
(601) 435-4227

Missouri

Easter Seal Society, Central Region
314 Jackson
Jefferson City, Missouri   65101

Robert M. Neely
Regional Director
(314) 634-2610

Easter Seal Society, Kansas City Region
7240 Wornall Road
Kansas City, Missouri   64114

Conrad Fassold
Regional Director
(816) 333-3223

Easter Seal Society, Southwest Region
1010 West Sunshine
Springfield, Missouri   65807

Rex Henderson
Regional Director
(417) 869-8116

Easter Seal Society of Missouri
Southeast Region
316 South Plaza Way
Cape Girardeau, Missouri   63701

Mrs. Rebecca Andrews
Regional Director
(314) 335-6626

The Easter Seal Society of Missouri
—St. Louis Region
4108 Lindell Boulevard
St. Louis, Missouri   63108

Daniel Henroid
Regional Director
(314) OL2-7342

Nevada

Reno Easter Seal Treatment Center
148 Richards Way
Sparks, Nevada   89431

Mrs. Linda S. Reid
Administrator

New Hampshire

The Easter Seal Rehabilitation Center of
    Greater Manchester, Inc.
80 Tarrytown Road
Manchester, New Hampshire   03103

Executive Director
(603) 623-8863

Portsmouth Rehabilitation Center, Inc.
P.O. Box 901
Interstate By-Pass
Portsmouth, New Hampshire   03801

Mrs. Jean Tufts
Executive Director
(603) 436-5716

New Jersey

The Easter Seal Society for Crippled Children
    and Adults of Burlington, Camden
    and Gloucester Counties
310 Ivywood Avenue
Haddonfield, New Jersey   08033

Mrs. John C. Young
    (Cecil Ann)
Executive Director

The Easter Seal Society for Crippled Children
    and Adults of Morris County
260 Tabor Road, Route 53
Morris Plains, New Jersey   07950

Mrs. Elizabeth McKenna
Executive Director
(201) 539-5636

The Easter Seal Society for Crippled Children and Adults
    of Union County
108 Eastman Avenue
Cranford, New Jersey   07016

John R. Mellin
Executive Director

New York

Northeastern New York Speech Center, Inc.
Room 155—Husted Hall
135 Western Avenue
Albany, New York   12203

Carolyn W. Harris
Acting Executive Director
(518) 472-3730

Nassau Society for Crippled Children and Adults, Inc.
I. U. Willets Road
Albertson, L.I., New York   11507

Judy Beckman
Interim Director
(516) 747-3553

Finger Lakes Society for Crippled Children, Inc.
117 East Elm Street
Penn Yan, New York   14527
c/o James Swart
18 Jefferson Avenue
Geneva, New York   14456

Chatauqua County Society for Crippled Children and
    Adults, Inc.
103 Hotel Jamestown
Jamestown, New York   14701

Mrs. Gen Manzel
Field Secretary

Suffolk county E. S. Society for Crippled Children and
Adults, Inc.
77 East Main Street
Bay Shore, New York   11706

Mrs. Josephine F. Florio
Executive Director
(516 665-0700

Crippled Children's Society of Monroe County, Inc.
55 St. Paul Street
Rochester, New York   14604

Mrs. Jean Vincent
Executive Secretary
(716) 232-5725

Tri-County Association for Crippled Children and
Adults, Inc.
3 Steuben Park
Utica, New York   13501

Mrs. James P. Heywood
Executive Secretary
(315) 732-3958

Westchester Society for Crippled Children and
Adults, Inc.
202 Mamaroneck Avenue, L.L.
White Plains, New York   10601

Mrs. Sidney Eaton Boyle
Executive Director

North Carolina

Southeastern Chapter
Easter Seal Society for Crippled Children and Adults
of North Carolina
P.O. Box 1259
Jacksonville, North Carolina   28540

Harold McNair
Executive Director

Blue Ridge Chapter
Easter Seal Society for Crippled Children and Adults of
North Carolina, Inc.
1000-C Haywood Road—Box 6128
Asheville, North Carolina   28806

David E. Cottengim
Executive Director
(704) 258-0782

Dogwood Chapter—Easter Seal Society for Crippled
Children and Adults of North Carolina, Inc.
P.O. Box 9412
Charlotte, North Carolina   28299

Miss Barbara Morgan
Executive Director
(704) 376-4439

North Central Chapter
Easter Seal Society for Crippled Children and Adults of
North Carolina, Inc.
R.4—Box 95, Highway 54
Durham, North Carolina   27703

Ms. Ann Campbell
Executive Director
(919) 544-1721

South Central Chapter
Easter Seal Society for Crippled Children and Adults
of North Carolina, Inc.
P.O. Box 1408
Southern Pines, North Carolina   28387

Mrs. Connie Henderson
Executive Director
(919) 692-6074

Tri-County Chapter
Easter Seal Society for Crippled Children and Adults
of North Carolina
1821 Pembroke Road
Greensboro, North Carolina   27408

Mrs. Peggy Clapper
Executive Director
(919) 378-9484

Northwest Chapter—Easter Seal Society for
Crippled Children & Adults of North Carolina, Inc.
3061 Trenwest Drive
Winston-Salem, North Carolina   27103

Robert C. Parrish
Executive Director
(919) 765-6035

Pine Valley Chapter—Easter Seal Society for Crippled
Children & Adults of North Carolina, Inc.
832 Wake Forest Road
Raleigh, North Carolina   27604

Charles Drake
Executive Director
(919) 834-1191

Northeast Chapter
Easter Seal Society for Crippled Children & Adults
of North Carolina, Inc.
P.O. Box 1391
Greenville, North Carolina   27834

Miss Susan Clark
Executive Director

Ohio
Mrs. Ellen Suydam
114—4th Street
Martin, Ohio   43445

The Easter Seal Society for Crippled Children
and Adults of Defiance Area
939 Perry Street
Defiance, Ohio   43512

Miss Joyce L. Parker
Executive Secretary
(419) 782-9346

Franklin County Society for Crippled Children, Inc.
P.O. Box 7166—565 Children's Drive
Columbus, Ohio   43205

T. William Taylor
Executive Director
(614) 228-5523

Greene County Easter Seal Society for Crippled
Children and Adults, Inc.
47 N. Galloway Street
Xenia, Ohio   45385

Mrs. Janida L. King
Executive Director
(513) 376-2271

Hamilton County Society for Crippled Children
and Adults, Inc.
The Easter Seal Society
3181 Linwood Rd.
Cincinnati, Ohio   45208

Emmett Carraher
Executive Director
(513) 241-2398 (answer-
ing service)
(513) 321-3705

The Easter Seal Society of Henry County
for Crippled Children and Adults, Inc.
Napoleon, Ohio   43545

Mrs. Mary D. Walker
Executive Secretary

Easter Seal Society for Crippled Children & Adults
of Lorain County, Inc.
43085 North Ridge Road East
Elyria, Ohio   44035

Mrs. Mary Jane Bloom
Executive Secretary
(216) Lorain—233-5909
Elyria—324-6121

Northeastern Ohio
Ohio Society for Crippled Children and Adults, Inc.
615 Crain Ave.
Kent, Ohio   44240

Miss Nancy Kiracofe

Montgomery County Society for Crippled Children
117 W. Monument Ave.
Dayton, Ohio   45402

George F. Sutermaster
Executive Director
(513) 222-9872

Easter Seal Society for Crippled Children & Adults
of Mahoning County
299 Edwards Street
Youngstown, Ohio   44502

James Vento
Executive Director
(216) 743-1168

Easter Seal Society for Crippled Children & Adults
of Seneca County, Inc.
P.O. Box 602
Tiffin, Ohio   44883

Springfield Rotary Club
503 First Nat'l Bank Building
Springfield, Ohio   45502

Mrs. James Gatten

Toledo Society for Crippled Children
630 West Woodruff Ave.
Toledo, Ohio   43624

Miss Dorothea Shock
Coordinator
(419) 244-4993

Easter Seal Society for Crippled Children & Adults of
    Trumbull County
6064 Village Center Mall
Youngstown Road
Niles, Ohio   44446

Miss Garnet Moyer

Wood County Society for Crippled Children, Inc.
500 Lehman Avenue
Bowling Green, Ohio   43402

(419) 352-1735

Pennsylvania

The Easter Seal Society for Crippled Children
    and Adults of Adams County
16 East Middle Street
Gettysburg, Pennsylvania   17325

Mrs. Lois Geib
Executive Director
(717) 334-8331

The Easter Seal Society for Crippled Children and
    Adults of Allegheny County
110—7th Street
Pittsburgh, Pennsylvania   15222

Andrew J. Wasko
Executive Director
(412) 281-1633 or 34

The Easter Seal Society for Crippled Children and
    Adults of Armstrong County, Pennsylvania, Inc.
910–4th Ave.
Ford City, Pennsylvania   16226

Miss Jennie Lee Morgan
Executive Director
(Full-time)
(412) 763-2881

Easter Seal Society for Crippled Children
    & Adults of Beaver County
P.O. Box 337—Dutch Ridge Road
Beaver, Pennsylvania   15009

Mrs. Karen S. Lynch
Executive Director
(412) 774-6494

The Easter Seal Society for Crippled Children & Adults
    of Bedford County, Inc.
P.O. Box 223
Bedford, Pennsylvania   15522

Mrs. Catherine Matulnes
Executive Secretary
(Part-Time)
(814) 623-8339

Easter Seal Society for Handicapped Children & Adults
    of Berks County, Inc.-Special Education Center
Box 76
Reading, Pennsylvania   19603

Miss Janet M. Dicks
Executive Director
(215) 775-1431

The Easter Seal Society for Crippled Children and Adults
    of Blair County, Inc.
501 Valley View Boulevard
Altoona, Pennsylvania   16602

Michael L. Weamer
Executive Director
(814) 944-5014

Bradford-Sullivan Counties Society for
    Crippled Children and Adults
301 York Avenue
Towanda, Pennsylvania   18848

Mrs. William Lafferty
Executive Director
(Part-Time)

Bucks County—(See Philadelphia Society)

The Easter Seal Society for Crippled Children and Adults
    of Butler County, Inc.
Deshone Veterans Hospital
P.O. Box 3—New Castle Road
Butler, Pennsylvania   16001

Joseph M. McDaniel
Executive Director
(412) 283-1010

Easter Seal Society for Crippled Children and Adults
    of Cambria County, Inc.
232 Walnut Street (P.O. Box 404)
Johnstown, Pennsylvania   15907

Richard L. Ryan
Executive Director
(814) 535-5508

Carbon County (See Luzerne County-Hazelton Area &
    Carbon County)

Easter Seal Society for Crippled Children and Adults
   of Central Pennsylvania
Child Development Center
R.D. 5—Box 84
Danville, Pennsylvania   17821

Mrs. Ann L. Lee
Executive Director
(717) 275-5502

Easter Seal Society for Crippled Children and Adults
   of Centre and Clinton Counties
1300 South Allen Street
State College, Pennsylvania   16801

Glenn Dunklebarger
Executive Director
(814) 238-4434

Chester County (See Philadelphia Society)

Clarion County (See Jefferson—Clarion County)

Easter Seal Society for Crippled Children and Adults
   of Clearfield County
P.O. Box 462
Clearfield, Pennsylvania   16830

Mrs. Mary B. McGoey
Executive Director
(Part-Time)
(814) 765-3794/4459

Columbia County—(See Central Pennsylvania Society)

Crawford County Society for Crippled Children and
   Adults
P.O. Box 193
Meadville, Pennsylvania   16335

Mrs. Elliot Lindquist
Executive Secretary
(Part-Time)
(814) 332-6244

Cumberland County—(See Tri-County Society)

Dauphin County—(See Tri-County Society)

Delaware County—(See Philadelphia Society)

Elk County Society for Crippled Children and Adults
P.O. Box 422
St. Mary's , Pennsylvania   15857

Mrs. Irene C. Wegemer

Erie County Crippled Children's Society Inc.
101 East Sixth Street, Box 1506
Erie, Pennsylvania   16507

Lawrence P. Rager, Jr.
Executive Director
(814) 459-2755

Fayette County Society for Crippled Children
   and Adults, Inc.
141 Oakland Avenue
Uniontown, Pennsylvania   15401

Mrs. Alice Young
Executive Director
(412) 437-4047

Franklin County Society for Crippled Children and
   Adults, Inc.
34 Roadside Avenue
Waynesboro, Pennsylvania   17268

Eric D. Boyer
Executive Director
(717) 762-5315

Fulton County Society for Crippled
   Children and Adults, Inc.
c/o Mrs. Faye Snyder
Star Route North
Box 85
Mc Connellsburg, Pennsylvania   17233

Mrs. Huldah Bain
Secretary

Green County (see Southwestern Pennsylvania Society)

Easter Seal Society for Crippled Children and
   Adults of Huntingdon County
510 Penn Street (P.O. Box 115)
Huntingdon, Pennsylvania   16652

S. Turner Jones
County Administrator
(814) 643-5724

Easter Seal Society for Crippled Children and
   Adults of Hazleton Area and Carbon County

John Seamon
Executive Director

S. Poplar St. and Gardner Beltway
Hazleton, Pennsylvania   18201

(717) 455-9511

Easter Seal Society for Crippled Children and Adults
    of Jefferson, Clarion and Indiana Counties, Inc.
P.O. Box 132, 103 North Gilpin Street
Punxsutawney, Pennsylvania   15767

Charles Wilhelm
Executive Director
(814) 938-6750

Juniata County Society for Crippled Children & Adults
Box 125, R.D. 1
Port Royal, Pennsylvania   17082

Mrs. Roy Armstrong
Secretary

Lackawanna County—(See Northeastern Society)

Easter Seal Society for Crippled Children and Adults
    of Lancaster County
630 Janet Avenue
Lancaster, Pennsylvania   17601

John A. Sippel, Jr.,
Executive Director
(717) 393-0425

Lawrence County Society for Crippled Children and
    Adults, Inc.
2715 Ellwood Road
New Castle, Pennsylvania   16101

Richard Chappell
Executive Director
(412) 658-4539

The Easter Seal Society for Crippled Children and
    Adults of Lebanon County
618 Cornwell Rd.
Lebanon, Pennsylvania   17042

William Trevor Swan, Jr.
Executive Director
(717) 273-7351

Lehigh County—(see Lehigh Valley Society)

Lehigh Valley Society for Crippled Children and
    Adults, Inc. (Serving Lehigh & North Hampton
    Counties)
2200 Industrial Drive
Bethlehem, Pennsylvania   18017

Harry S. Diehl
Executive Director
(215) 866-8092

McKean County Easter Seal Society for Crippled
    Children and Adults
407 Odd Fellows Building
Bradford, Pennsylvania   16701

Mrs. Anna L. Confer
Executive Secretary
(814) 362-4621

Mercer County Crippled Children's Society, Inc.
900 North Hermitage Road
Sharon, Pennsylvania   16146

Kenneth Delahunty
Secretary
(412) 342-3738

Mifflin County Society for Crippled Children and
    and Adults, Inc.
401 Yale Street
Lewiston, Pennsylvania   17044

Mrs. Donna Baer
Executive Director
(Part-Time)
(717) 248-6261

Easter Seal Society for Crippled Children and Adults
    of Monroe County, Inc.
2020 Laurel Avenue
Stroudsburg, Pennsylvania   18360

Mrs. Virginia Gerek
Executive Secretary
(Part-Time)
(717) 421-1254

Montgomery County—(See Philadelphia Society)

Montour County—(See Central Pennsylvania Society)

Northeastern Pennsylvania Society for Crippled Children
    & Adults, Inc. (Serving Lackawanna, Susquehanna,
    Wayne & Wyoming Counties)
R.D. 1,—Scranton-Carbondale Highway
Olyphant, Pennsylvania   18447

Miss Edith E. Wilson, RP
Executive Director
(717) 489-8691

Northhampton County—(see Lehigh Valley Society)

Northumberland County—(See Central Pennsylvania
Society

Perry County—(See Tri-County Society)

Easter Seal Society for Crippled Children and Adults
of Philadelphia (Serving Bucks, Chester, Delaware,
and Montgomery Counties)
371 Baltimore Pike
Springfield, Pennsylvania 19064

James S. Fiske
Acting Executive Vice
President
(215) 328-1900

Pike County Committee for Crippled
Children and Adults
Matamoras, Pennsylvania 18336

Mrs. Charlotte Zulick
Secretary

Potter County Society for Crippled
Children and Adults
202 W. Maple Street
Coudersport, Pennsylvania 16915

Mrs. Marjorie J.
Hamilton
Secretary

Schuylkill County Easter Seal Society for Disabled
Children and Adults
127 So. Center Street
Frackville, Pennsylvania 17931

Mrs. Isabel Watkins
Executive Director
(Part-Time)
(717) 874-0862

Snyder County—(See Central Pennsylvania Society)

Easter Seal Society for Crippled
Children and Adults of Somerset County
124 Center Street
Scull Building—Room 228
Somerset, Pennsylvania 15501

Mrs. Pauline Davis
Executive Secretary
(814) 445-4834

The Southwestern Pennsylvania Easter Seal Society for
Crippled Children and Adults, Inc.
Brownson House—1415 Jefferson Avenue
Washington, Pennsylvania 15301

Robert A. Kerr
Executive Director
(412) 225-2226

Sullivan County—(See Bradford County)

Susquehanna County—(See Northeastern Pennsylvania
Society)

Tri-County Society for Crippled Children and Adults, Inc.
(Serving Cumberland, Dauphin and Perry Counties)
2930 Derry Street
Harrisburg, Pennsylvania 17111

Harry C. Patchin
Executive Director
(717) 564-6500

Union County—(See Central Pennsylvania Society)

The Easter Seal Society for Crippled Children and Adults
of Venango County
Venango Human Services Center, Inc.
Route 322-East, Box 231
Franklin, Pennsylvania 16323

Mrs. Wayne (Mary Lou)
E. Mook
Executive Director
(814) 437-6821

Crippled Children Committee of Warren County, Inc.
Court House
P.O. Box 966
Warren, Pennsylvania 16365

Mrs. Jean C. Proud, R.N.
Executive Director
(814) 723-5730

Wayne County—(See Northeastern Pennsylvania Society)

The Easter Seal Society for Crippled Children
and Adults of Westmoreland County, Inc.
Mellon National Bank Building, Room 410
New Kensington, Pennsylvania 15068

Mrs. Carol Greco
Executive Director
(412) 335-7117

Wyoming County—(See Northeastern Pennsylvania
 Society)

Wyoming Valley Crippled Children's Association, Inc.   Bernard Kolodziej
71 North Franklin Street   Executive Director
Wilkes-Barre, Pennsylvania 18701   (717) 829-2453

The Easter Seal Society for Crippled Children and Adults   Bruce T. Bobb
 of York County, Inc.   Executive Director
2201 South Queen Street (Rear)   (717) 741-3891
York, Pennsylvania 17402

South Carolina
Easter Seal Society for Crippled Children and Adults of   Forrest H. Norvell, Jr.
 Berkeley, Charleston and Dorchester Counties   Executive Director
Charles Webb Easter Seal Rehabilitation Center   (803) 723-7224
325 Calhoun Street
Charleston, South Carolina 29401

Tennessee
Easter Seal Society for Crippled Children & Adults   Spencer L. Davis
 of Tennessee, Inc. Volunteer Regional Chapter   Executive Director
3011 Broadway N.E.   (615) 688-5080
Knoxville, Tennessee 37917

Easter Seal Society for Crippled Children and Adults   E. H. Wright, Jr.
 of Tennessee, Inc.—West Tennessee Regional   Executive Director
 Chapter   (901) 324-3731
P.O. Box 11532
Memphis, Tennessee 38111

Easter Seal Society for Crippled Children and Adults of   Neeley E. Butler
 Tennessee, Inc.—Middle Tennessee Regional   Executive Director
 Chapter   (615) 292-6639
2001 Woodmont Blvd.—P.O. Box 15581
Nashville, Tennessee 37215

Texas
Bell County Rehabilitation Center   Richard Schaub
2000 West Marland Wood Road   Executive Director
Temple, Texas 76501   (817) 773-5845

The Easter Seal Society for Crippled Children and   Randel Aaron
 Adults of Bexar County—Easter Seal Treatment   Executive Director
 Center   (512) 532-4295
2818 South Pine Street
San Antonio, Texas 78210

Temple Memorial Easter Seal Society for Crippled   Mrs. Janet Hoag
 Children and Adults of Texarkana   Executive Director
 Bowie-Miller County   (501) 772-3789
304 East Fifth Street
Texarkana, Arkansas-Texas 75501

Brazos Valley Rehabilitation Center   James Thompson
3300 East 29th Street   Executive Director
Bryan, Texas 77801   (713) 822-0193

Dallas Society for Crippled Children and Adults   Lloyd F. Martin
5701 Maple at Inwood   Executive Director
Dallas, Texas 75235   (214) 358-5261

Easter Seal Society for Crippled Children and Adults
    of Grayson County
1216 Hill Crest—P.O. Box 453
Sherman, Texas   75090

Mrs. Al Norrell
Executive Director
(214) 893-0604

The Easter Seal Society for Crippled Children and Adults
    of Harris County, Inc.
P.O. Box 13399—3630 West Dallas
Houston, Texas,   77019

Jacqueline Gleckler,
    Ph.D.
Executive Director
(713) 526-1651

Easter Seal Society for Crippled Children and Adults
    of Hidalgo County Treatment Center
P.O. Box 489
McAllen, Texas   78501

Miss Ruth Glover
Executive Director
(512) 682-3436

McLennan County Rehabilitation Center for
    Children and Adults
1501 North 18th Street
Waco, Texas   76707

Mrs. Irvin (Elizabeth)
    Pettis
Executive Director
(817) 756-4447

The Easter Seal Society for Crippled Children and Adults
    of Tarrant County, Inc.
617 Seventh Avenue
Fort Worth, Texas   76104

Robert F. Scott, R.P.T.
Executive Director
(817) 336-8693

Easter Seal Society for Crippled Children & Adults
    of North Texas
North Texas Rehabilitation Center
516 Denver Street
Wichita Falls, Texas   76301

Mrs. Bettye Wages
Executive Director
(817) 322-0771

Virginia
Virginia Easter Seal Center
Region 1
5232 Lee Highway
Arlington, Va.   22207

(703) 536-9400

Virginia Easter Seal Center
Region II
116 North Boulevard
Richmond, Virginia   23220

(804) 355-7166

Virginia Easter Seal Center
Region III
3101 Magic Hollow Boulevard
Virginia Beach, Va.   23456

(804) 427-1480

Virginia Easter Seal Center
Region IV
126 Buena Vista Circle, Box 7
South Hill, Va.   23970

(804) 447-4461

Virginia Easter Seal Center
Region VII
1732 Euclid Avenue
Bristol, Virginia   24201

(703) 669-5433

Washington (State of)
Easter Seal Society for Crippled Children
    and Adults of Washington
510 Second Avenue, West
Spokane, Washington   99204

Paul Hammond
(509) 838-8353

West Virginia

Monongalia County Easter Seal Society
15 Cottage St., W.O.
Morgantown, West Virginia   26505

Mrs. Patricia Poston
Executive Secretary
(304) 296-0150

Harrison County Society for Crippled Children
Box 2366
Clarksburg, West Virginia   26301

Harry E. Dean, Jr.
Executive Director
(304) 624-5009

Wheeling Society for Crippled Children
1316 National Road
Wheeling, West Virginia   26003

Miss Rosemary Front
Executive Director
(304) 242-1390

Logan County Society for Crippled Children
P.O. Box 178
Logan, West Virginia   25601

Mrs. Alice L. Cooke
Executive Secretary
(304) 239-2211

Easter Seal Society for Crippled Children
    and Adults—Wood County Rehabilitation Center
700 18th Street
Parkersburg, West Virginia   26101

Ron D. Somerville
Executive Director
(304) 422-7243

Wisconsin

Easter Seal Society for Crippled Children and Adults
    of Milwaukee County, Inc.
5225 West Burleigh Street
Milwaukee, Wisconsin   53210

Scott L. Defebaugh
Executive Director
(414) 871-1270

APPENDIX IX

Directory of Colleges and Universities With Facilities for Handicapped Students

The colleges and universities included in this directory provide certain basic facilities necessary for handicapped students. The selection was based on a research project completed by Kansas State Teachers College, Emporia, Kansas, which was supported in part by a research and demonstration grant, Number 812, from the Vocational Rehabilitation Administration, Department of Health, Education, and Welfare, Washington, D.C. (Permission has been received to extract.)

In the initial survey, conducted during the period 1961–1963, all institutions of higher learning having enrollments over 1,000 were contacted and the results published. We have, however, employed certain criteria in our selection and have included only those institutions evidencing at least two of these six conveniences. They are: On-Campus Housing Ramps (indicated as HR), Classroom Ramps (CR), Library Ramps (LR), Beveled Curbs (BC), Reserved Parking (RP), and Modified Toilet Facilities (MT). After employing this standard for selection, other services such as Special Counselor (SC), Regular Vocational Rehabilitation Service Visits (VR), and Adapted Physical Education (PE) were listed.

In addition to the name of the institution, we have added its location, whether public or private, length of program offered and type of student body.

Sources of Financial Information

The following chart indicates if the institution is participating in the program for the preparation of professional personnel in the education of handicapped children sponsored by the Office of Education under Public Law 85-926, as amended. Under this program, senior year traineeships, summer traineeships and graduate fellowships are awarded to encourage the expansion of teaching and research in the education of handicapped children.

Federal financial aid programs are available at most of the institutions listed. Frequently students can work out package financial plans that may include the Work-Study Program, the National Defense Student Loan Program and the Educational Opportunity Grants Program, together with other sources of help that may be available through the college.

The College Work-Study is a program of *employment* in which the student, particularly one from a low-income family, is compensated for the number of hours he works for the institution or for an eligible off-campus agency.

The National Defense Student Loans is a program of *borrowing,* primarily for needy students, in which the student has an obligation to repay his loan, with 3% interest within a ten year period following college attendance.

The Educational Opportunity Grants is a program of direct *grants* in which the student receives a non-obliging award of funds, based on exceptional financial need and evidence of academic creative promise.

The Guaranteed Loans is a program of *borrowing,* primarily for students from middle- or upper-income families. The student has an obligation to repay his loan with 3% (middle income) or 6% (upper income) interest.

Many institutions offer other types of scholarships, student loan, employment and work-study plans.

Students interested in applying for any of these benefits should apply directly to the college or university of their choice.

Each of the fifty State education agencies participate in the Federal program for the preparation of professional personnel in the education of handicapped children. In addition, many States offer local scholarships and loans. For further information regarding State financial assistance, one should communicate with the state Department of Education.

The National Society for Crippled Children and Adults, 2023 West Ogden Avenue, Chicago, Illinois 60612, and the United Cerebral Palsy Research and Education Foundation, 321 West 44th Street, New York, New York 10036, have available scholarships.

Key to Abbreviations

HR—On-Campus Housing Ramps	MT—Modified Toilet Training
CR—Classroom Ramps	SC—Special Counselor
LR—Library Ramps	VR—Regular Vocational Rehabilitation
BC—Beveled Curbs	Service Visit
RP—Reserved Parking	PE—Adapted Physical Education

INSTITUTION, CITY & STATE	Public	Private	2 Year	4 Yr. or more	P.L. 85–926	Coed	Men	Women	HR	CR	LR	BC	RP	MT	SC	VR	PE
ALABAMA																	
Troy State College, Troy	X			X		X				X			X			X	X
ARIZONA																	
Arizona State College, Flagstaff	X			X		X			X	X		X			X	X	X
Arizona State University, Tempe	X			X		X					X		X				X
Grand Canyon College, Phoenix		X		X		X			X	X	X		X			X	
Phoenix College, Phoenix	X		X			X				X			X				
ARKANSAS																	
State College of Arkansas, Conway	X			X	X	X			X		X	X				X	
Little Rock University, Little Rock		X		X		X				X			X				
University of Arkansas, Fayetteville	X			X	X	X			X				X				
CALIFORNIA																	
Bakersfield College, Bakersfield	X		X			X				X	X		X			X	X
California State Polytechnic College Pomona-San Dimas	X			X		X				X	X	X	X	X		X	X
California State Polytechnic College San Luis Obispo	X			X		X			X	X	X	X		X		X	X
Cerritos College, Norwalk	X		X			X				X	X	X				X	X
Citrus Junior College, Azusa	X		X			X				X	X	X	X		X	X	X
College of San Mateo, San Mateo	X		X			X				X			X			X	X
Compton College, Compton	X		X			X						X	X		X	X	
Contra Costa College, San Pablo	X		X			X				X			X	X	X	X	
Diablo Valley College, Concord	X		X			X				X			X			X	
East Los Angeles College, Los Angeles	X		X			X				X	X					X	
El Camino College, El Camino	X		X			X				X			X				X
Fresno City College, Fresno	X		X			X				X		X	X			X	
Hartnell College, Salinas	X		X			X				X	X					X	X
Los Angeles Harbor College, Wilmington	X		X			X				X	X	X	X		X	X	
Los Angeles State College, Los Angeles	X			X	X	X				X			X	X			X
Los Angeles Valley College, Van Nuys	X		X			X				X	X		X		X	X	X
Long Beach State College, Long Beach	X			X	X	X				X	X	X	X	X	X	X	X
Modesto Evening Junior College, Modesto	X		X			X							X	X		X	
Mt. San Antonio College, Pomona	X		X			X				X	X						
Napa College, Napa	X		X			X				X	X						
Orange Coast College, Costa Mesa	X		X			X				X	X	X					
Pomona College, Claremont		X		X		X				X		X					
Riverside City College, Riverside	X		X			X				X	X		X		X	X	
Sacramento City College, Sacramento	X		X			X						X	X	X	X		X
San Diego Junior College, San Diego	X		X			X				X	X				X	X	X
San Diego State College, San Diego	X			X	X	X			X	X	X	X	X	X		X	X
San Fernando Valley State College Northridge	X			X		X				X					X	X	X

INSTITUTION, CITY & STATE	Public	Private	2 Year	4 Yr. or more	P.L. 85–926	Coed	Men	Women	HR	CR	LR	BC	RP	MT	SC	VR	
CALIFORNIA (CONTINUED)																	
San Francisco State College, San Francisco	X			X	X	X				X	X	X	X	X		X	X
San Jose City College, San Jose	X			X	X	X				X	X		X	X			
San Jose State College, San Jose	X			X	X	X				X	X	X	X	X			X
Santa Monica City College, Santa Monica	X		X			X				X	X	X	X				X
Santa Rosa Junior College, Santa Rosa	X		X			X				X	X		X				
Stanford University, Stanford		X		X		X			X	X	X	X	X				X
San Joaquin Delta College, Stockton	X		X			X				X	X		X				X
University of California, Berkeley	X			X		X			X	X	X		X	X	X	X	X
University of California, Davis	X			X		X						X	X	X			
University of California, Los Angeles	X			X	X	X			X	X	X	X	X	X	X	X	X
University of California, Riverside	X			X		X			X	X	X	X	X	X		X	X
University of California, Santa Barbara	X			X		X			X	X	X		X	X	X		X
Vallejo Junior College, Vallejo	X		X			X				X			X			X	
Ventura College, Ventura	X		X			X					X	X	X			X	X
COLORADO																	
Adams State College, Alamosa	X			X		X				X			X			X	X
University of Colorado, Boulder	X			X	X	X						X	X			X	X
CONNECTICUT																	
Hartford State Technical Institute, Hartford	X		X			X			X	X	X		X			X	
University of Connecticut, Storrs	X			X	X	X						X	X		X	X	
University of Hartford, Hartford		X		X		X				X		X		X			
DISTRICT OF COLUMBIA																	
Dunbarton College of Holy Cross, Washington, D.C.		X		X				X	X				X				
FLORIDA																	
Central Florida Junior College, Ocala	X		X			X						X	X			X	X
North Florida Junior College, Madison	X		X			X					X	X				X	
St. Petersburg Junior College, St. Petersburg	X		X			X				X	X	X	X			X	
University of Florida, Gainesville	X			X	X	X	X					X		X		X	
University of Miami, Coral Gables		X		X	X	X				X	X	X	X	X			
University of South Florida, Tampa	X			X	X	X				X	X	X	X	X		X	X
University of Tampa, Tampa		X		X		X				X	X	X	X	X	X		X	X
GEORGIA																	
Augusta College, Augusta	X		X			X					X	X	X				X
Emory University, Atlanta		X		X	X	X							X	X			X
Georgia State College, Atlanta	X			X	X	X					X	X	X				X
Oglethorpe University, Atlanta		X		X		X							X	X			
South Georgia College, Douglas	X		X			X			X				X				

INSTITUTION, CITY & STATE	Public	Private	2 Year	4 Yr. or more	P.L. 85-926	Coed	Men	Women	HR	CR	LR	BC	RP	MT	SC	VR	PE
GEORGIA (CONTINUED)																	
Tift College, Forsyth		X		X				X	X	X						X	
The Women's College of Georgia, Milledgeville	X			X				X	X	X	X				X	X	X
IDAHO																	
Boise Junior College, Boise	X		X			X			X	X	X	X	X				
College of Idaho, Caldwell		X		X		X			X			X				X	X
North Idaho Junior College, Coeur d'Alene	X		X			X				X	X		X			X	
ILLINOIS																	
Northern Illinois University, DeKalb	X			X	X	X						X	X			X	X
Southern Illinois University, Carbondale	X			X	X	X			X	X	X	X	X	X	X	X	X
University of Illinois, Urbana	X			X	X	X			X	X	X	X	X	X	X	X	X
Western Illinois University, Macomb	X			X		X						X	X		X	X	X
INDIANA																	
Ball State Teachers College, Muncie	X			X	X	X						X	X		X	X	X
Earlham College, Richmond		X		X		X			X	X	X	X					
Indiana University, Bloomington	X			X	X	X			X				X		X	X	X
IOWA																	
Drake University, Des Moines		X		X	X	X			X				X				
Graceland College, Lamoni		X		X		X			X	X			X		X	X	X
Luther College, Decorah		X		X		X				X		X	X			X	
KANSAS																	
Kansas State Teachers College, Emporia	X			X	X	X			X	X	X	X	X	X	X	X	X
Southwestern College, Winfield		X		X		X			X		X		X			X	
University of Wichita, Wichita	X			X	X	X				X	X		X				X
Washburn University, Topeka	X			X		X				X	X	X	X				
KENTUCKY																	
Morehead State College, Morehead	X			X	X	X							X	X		X	X
Murray State College, Murray	X			X	X	X			X			X	X	X	X		
University of Kentucky, Lexington	X			X	X	X				X			X			X	
LOUISIANA																	
F.T. Nicholls State College, Thibodaux	X			X		X						X	X			X	
Louisiana State University, Baton Rouge	X			X	X	X			X	X	X		X			X	X
Louisiana State University, New Orleans	X			X	X	X				X			X			X	
McNeese State College, Lake Charles	X			X		X			X			X	X				
MAINE																	
Colby College, Waterville		X		X			X	X			X		X				

INSTITUTION, CITY & STATE	Public	Private	2 Year	4 Yr. or more	P.L. 85-926	Coed	Men	Women	HR	CR	LR	BC	RP	MT	SC	VR	PE
MASSACHUSETTS																	
College of the Holy Cross, Worcester		X		X			X		X		X	X	X		X		
Harvard University, Cambridge		X		X		X	X		X		X		X				
Massachusetts Institute of Technology Cambridge		X		X		X			X	X	X	X	X				
MICHIGAN																	
Ferris State College, Big Rapids	X			X		X			X	X	X	X	X	X	X	X	
Henry Ford Community College, Dearborn	X		X			X				X	X	X	X				
Kellogg Community College, Battle Creek	X		X			X				X	X		X			X	
Lansing Community College, Lansing	X		X			X				X	X					X	X
Wayne State University, Detroit	X			X	X	X			X	X	X	X	X	X	X	X	
MINNESOTA																	
Austin Junior College, Austin	X		X			X						X	X				
College of St. Catherine, St. Paul		X		X				X				X	X				
Gustavus Adolphus College, St. Peter		X		X		X			X	X	X				X	X	X
St. Cloud State College, St. Cloud	X			X	X	X			X	X		X				X	X
MISSOURI																	
Culver-Stockton College, Canton		X		X		X						X	X			X	X
St. Louis University, St. Louis		X		X	X	X				X			X				
Southeast Missouri State College, Cape Girardeau	X			X	X	X						X	X			X	X
University of Missouri, Columbia	X			X	X	X			X	X	X	X	X	X	X	X	
Washington University, St. Louis		X		X	X	X						X	X			X	X
MONTANA																	
Montana State University, Missoula	X			X	X	X			X	X	X		X	X		X	
NEBRASKA																	
Creighton University, Omaha		X		X		X			X	X	X		X				
Nebraska State Teachers College, Kearney	X			X		X					X	X	X			X	
Nebraska State Teachers College, Peru	X			X		X					X	X	X		X	X	
University of Nebraska, Lincoln	X			X	X	X				X		X	X			X	X
University of Omaha, Omaha	X			X	X	X				X	X	X	X	X			X
NEVADA																	
University of Nevada Southern Regional Division, Las Vegas	X			X		X				X	X	X	X			X	X
NEW JERSEY																	
Monmouth College, West Long Branch		X		X		X			X	X			X			X	
NEW MEXICO																	
St. Michael's College, Santa Fe		X		X			X		X	X							
University of New Mexico, Albuquerque	X			X	X	X						X	X				

INSTITUTION, CITY & STATE	Public	Private	2 Year	4 Yr. or more	P.L. 85-926	Coed	Men	Women	HR	CR	LR	BC	RP	MT	SC	VR	PE
NEW YORK																	
Barnard College of Columbia University, New York City		X		X				X	X	X	X	X					
Brooklyn College, Brooklyn	X			X		X				X	X		X	X	X		X
Columbia University, New York City		X		X	X	X			X	X	X	X	X				
The City College of the City University of New York, New York City	X			X	X	X				X	X		X		X	X	X
Hofstra University, Hempstead, Long Island		X		X	X	X						X	X		X	X	X
Marymount College, Tarrytown		X		X				X	X	X			X				X
NORTH CAROLINA																	
Agricultural and Technical College of North Carolina, Greensboro	X			X		X				X		X	X		X	X	X
Atlantic Christian College, Wilson		X		X		X				X	X					X	X
Methodist College, Fayetteville		X		X		X			X	X	X		X	X			
North Carolina Wesleyan College, Rocky Mount		X		X		X			X	X	X	X		X		X	
Pfeiffer College, Misenheimer		X		X		X						X	X			X	X
St. Andrews Presbyterian College, Laurinburg		X		X		X			X	X	X	X		X			
University of North Carolina, Chapel Hill	X			X	X	X			X	X	X	X	X			X	
OHIO																	
Baldwin-Wallace College, Berea		X		X		X				X	X				X	X	
University of Cincinnati, Cincinnati	X			X	X	X				X			X				
University of Dayton, Dayton		X		X		X	X						X				
University of Toledo, Toledo	X			X		X	X						X	X		X	
Wittenberg University, Springfield		X		X		X						X	X			X	X
OKLAHOMA																	
Central State College, Edmond	X			X	X	X						X	X		X	X	X
East Central State College, Ada	X			X		X							X	X		X	
Northeastern State College, Tahlequah	X			X		X							X	X		X	
Oklahoma State Technical Institute, Oklahoma City	X			X		X			X	X	X	X	X	X	X		
Oklahoma State University, Stillwater	X			X	X	X				X	X		X			X	
Southwestern State College, Weatherford	X			X		X							X	X	X	X	
University of Oklahoma, Norman	X			X	X	X			X	X	X	X	X			X	X
OREGON																	
Lewis and Clark College, Portland		X		X	X	X			X			X	X			X	X
Oregon State University, Corvallis	X			X		X			X	X	X		X			X	X
Oregon Technical Institute, Klamath	X		X			X			X	X	X	X	X			X	
Portland State College, Portland	X			X	X	X				X				X			X
Reed College, Portland		X		X		X				X		X					

INSTITUTION, CITY & STATE	Public	Private	2 Year	4 Yr. or more	P.L. 85–926	Coed	Men	Women	HR	CR	LR	BC	RP	MT	SC	VR	DF
PENNSYLVANIA																	
California State College, California	X			X	X	X				X			X		X	X	
Duquesne University, Pittsburgh		X		X	X	X					X		X			X	
Temple University, Philadelphia		X		X	X	X			X	X	X	X					X
SOUTH CAROLINA																	
University of South Carolina, Columbia	X			X	X	X				X			X				
SOUTH DAKOTA																	
South Dakota State College, Brockings	X			X		X				X		X	X	X	X	X	X
TENNESSEE																	
George Peabody College for Teachers Nashville		X		X	X	X							X	X		X	X
Memphis State University, Memphis	X			X	X	X				X	X	X	X				X
Tennessee A & I State University Nashville	X			X		X				X	X			X		X	X
TEXAS																	
Del Mar College, Corpus Christi	X		X			X				X			X			X	
East Texas State University, Commerce	X			X	X	X				X			X			X	
Kilgore College, Kilgore	X		X			X			X	X		X		X	X	X	
Lamar State College of Technology Beaumont	X			X	X	X				X	X	X		X		X	X
Midwestern University, Wichita Falls	X			X		X							X	X		X	X
Pan American College, Edinburg	X			X		X				X	X		X			X	
San Angelo College, San Angelo	X		X			X				X	X			X			
Southern Methodist University, Dallas		X		X	X	X							X	X			X
South Texas College, Houston		X	X			X				X	X						
Texas Technological College, Lubbock	X			X	X	X					X		X				X
Texas Woman's University, Denton	X			X	X			X	X				X	X	X	X	X
University of Houston, Houston	X			X	X	X			X	X	X	X	X		X		
University of Texas, Austin	X			X	X	X			X	X	X	X	X		X		X
UTAH																	
Brigham Young University, Provo		X		X	X	X							X	X		X	X
Westminster College, Salt Lake City		X		X		X			X			X	X				
VERMONT																	
University of Vermont, Burlington	X			X	X	X							X	X			
WASHINGTON																	
Central Washington State College Ellensburg	X			X	X	X			X	X		X	X		X	X	X
Columbia Basin College, Pasco	X		X			X				X	X	X	X	X	X	X	X
Eastern Washington State College, Cheney	X			X		X			X				X		X	X	X
Everett Junior College, Everett	X		X			X					X		X				
Grays Harbor College, Aberdeen	X		X			X				X	X		X			X	

INSTITUTION, CITY & STATE	Public	Private	2 Year	4 Yr. or more	P.L. 85–926	Coed	Men	Women	HR	CR	LR	BC	RP	MT	SC	VR	PE
WASHINGTON (CONTINUED)																	
University of Puget Sound, Tacoma		X		X		X			X	X	X	X	X	X	X	X	
University of Washington, Seattle	X			X	X	X			X				X		X		X
WEST VIRGINIA																	
Marshall University, Huntington	X			X	X	X			X	X		X	X			X	X
WISCONSIN																	
Marquette University, Milwaukee		X		X	X	X				X			X	X			
University of Wisconsin, Madison	X			X	X	X				X			X		X		
Wisconsin State University, Eau Claire	X			X	X	X			X		X	X	X			X	X
Wisconsin State University, Oshkosh	X			X		X				X	X				X		
Wisconsin State University, River Falls	X			X		X							X	X		X	X
Wisconsin State University, Stevens Point	X			X	X	X							X	X			

APPENDIX X

Ways to Be Independent

I. SELF-HELP GENERAL

A. *Device for Putting on Stockings*
   1. This device consists of a 2½-foot wooden handle to which is attached a "U" shaped spreader. This spreader is made of polished wire, and there are two curved loops on each end of the spreader to hold a rolled stocking. The stocking, unrolling under proper tension, is then drawn over the foot and leg.
   2. The device makes it possible for a woman to put on her own stockings even though she is unable to bend or stoop.

B. *Garter Tape*
   1. A corset garter is attached to either end of a 5–6 foot length of cotton tape. Length of tape will depend upon height of user, especially length of leg.
   2. A garter is fastened to either side of the stocking. Holding the tape, the seated patient can drop the stocking and draw it over her foot. Then, using great care, she pulls the top of the stocking over her leg until it reaches the place where it can be grasped in either hand while the operation is completed. Garters are then detached and stocking is drawn on the other leg in the same manner.
   This method of putting on stockings is used by women unable to bend over

or to lift their feet to use any of the usual methods. It is helpful to arthritics and others in similar condition.

C. *Long Handled Shoe Horn—Elastic Shoe Laces*
1. The equipment consists of a metal shoe horn, soldered to a 22-inch length of ⅝-inch aluminum tubing. Some patients prefer the shoe horn to have some flexibility of movement, in which case it may be attached to the rod with a ball and socket joint. If used by patient wearing a zipper-fastened shoe, the other end may be fashioned so as to form a small hook to open and close zipper.
2. This shoe horn is designed to facilitate putting on shoes when the patient is unable to reach his feet, as in the case of fused hips or fractured hips. If used with elastic shoe laces or the zipper shoe, the patient is able to put on shoes entirely unassisted.

D. *Clip-on Ties—Esquire Tie Clasp*
1. These are ordinary men's bow and four-in-hand ties, having on the back, behind the knot, metal clips that can be inserted under the collar. The tie clasp has spring clips on both ends.
2. The purpose of ties and clasp is to enable those having the use of only one arm such as the polio, hemiplegia or c.p. patient, to put on their ties unaided.

E. *E-Z Reach Suspenders*
1. The suspenders are made of a single length (about 60 inches) of nylon parachute cord, to each end of which is fastened an alligator radio clamp. The cord is placed under the shirt collar with the ends run through the front belt-loops of trousers and doubled back and clamped to the cord on either side near the tip of the collar. This arrangement is neat and inconspicuous.
2. This device was designed to solve the self-care problem of lowering trousers without letting them drop to the floor when wearer finds difficulty in this matter due to arm amputation, partial paralysis, or other disability affecting his dexterity. When the wearer stands up—with suspenders still at full extension—the trousers are knee-high and within reach of being pulled up without danger of a struggle to retrieve them from the floor. The suspenders can be helpful to an amputee, a hemiplegic, or other unilaterally disabled person.

F. *Long-Handled Comb*
1. The handle is made from a 24-inch length of ⅜-inch hollow aluminum tubing. The rod is bent about 4 to 5 inches from the end, to form a right angle. The end of a rat-tailed comb made of either nylon or hard rubber is inserted into the rod. A word of warning is given against using plastic rod or comb as they do not hold up.
2. The long-handled comb is designed to enable those patients who have limitation of shoulder and elbow flexion to comb their hair. It can also assist patients who have weakness of shoulder or elbow flexors; if accompanied by weak finger flexors, a built-up handle may have to be added.

G. *The Comb Adjustment*

    1. This device consists of a comb set on a light-weight aluminum handle. The long handle can be bent to desired angle and the comb is bent into a less than right angle. Comb may also be attached perpendicular to the handle by first riveting it to a strip of light-weight aluminum which has been attached to handle.

    2. This is a variant of the long-handled comb. It will be very helpful to anyone unable to raise hands high enough to use comb held in hand.

H. *Suction Cup Brush*

    1. This is a standard surgeon's hand brush, on either wood or plastic back, with two rubber suction cups secured to the back of brush. It can be fastened on any surface, metal, wood, tile, etc., in any location most convenient to use.

    2. This device is used for assisting in the washing of remaining hand and arm when person has sustained either temporary or permanent loss of the use of one hand.

I. *Foot Controlled Nail Clipper*

    1. This device is made from two pieces of plywood ($1\frac{1}{2}''$ x $5''$ x $\frac{1}{4}''$ and $1\frac{1}{2}''$ x $3''$ x $\frac{3}{8}''$) which are nailed together. A piece of $1\frac{1}{2}$-inch spring steel is screwed on top to hold nail clippers. A piece of mesh wire, soldered to lever of nail clippers, descends through a hole drilled directly beneath same. Foot cuff is made from a $9''$ x $5''$ piece of leather, and a spring clamp is used to adjust to proper length.

    To use: The base of clipper is slipped into an open drawer which is then closed to hold device, or it may be clamped to a table; the foot is placed in the leather foot cuff; the spring clip is adjusted so that heel rests upon the floor; the clipper is opened and closed by the extension and flexion of the foot.

    2. The device enables a patient to cut his finger nails without using his other hand.

J. *Long Handled Toothbrush*

    1. Two pieces of telescoping metal tubing are used for the handle, the length according to the need (approx. $14''$ x $18''$). A solid block of aluminum is inserted into the open end of the smaller piece of tubing to provide a means of attaching toothbrush to tubing. The toothbrush handle is cut short and the end is attached to the tubing with a small strip of aluminum. The toothbrush is attached in this way to provide swiveling—for use in either right or left side of mouth.

    Since both aluminum and plastic are soft materials that wear easily, it is recommended to use spring washers where the pieces are riveted together (only the top rivet need be loose). This maintains the desired tension, so that toothbrush can be moved into various positions yet will not flop loosely.

    2. The long, extendable handle makes it possible for toothbrush to be used independently.

K. *Toothbrush Holder for Cleaning Dentures*

    1. The toothbrush holder is composed of two small blocks of wood, one thick enough to permit drilling of hole to accommodate toothbrush handle (1), the other thin enough to accommodate bolts in suction cups (2). The two blocks are nailed together with the suction cups attached to the thin block so that a nail, thrust through this hole, will catch the hole in the toothbrush handle to hold the toothbrush in position. The suction cups hold the blocks and toothbrush firmly in place while the patient cleans his dentures with his functional hand.

        (1) approx. 2″ x 1½″ x ⅝″

        (2) approx. 3″ x 1½″ x ¼″

    2. This holder makes it possible for a person having only one functional hand to clean his dentures. It might be used by hemiplegics or others who wear dentures and face the problem of cleaning them with the use of only one hand.

L. *Denture Cleaner*

    1. This device consists of a hand clip and a forearm clip connected by a bar on the dorsal surface of the hand, with circular holders for toothbrush attached on each clip at medial side.

    2. For a flaccid hand, the holder serves to stabilize wrist, substitute for grasp, and allow shoulder motion to be used. By the addition of circular holders on the other side, the device could be adapted for holding other utensils, such as comb or razor.

M. *Bathtub Rail*

    1. This strong rail of chromium steel extends the full length of the bathtub about 12″ above the top on the wall side. It is supported in the middle as well as at the ends for extra strength.

    2. The bath rail helps any bather to get in and out of the tub, especially a tub built directly against the wall. It makes independent use of the tub possible for persons with paralyzed or weak legs, or for bilateral amputees, provided their upper extremities are strong.

N. *Bath Bench*

    1. The bath bench is a plain wooden bench about 3½ feet long and a little less than a foot wide, its height level with the seat of standard wheel chair. It should be sturdy and entirely steady.

    2. The bath bench is designed to facilitate transfer from wheel chair to tub by patients with paralysis of lower extremities and with strong upper extremities. The bench is placed alongside of the bathtub, and the wheel chair is brought directly up to the end of the bench. Patient slides on to the bench, turns towards tub and places his legs over the side. With one hand on arm of chair and the other flat on the bench, he slides to the edge of tub. Grasping edge of tub with one hand and rail with the other hand, he lowers himself into the bathtub. In getting out of the tub, the process is reversed. The bench can also be used at end of tub.

O. *Chair for Bathtub Use—Bathtub Board*

    1. Two ordinary light weight chairs in wood or metal—one inside and one outside the tub—offer another solution to the bathing problem. The legs of

the chair inside the tub are shortened and supplied with rubber crutch tips; the legs of the outside chair are fitted with lock casters and adjusted to tub height.

The bathtub board for transfer consists of two pieces of wood, 25″ by 8″ and 32″ by 8″, with plastic and latex cover, center hinge and block. It is hinged in the center with butler tray hinges so that the outside end can be raised at a right angle and thus kept inside the shower curtain. The board has a wooden block under the hinge to support board at chair height. This board is covered with a plastic material lined with a thin piece of latex.

2. For the patient too weak, too uncertain, or too heavy to use either of the backless tub seats, it is often possible to slide from the chair outside the tub to the inside chair and there, in the security of the chair's ample seat and back, use shower or bath spray safely. This method of bathing is especially suitable for hemiplegia patients.

The bathtub board permits the patient to slide or edge from chair to chair. It is used for patients who are unable to lift themselves across even such a narrow space.

P. *Bath Lounge—Suction Cup Bath Mat—Bathtub Master*

1. *The Bath Lounge,* with back and head rest, is an inflatable seat made of Vinylite plastic suction cups on the bottom to hold it in place. After being blown up, it is placed in position in the tub, and the tub is then filled with water.

The suction cup bath mat is made of rubber, molded to form a continuous series of shallow suction cups that hold the mat firmly in place with their concave side while their convex sides provide a non-skid surface for the bather's feet. Small holes between the cups release any water under mat.

The Bathtub Master is a long-handled scrubber with foam rubber head curved to fit tub inclines and a 24-inch aluminum handle with non-skid Lucite gripper.

2. *The Bath Lounge* gives comfortable support in the tub to persons who need it. Many paraplegics can get in and out of the tub, yet would find a backrest and cushioned seat desirable. And some children, although lifting them in and out presents no problem, may need support in the tub.

The suction cup bath mat prevents slipping on the bottom of the tub and should be used with any of the bathtub seats and with the bath rail.

The Bathtub Master makes it possible to clean the tub without kneeling or leaning over into the tub.

Q. *Shower Benches*

1. The shower benches are plain wooden benches about 3½ feet long and a little less than a foot wide, in height level with the seat of the wheel chair.

2. One bench is placed in the stall shower and one outside but touching the inside bench. The wheel chair seat is brought directly next to the outside bench, its brakes are locked, and the patient slides across the outside bench and thence into the shower. He returns to his chair in the same manner. The shower benches can be used in connection with the stall shower in cases of weakness or paralysis of the lower extremities.

R. *Ever-ready Portable Wall Shower*

1. The powerful 2¾" suction cup attaches securely to any surface without marring wall and can be detached when the spray is to be used for shampoo. The rust-proof swivel head permits spray to be adjusted to any angle. Adjustable faucet connection fits all size faucets. The hose consists of 5½ feet of rubber tubing. Detached from the wall, the spray head makes a 3¾" rubber massage brush.

2. A portable wall shower makes it possible to take a shower when only a tub is available. This is of special advantage when the bather cannot get down into the tub and must use one of the bathtub seats. It is convenient to be able to place the shower head at different heights so that spray can be kept from head and face if desired. The swivel helps send the spray in the desired direction. It can also be held in the hand by patient or attendant and used like hose.

S. *Lavatory With Extended Brackets*

1. A wall hanger lavatory has neither legs nor pedestal and is supported by extended brackets. The brackets are extra heavy in anticipation of possible weight bearing. This arrangement is standard equipment made especially for the Institute of Physical Medicine and Rehabilitation.

2. The absence of legs or pedestal allows a wheel chair to approach the lavatory unimpeded and the extended brackets increase its accessibility. Some persons find that the swan-neck faucet offers special advantages, too.

T. *Bathroom Cabinet For Wheel Chair User*

1. The bathroom medicine cabinet with mirror is placed in the wall at a height convenient for use from the wheel chair. It can be placed at the side of the lavatory rather than over it.

2. With the cabinet in this position the wheel chair user can easily look into the mirror. Not only is the height correct for him, but the lavatory is conveniently at hand, to one side instead of in front of him. The interior of cabinet also is easily accessible to him.

U. *Schick Electric Razor Holder*

1. This device is a clamp, or bracket, of metal, designed to hold a Schick electric razor Model 20. It can be connected to an artificial arm by means of a 20½-inch thread connector and will fit all standard arms.

2. The razor holder is designed for use by one arm or hand of a c.p., both bilateral and unilateral, and enables him to shave without assistance. Since it is extremely difficult to lather the face with one or both hands gone, the electric razor, which requires no lather, is by far the best razor for an arm amputee to use.

V. *Safety Razor Holder*

1. This device consists of an aluminum hand-piece shaped to fit the hand comfortably and having on the palmar surface a small screw clip (such as is used for intravenous clamps) attached with aluminum rivets.

2. The holder is designed to substitute for hand grasp and enable the patient to care for his own shaving needs. It is easily made, inexpensive, easy to keep clean, is not rusted by water, and patient can slip in and out of it himself. It is especially helpful in cases of quadriplegia.

W. *Celastic Combination Self-Care Cock-Up Splint*

    1. This is a cock-up splint made of three layers of laminated celastic. An 18-gauge metal strip bent to a 40-degree angle is inserted between the two outside layers to reinforce the cocked up portion; webbing straps are inserted and laminated between bottom and middle layers. While still wet the entire splint is molded to the patient's arm. At the palm end of the splint, on the outer layer, various tunnels and slits are made while the device is still wet. The pencil, tongue depressor, and dowel stick, to which the attachments are taped, are inserted in splint and left until dry to insure proper fit. The device is given two coats of finishing lacquer.

    2. This splint is of use where there is inability to grasp and weakness or spasticity. A small amount of motion in the shoulder is necessary for successful manipulation, however. It enables the severely disabled patient to eat, shave, brush teeth, telephone, write, stencil, and type with the aid of typing strap.

X. *Toilet Bench*

    1. The toilet bench is about three feet long and in height is level with the seat of the wheel chair. The opening is towards one side rather than in the middle.

    2. This bench enables wheel chair patients to use the toilet even though they may not be able to get from chair to toilet in the usual manner, for with this bench it is possible to slide from the wheel chair seat and back again.

Y. *Free Standing Hand Bars For Toilet*

    1. This frame is made of chromium plated steel tubing and can be lifted over a toilet and set around it to form arms, as if for a chair. The base is 18 inches wide and 21 inches deep, with a flat strip of steel with tread-rubber base under either side for added stability. The 13-inch arm pieces are supported on rectangular loops attached to the base at either side and reinforced by a double-L length of tubing across the back, fastened with two bolts at each side. These arm pieces can be moved forward or backward so that frame will fit various models of toilets. The arms are also adjustable in height from 25 inches high to 30 inches high. If further stability is desired, the two attachments on rear bar can be placed under seat bolts to hold frame in place.

    2. This frame has been designed for persons who need side bars to assist them in getting to and from toilet when the installation of permanent bars is not feasible.

Z. *Toilet Care Device*

    1. This device consists of two plastic rods joined by an aluminum strip, fitted into slots, with one end of the rods formed to make handles and the other end smooth-edged interlocking teeth. The outer rod is fastened at both ends of the strip, the inner rod at only the center of the slot, thus permitting a certain degree of play in both directions with the fastening point as fulcrum. A small spring placed between the rods about 2 inches on the hand-grip side of the fulcrum is under expansile tension and tends to maintain the teeth ends clamped.

    2. This device is intended to facilitate self-care in toilet activities by persons

unable to reach perineum because of limitation of upper extremity function. This condition may exist in cases of orthopedic conditions, and congenital deformities. To operate, the handle ends are compressed, thereby separating the teeth. Toilet paper is placed between the teeth, then wrapped around one or both ends. Relaxing the hand grip permits the device to grasp the paper firmly, and it is then used by holding the longer of the two handle ends and directing the device.

Za. *A Wheel Chair Bathroom*

1. This bathroom was designed especially for wheel chair users and contains the following special features: low tub with corner ledge forming a seat, low fold-back shower curtain rod, low shower controls, medicine cabinet placed low on wall and to side of lavatory, lavatory with set-back drain pipe that does not impede close approach, towel racks at either side of lavatory, and an extra rod at side of toilet for assistance in getting to and from toilet seat. As throughout the house, the casement window is controlled by handle at the sill.

2. All fixtures in this bathroom can be approached and controlled by a person in a wheel chair. Even the shower curtain is easily pulled forward or pushed back from that position. In entering the tub, it is possible to slide from chair to ledge seat and then, grasping either side of tub, lower body into water. Or, bather can sit in tub and use shower. The medicine cabinet is freely accessible and the mirror can be used at close range. Towel racks at lavatory sides obviate extra moving about.

II. SELF-HELP FEEDING DEVICES

A. *Adapted Eating Utensils*

1. Conventional spoons and forks are adapted for special use by attaching metal strips of various shapes and sizes.

2. The adapted spoons and forks are used to facilitate eating for patients who have weakness or loss of grasp, or general weakness of hands and arms. They are usable in various positions, since the metal pieces are so attached that the utensils will accommodate hand and arm during feeding motions even when these motions and the grasp vary from the normal.

B. *Joined Fork and Spoon*

1. A long-handled spoon, such as an iced tea spoon, and a fork, are joined together by drilling a hole in the ends of the handles and inserting a small bolt and nut.

2. The purpose of this device is to give extra length to a spoon and fork without having to have a special long handle made. They may also be folded together for carrying purposes. This device was set up for patients like the arthritic, or anyone having limitation of joint motion or insufficient muscle power to bring the spoon close enough to the mouth.

C. *Plastic Food Holder*

1. The holder is made from three pieces of Plexiglas: one strip 1″ by desired length, from ⅛″ plexiglas, for the handle, and two half-circles 5″ in diameter (one slightly smaller)—the larger piece from ⅛″ plexiglas, the

smaller from ¹/₁₆″. The larger half-circle is riveted to the handle. The small end is attached by a rubber band inserted through matching ⅛″ holes.

The attachment for holding hard-boiled eggs is made from aluminum, curved as indicated in diagram. It is also attached by means of the rubber band.

2. This implement was designed primarily to assist the patient unable to raise his arms to eat types of food ordinarily held in the hand, i.e., toast, hard-boiled eggs, etc.

D. *Kant-Spill Training Cup*
  1. The Kant-Spill Training Cup is a plastic cup with a transparent lock-on lid. The lid is perforated with six small holes along one side and two holes on the opposite side.
  2. This cup is recommended when there is difficulty in using an ordinary cup because of involuntary movements. It is adapted to the training of the cerebral palsy patient and also to the quadriplegic or arthritic person. More holes can easily be drilled in the lid to permit the desired flow of liquid.

E. *Drinking Tube Holder*
  1. The holder is made of light-weight aluminum. The center piece is then curved to hold the glass or plastic drinking tube and the side pieces are bent forward to grasp the rim of the drinking vessel.

     Although a straw can be used with holder, it is suggested that a plastic tube is preferable to the usual glass tube. It is often impossible for the patient to lift the glass at all, and plastic tubing can be cut in longer lengths and is easily bent to suit the needs of the patient.
  2. This holder was made for the convenience of any patient unable to lift a drinking glass to the mouth. It is a convenience for anyone obliged to use a drinking tube and it greatly reduces the danger of breaking the tube or spilling the liquid.

F. *The Hoyer Lifter*
  1. This lifter is constructed of gray-painted steel and consists of a U-shaped base mounted on four hard rubber swivel casters, two of which are provided with locks, with an upright rising from closed end of U. A horizontal arm (which is raised and lowered as desired) is equipped with web lifting slings. Power is provided by a hydraulic pump, easily operated with little physical effort.

     A canvas seat and back—for use instead of the slings—may be purchased at small additional cost. New models are equipped also with a steering bar which is attached to the upright. The upright piece can be lifted out of the U-shaped base for storage or transportation, or for transfer to the special base when this has been installed in the bathroom.
  2. The web lifting slings are slipped under his knees and behind his back, the "D" rings hooked onto the swivel bar. A few strokes of the hydraulic pump will raise the patient, who is comfortable and entirely relaxed in slings. The attendant rolls the lifter clear of the bed and steers it toward wheel chair (arm chair, couch etc.). When release valve knob is turned, the patient sinks down gently—full length or sitting position, as the

case may be. The lifter is able to lower the patient to the floor (for exercise) or to raise him to a height several inches above hospital-type bed. It can transfer him to a toilet, bathtub, easy chair, hammock, boat or car. The special floor attachment for bathroom use is available if needed.

III. SELF-HELP COMMUNICATION

A. *Telephone Holder*

1. This device consists of a wooden base (approximately 4″ x 6″) and an upright arm to which is attached a cradle, or seat, for receiving the mouthpiece. It is light-weight and easily pushed out of the way when not in use. A similar device made of metal is on the market.
2. The purpose of the telephone holder is to enable hemiplegia or quadriplegia patients, or anyone having the use of only one arm, to use the telephone and have the hand free to make notations, or for other necessary purposes.

B. *Magnetized Bulletin Board*

1. Small magnetized cubes hold paper in place on this magnetized board. Although the cubes hold paper firmly, they are easily detached for replacement in any desired position.
2. The board and cubes serve to hold writing paper for persons having the use of only one arm, whether from hemiplegia or c.p.

C. *Writing Aid*

1. The writing aid consists of a ¾-inch wide strip of metal, curved to fit over the hand, with a slot to hold the pencil.
2. The device is designed to assist in writing when there is insufficient muscle power to hold pencil in ordinary manner. It is suitable for such patients as the quadriplegic and hemiplegic.

D. *Leather Writing Device*

1. This holder for pencil or pen is formed of two pieces of leather, one approximately 1½ × 2¼ inches, the other approximately 6¼ × 1⅝ inches, depending on size requirements. The shorter length is slit to admit the long strap and the ends are fastened by snaps.
2. This device is intended to allow persons to write with a hand having insufficient power to grasp pen or pencil. It will be a help to many patients with paralysis or other neurological conditions involving the fingers. Placed over thumb and index fingers, the device maintains the writing implement in proper position. It is small enough to be carried in the pocket.

E. *Pencil Holder For Hands With Unsteady Grasp*

1. A piece of broomstick (or wooden dowel) 5-6 inches long (or whatever length is desired) is bored about half an inch from one end to make hole to fit a pencil. The pencil is made secure by a picture hook or wing bolt passed through nut which has been inserted in hole made for it midway between pencil hole and end elastic band which is slipped over pencil.
2. This device was designed particularly for the athetoid cerebral palsied; it has been used successfully by the spastic, the rigid and other types of cerebral palsy cases. The rubber band secures the pencil and assists the athetoid in holding it.

F. *Typing Sticks With Fiberglass Handles*

1. Two cylindrical sticks $5/16$-inch in diameter are fastened to fiberglass cuffs made to fit the natural grasp of this quadriplegia patient. The tips are covered with slip-on pencil erasers. The fiberglass offers just enough resistance to make squeezing the cuffs a profitable hand exercise and the rubber tipped sticks make possible two-finger typing while strength is developed for the beginning of ten-finger typing.

2. The typing sticks might be used by anyone with enough hand power to manage them but not enough to attempt conventional typing. They may be particularly helpful to the patient for whose hands some strength is expected, for they encourage exercise and permit the patient to type while he awaits return of function.

G. *Leather Typing Device*

1. This is a light-weight cowhide cuff fitting under palm of hand and buckling snugly on dorsal side. The underside piece is riveted on. This has one-third of a wire coat hanger bent to picture shape with the ends woven through side holes and tacked in place with waxed thread. A piece of a pencil eraser is cut halfway down the middle, then end of the wire is inserted, and eraser is taped tightly.

2. This device permits a patient without use of the fingers to type. It does require, however, a small amount of wrist, elbow and shoulder motion. It is most valuable to persons suffering from the effects of high lesion spinal cord injuries.

H. *Remote Control Keyboard for Electric Typewriter*

1. This light keyboard is used as a selector for the electric typewriter, to which it is connected by a rubber-covered wire. The typewriter, which does the actual typing, can remain on the desk or table while the keyboard is placed on a bed table, wheel chair tray, lapboard, or wherever it can be used most conveniently.

2. The remote control keyboard permits the use of the electric typewriter by persons who would be unable to approach the typewriter itself, either by reason of weakness or because of the position to which they are confined.

I. *Reading Rack for Wheel Chair Tray*

1. This plywood rack is held in place on the wheel chair tray by a clamp at either side. It is easily detached and folds flat for storage. The angle at which it stands when in place can be adjusted from either side, so that either hand can be used, accordance with patient's convenience.

2. The rack was designed for reading and painting to meet the needs of wheel chair patients. It would be suitable for any wheel chair user, especially those with hands too weak to hold a book comfortably, such as a quadriplegic or person with hands affected by multiple sclerosis or c.p.

J. *"Read'N Bed"*

1. "Read'N Bed" holds book or magazine for reader reclining in bed. It can be adjusted to any desired angle and will hold book even when inclined toward the reader. The board is made of a light-weight building material, the legs of aluminum, and an acetate film strip secured by elastic holds book in place. When not in use, legs can be folded back against the board

and the entire device can be stored flat in a drawer. Total weight is just over one pound.

    2. "Read'N Bed" will be a convenience and a comfort to anyone able to read and confined to bed for a long or short period. It eliminates the fatigue of holding book and the difficulty of keeping it at proper reading angle. It can be used independently by anyone, even by a patient confined to the supine or slight hyper-extension position.

K. *Page Turner*

    1. The construction of the page turner utilizes spools, scraps of wood, and paper clips. The book is prepared by attaching a paper clip to each page and a continuous thread to each clip and winding the thread around the spool at the side of the turner. Patient can turn or "swat at" a rod that is fastened to the small drum (or spool) which will continually wind up the thread and so turn the pages.

    2. The purpose of the page turner is to make it possible for the athetoid to turn the pages of his book unassisted.

IV. SELF-HELP HOMEMAKING AIDS

A. *Kitchen Utensils For The One-Handed*

    1. The eggbeater is operated by an up-and-down motion of one hand.

        This pot lid has a handle into which fingers can be slipped to lift the lid—even weak fingers or fingers stiffened and deformed by arthritis and unable to grasp the usual knob.

        With this long-handled dipper, serving is accomplished by many who could neither lift the pot nor manage the ordinary ladle.

        This rolling pin, consisting of many small rollers held together in a ring, with attached handle over the top, can be used effectively entirely by one hand.

        This slicer and grater for eggs, cheese or vegetables requires only one hand for successful use, since when base is pressed against a bar, as shown, no other hold is needed. It can be used also to peel fruit.

        The double suction cup holds the mixing bowl steady at any angle desired, so that only a hand to hold fork or one-hand beater is necessary.

    2. All of these utensils are usable by persons having only one hand, or whose hands are crippled.

B. *One Armed Can Opener*

    1. The can opener is solidly constructed of a rustproof metal. To make it suitable for use with one arm only, a special arrangement is attached to the wall, consisting of an iron rod bent at a 90-degree angle with attached plate. This holder can be turned sideways and can be elevated and lowered so that cans of different dimensions may be accommodated.

    2. Adjustment of holder and placement of can are accomplished easily using one hand only. This means that the device can be operated by persons who have lost the use of a hand or arm. Opening cans—an operation almost essential in preparing meals daily—is made possible to amputees and others who have one arm.

C. *Kitchen Range*

1. The wheel chair house has a gas range, and the Welbilt, four burner style, is used.

2. The requirements for a kitchen range are simply that oven, broiler, and burners be accessible from the wheel chair. If an electric range is used, it is important to make sure that the cocks controlling the burners are all at the front of the stove.

D. *Kitchen Sink for Wheel Chair User*

1. The sink is at a height to be usable from the wheel chair and the drain pipe is set back where it cannot prevent a close approach. Also, the sink is not too deep for convenient use from wheel chair.

2. A wheel chair user finds no difficulty in washing dishes or preparing vegetables at this sink for it was chosen with her comfort in mind.

E. *Kitchen Cupboards in Wheel Chair House*

1. These kitchen cupboards for china, glassware, and cooking utensils have sliding wooden doors and the shelves are spaced about a foot apart. There can be as many shelves as desired. The depth should be about 9 inches, so that everything is within easy reach.

2. All of these shelves can be reached from the wheel chair except the top, and that is accessible from a standing position. The sliding doors save space and can be opened with minimal maneuvering of wheel chair.

F. *Fold-Away Dining Table*

1. This fold-up table, released from its position as cupboard door by a pull of the hanging chain, has a folding leg to hold it steady when in use. It is at exact height to be used sitting in wheel chair.

2. This folding table provides a convenient place for meals in the kitchen. The height is suitable for use from wheel chair. When folded, the table doubles as a cupboard door and saves kitchen space. It can be used also as a work table for preparing food. A convenient wall outlet located close by will accommodate electric toaster or coffee percolator.

G. *Office Chair With Raised Arms*

1. The arms of an office posture chair (made by the Ohio Chair Company) have been raised to the desired height with pieces of specially ground angle iron to support arms for typing and general office work.

2. This inconspicuous adaptation of a standard chair has served the same purpose satisfactorily. It could be useful to others with the same problem, always provided that their arm weakness was not so great as to make it difficult to keep the arms in place.

H. *Chair for Ankylosis of One Hip*

1. This chair was designed to meet the particular needs of an individual with one fused hip who is unable to sit in any conventional chair. The chair is made of light-weight welded steel tubing painted as desired, with extra wide leg spread to provide good balance. Legs are tipped with rubber crutch tips or furnished with sliding domes, as circumstances suggest. Seat and back are made of plain half-inch hardwood plywood upholstered in

foam rubber and covered with imitation leather, plastic fabric, or a cloth material. (Cloth is less slippery than the other coverings and therefore preferable.)

The back piece can be moved on its clamps from side to side and backward and forward and its angle can be adjusted fully from vertical to horizontal.

The seat is cut to accommodate the loss of flexion of one hip, and the side piece on the chair leg has been added to make a knee rest. This rest is adjustable in height and controlled by lever on side of chair. It also tilts on a center bar to provide angle for best comfort.

If the patient's left hip is locked in extension, the use of strong springs under the seat, front and back, gives a slightly pivotal motion. This permits some change of position so that sitting is less tiring, and also makes possible slight shift of position which may be necessary for working purposes.

2. While it is desirable for anyone to be able to sit down, it is doubly important for one whose gainful employment depends upon his ability to assume a sitting position. And sitting is necessary in almost any occupation, even those where standing much of the time is common. This type of chair is especially suitable for conditions which may leave the individual with one stiff hip.

I *The Front Door*

1. The wheel chair house has no doorstep, only a low sill. Sloping grade of the lot takes care of drainage. In this house all doorways are 36 inches wide and halls are 51 inches wide.

2. Absence of a step makes it easy to propel wheel chairs in and out of the front door and the width of 36 inches is more than enough to accommodate the chair.

J. *Casement Windows*

1. The wheel chair house is fitted throughout with casement windows and screens, made as a unit and controlled from near the sill.

2. Windows of this type can be opened and closed while one remains in the sitting position, and with very little physical effort. The screens—which are furnished with the windows—are managed with equal ease since they are made of aluminum and are very light in weight. They are installed on the inside and easily removed. The catch at side also acts as a lock.

K. *Convenient Electric Outlets*

1. Electric light outlets in the wheel chair house are placed 12 to 18 inches from the floor instead of in the baseboards.

2. At this height from the floor the outlets can be reached from the wheel chair without risk of a fall. Whether the attachment is to be made for vacuum cleaner, electric iron, toaster, heating pad, or lamp, a more conveniently placed outlet adds to living comfort.

L. *Stair Climber*

1. This climber—a portable wooden step with side handle—differs from similar devices in that the handle side of the step is 1-¾ inches in height, while

the other side is 5-¼ inches high. Thus to go from one riser to another requires that the user take not half but quarter the usual step at a time.

2. The stair climber could be useful to anyone who finds steps of standard height difficult to climb, either because of weak muscles or stiffened joints. (But note that a certain minimal strength in arms is needed to lift the climber and keep a firm grasp on the stair rail.) The device is suitable for persons affected by muscular dystrophy, multiple sclerosis and other conditions involving the lower extremities.

M. *Retractable Key Chain*
1. This is a small reel with an automatic retractable fine chain. It is fastened to lapel or handbag by means of a safety clasp on the back of reel.
2. Key or pencil may be attached to the chain. Its purpose is to make them always available and to lend assistance to weak or unsteady hands, as in the case of quadriplegia or palsy patients.

N. *Paulo Pick-Up Stick*
1. This is a 2½ inch light-weight rod with a wire loop and point on one end and a magnet on the other.
2. This device enables patients confined to bed or wheel chair, or patients who cannot stoop or reach to pick up objects at a distance.

O. *Reaching Tongs*
1. These tongs—fashioned after a pair pictured in the March 1950 issue of *Popular Mechanics* are made of light-weight Duralumin and weigh less than 10 ounces. The metal is bent and the two parts are riveted in the center. (A washer can be inserted between them for smooth operation.) In this way a positive gripping action is attained, causing the arms to grasp firmly when the handles are held closely. Note that the arms of the tongs are curved slightly and that a piece of rubber tubing is pressed over the ends. There is also on the market a similar device in wood.
2. The tongs enable persons with limited joint motion, or persons confined to a wheel chair, to grasp and pick up objects otherwise out of their reach. They are especially useful in lifting cans from cupboard shelves or clothing from closets. The tongs will assist patients with paraplegia, incomplete quadriplegia, multiple sclerosis, or any condition requiring wheel chair living.

P. *Special Appliance for Sewing Machine*
1. The appliance is made of nickel-plated steel and has a pressure plate of polished birch or ash. The arm of the appliance is placed under top of table and screwed to same so that pressure plate extends slightly higher than top of table to be comfortable for patient's underarm or elbow. An extension connects with foot pedal.
2. This appliance affords a means whereby the speed of a sewing machine can be regulated by a relatively slight pressure of the forearm. It is intended for persons with weakness of the lower extremities.

V. A FEW SELF-HELP VOCATIONAL AIDS

A. *Knee Clamp Holder For Embroidery Rings Or Darning Egg*

1. The holder itself is constructed of stainless steel; the brackets are partly covered by rubber; and the darning egg is made of polished hardwood with felt-covered sides. The holder can be raised or lowered or turned in various directions.

2. This holder makes it possible for persons having the use of only one hand to embroider or darn. It may be helpful to hemiplegics and those with a hand disabled.

B. *Scissors Board*

1. The scissors are attached to table at axis with C-clamp and at end of lower blade with a screw. Scissors screw onto the right side for a right-handed child; for the left-handed, attachment would be at left side of table. The scissors are fixed and the paper is fed to them.

2. The scissors board was designed to aid persons suffering from weakness, incoordination or spasticity who cannot handle scissors in the ordinary manner. This provides a safe way of handling a tool that might otherwise be too difficult or dangerous to handle. An assistant may guide the paper into the scissors for a person unable to guide with his own other hand. The board may offer finger exercise and help in gaining some skill and the pleasure of accomplishing something almost alone. It can be used by the cerebral palsied, especially the athetoid, the multiple sclerosis patient and patients with conditions causing similar disability. It might also be helpful to those with hand weakness resulting from poliomyelitis.

C. *Plastic Tool Holder*

1. This therapeutic adjunct is made from three pieces of plastic:

    1 piece 3-inch dowling 4 inches long
    2 pieces plastic rod—½ inch x 6   inches
    ½ inch x 1½ inches

    The three pieces are cemented together as shown and a hole is drilled through the plastic rods.

2. This device is used in leather work when co-ordination and finger dexterity are limited and not likely to improve. In such cases the problem of maintaining a normal working position of the affected extremity is ever present. Use of this holder permits the patient to achieve the correct position. The repetitious use of this position forms a good habit pattern.

    Motivation of the patient is increased when his skill is comparable to that of others without his handicap and permits him to identify himself as one of the group.

    The advantage of using plastic in the construction of this device lies in its transparency, which allows the work to be seen through the holder. The device was originated for the hemiplegic patient and can be altered to meet the specific needs of those who have difficulty with dexterity and stabilization in one hand.

D. *Slide-Rule Holder And Operating Device*
  1. A plastic hand band is fastened to the back of slide rule. To each end of the slide rule. For persons with marked limitation of motion in their hands and fingers.
  2. This device permits patients with insufficient function of the fingers, particularly those having poliomyelitis, paralysis due to cervical cord injury, or other neurological or neuromuscular dysfunction, to hold and use a standard slide rule. For persons with marked limitation of motion in their hands and fingers.

E. *Worktable With Support For Standing*
  1. This adjustable standing table consists of a flat top of wood with wide, hinged arm-rests and a safety belt to prevent the worker from falling. Four adjustable metal pipes serve as legs, which are run through the ordinary wooden work bench.
  2. This worktable is used primarily for lower extremity paraplegics, to improve their balance.

APPENDIX XI

Occupational Therapy—State Offices

Programs listed are approved by the Council on Medical Education of the American Medical Association, 535 N. Dearborn St., Chicago, IL 60610, in collaboration with the American Occupational Therapy Association, 6000 Executive Blvd., Rockville, MD 20852.

ALABAMA
Birmingham: University of Alabama

ARKANSAS
Conway: University of Central Arkansas

CALIFORNIA
Downey: University of Southern California
Loma Linda: Loma Linda University
San Jose: San Jose State University

COLORADO
Fort Collins: Colorado State University

CONNECTICUT
Hamden: Quinnipiac College

FLORIDA
Gainesville: University of Florida

GEORGIA
Augusta: Medical College of Georgia

ILLINOIS
Chicago: University of Illinois College of Medicine

INDIANA
Indianapolis: Indiana University

KANSAS
Lawrence: University of Kansas

LOUISIANA
Monroe: Northeast Louisiana University

MASSACHUSETTS
Boston: Boston University. Tufts University

MICHIGAN
Detroit: Wayne State University
Kalamazoo: Western Michigan University
Ypsilanti: Eastern Michigan University

MINNESOTA
Minneapolis: University of Minnesota
St. Paul: College of St. Catherine

MISSOURI
Columbia: University of Missouri
St. Louis: Washington University

NEW HAMPSHIRE
Durham: University of New Hampshire

NEW YORK
Brooklyn: State University of New York, Downstate Medical Center
Buffalo: State University of New York at Buffalo
New York: Columbia University · New York University
Utica: Utica College of Syracuse University

NORTH CAROLINA
Greenville: East Carolina University

NORTH DAKOTA
Grand Forks: University of North Dakota

OHIO
Columbus: Ohio State University

OKLAHOMA
Oklahoma City: University of Oklahoma

PENNSYLVANIA
Philadelphia: Temple University · University of Pennsylvania

TEXAS
Denton: Texas Woman's University
Galveston: University of Texas Medical Branch

VIRGINIA
Richmond: Virginia Commonwealth University

WASHINGTON
Seattle: University of Washington
Tacoma: University of Puget Sound

WISCONSIN
Madison: University of Wisconsin
Milwaukee: Mount Mary College

APPENDIX XII

Physical Therapy—State Offices

ALABAMA
Birmingham: University of Alabama in Birmingham

ARKANSAS
Conway: State College of Arkansas

CALIFORNIA
Fresno: California State University
Loma Linda: Loma Linda University
Long Beach: California State University
Los Angeles: Childrens Hospital of Los Angeles · University of Southern California
Northridge: California State University
San Francisco: University of California at San Francisco
Stanford: Stanford University School of Medicine

COLORADO
Denver: University of Colorado Medical Center

CONNECTICUT
Hamden: Quinnipiac College
Storrs: University of Connecticut

FLORIDA
Gainesville: University of Florida

GEORGIA
Atlanta: Georgia State University
Augusta: Medical College of Georgia

ILLINOIS
Chicago: Chicago Medical School/University of Health Sciences · Northwestern University Medical School · University of Illinois Medical Center

INDIANA
Indianapolis: Indiana University School of Medicine

IOWA
Iowa City: University of Iowa

KANSAS
Kansas City: University of Kansas Medical Center

KENTUCKY
Lexington: University of Kentucky Medical Center

LOUISIANA
New Orleans: Louisiana State University Medical Center

MARYLAND
Baltimore: University of Maryland

MASSACHUSETTS
Boston: Boston University, Sargent College of Allied Health Professions · Northeastern University · Simmons College

MICHIGAN
Ann Arbor: University of Michigan Medical Center
Detroit: Wayne State University

MINNESOTA
Minneapolis: University of Minnesota
Rochester: Mayo Foundation

MISSOURI
Columbia: University of Missouri
St. Louis: St. Louis University · Washington University School of Medicine

NEBRASKA
Omaha: University of Nebraska

NEW YORK
Albany: Albany Medical Center
Brooklyn: Downstate Medical Center, State University of New York
Buffalo: State University of New York at Buffalo
Ithaca: Ithaca College
New York: Columbia University College of Physicians and Surgeons · Hunter College · New York University
Stony Brook: State University of New York at Stony Brook
Syracuse: State University of New York-Upstate Medical Center

NORTH CAROLINA
Chapel Hill: University of North Carolina
Durham: Duke University Medical Center
Greenville: East Carolina University

NORTH DAKOTA
Grand Forks: University of North Dakota School of Medicine

OHIO
Columbus: Ohio State University

OKLAHOMA
Oklahoma City: University of Oklahoma

PENNSYLVANIA
Philadelphia: Temple University · University of Pennsylvania
Pittsburgh: University of Pittsburgh

TENNESSEE
Memphis: University of Tennessee

TEXAS
Dallas: University of Texas
Denton: Texas Woman's University
Fort Sam Houston: Academy of Health Sciences, U.S. Army
Galveston: University of Texas Medical Branch at Galveston

UTAH
Salt Lake City: University of Utah

VERMONT
Burlington: University of Vermont

VIRGINIA
Richmond: Virginia Commonwealth University

WASHINGTON
Seattle: University of Washington

WEST VIRGINIA
Morgantown: West Virginia University

WISCONSIN
Madison: University of Wisconsin
Milwaukee: Marquette University

APPENDIX XIII

Speech Pathology and Audiology—State Offices

All master's degree programs listed are accredited by the American Speech and Hearing Association, 9030 Old Georgetown Rd., Washington, DC 20014.

ARIZONA
Tempe: Arizona State University

CALIFORNIA
Fullerton: California State University
Long Beach: California State University
San Jose: California State University

Santa Barbara: University of California
Stockton: University of the Pacific

CONNECTICUT
New Haven: Southern Connecticut State College

DISTRICT OF COLUMBIA
Washington: Catholic University of America

GEORGIA
Athens: University of Georgia

ILLINOIS
Carbondale: Southern Illinois University
Charleston: Eastern Illinois University
Peoria: Bradley University

INDIANA
Terre Haute: Indiana State University

IOWA
Cedar Falls: University of Northern Iowa

KANSAS
Manhattan: Kansas State University

LOUISIANA
Baton Rouge: Louisiana State University
New Orleans: Tulane University Speech and Hearing Center

MASSACHUSETTS
Amherst: University of Massachusetts

MICHIGAN
Detroit: Wayne State University
Marquette: Northern Michigan University
Ypsilanti: Eastern Michigan University

MINNESOTA
Minneapolis: University of Minnesota

MISSOURI
Columbia: University of Missouri
Kirksville: Northeast Missouri State College

St. Louis: St. Louis University
Warrensburg: Central Missouri State College

NEW MEXICO
Albuquerque: University of New Mexico

NEW YORK
Brooklyn: Brooklyn College
Garden City: Adelphi University
Geneseo: State University College
New York: City College

NORTH DAKOTA
Minot: Minot State College

OKLAHOMA
Enid: Phillips University

OREGON
Portland: Portland State University

SOUTH DAKOTA
Vermillion: University of South Dakota

TEXAS
Houston: University of Houston
San Antonio: Our Lady of the Lake College
San Marcos: Southwest Texas State College

WASHINGTON
Pullman: Washington State University

WISCONSIN
Milwaukee: Marquette University · University of Wisconsin